Hustlers, Heroes and Hooligans

Reporting on the New York Experience

To Donna,
who put up with it all.

Hustlers, Heroes and Hooligans

Reporting on the New York Experience

Dan Lynch

Whitston Publishing Company, Inc.
Albany, New York
2003

Copyright © 2003
Lynch Productions, LLC

Library of Congress Control Number 2002109292

ISBN 0-87875-541-1

Printed in the United States of America

Also by Dan Lynch . . .

Deadly Ernest

A Killing Frost

Deathly Pale

Brennan's Point

Bad Fortune

Yellow

*Running With The Machine:
A Journalist's Eye-Opening Plunge Into Politics*

Lakeside Stories

Contents

Acknowledgments vii

Introduction 1

Everyday Heroes 3

There's No Business Like Show Business 21

Politicians, Perverse Priorities and Puzzled People 41

Battered and Bullied by the Brusque, Brutal Bureaucracy .. 79

Law and Order 105

The New York State of Mind 161

The Uniquely Albany State of Mind 185

The Color of Disharmony 219

The Four Seasons 235

Animal Companions 259

Family Matters, and the Stuff That Truly Counts 269

Acknowledgments

Nobody really does anything alone.
Work in the newspaper business, and you'll figure that out early on. You'll realize that however brilliant you may view your reporting and writing, the act of producing and distributing the Daily Miracle is the ultimate exercise in teamwork. Every day, reporters report, photographers photograph, editors edit, artists produce alchemy, the guys in the shop put it all together and truck drivers get the thing out into the neighborhoods for carriers to plop on civilians' doorsteps as the sun sneaks up over the eastern horizon.
Yeah, sure, the newspaper also goes out on-line, but the daily paper product—that ink-reeking relic of the industrial past—remains the beating heart of American journalism, and probably always will.
Meanwhile, as all this occurs, the newspaper building is unendingly abuzz with receptionists receiving, computer geeks computing, salespeople selling ads, bean counters crunching numbers, maintenance people cleaning up and, in the words of a publisher under whom I once served, publishers pubbling. All this frantic activity centers on a single ceaseless chore—that of delivering daily to the newspaper's readers the best available version of truths minor and momentous—from births to deaths, from marriages to bankruptcies, from Afghanistan to Albany, from tragedy to triumph.
So, while this book bears my name, it also bears the imprint of Jim McGrath, who deftly copy-edited most of these

pieces on deadline; of Bob Williams, who tutored a much younger me in journalistic values; of Nick Lederer, Harry Rosenfeld, Dave Laventhol, John McMullan, Gene Roberts and Tony Insolia—admired bosses whose uncompromising journalistic standards shaped my own; of gifted publishers like Roger Grier and Joe Lyons, hard-nosed businessmen who appreciated profit but who also wanted the newspapers they led to make a positive difference in the communities they served; of treasured, longtime friends in the business, like Terry Bitman and Larry Levy; of Mike Laddin, who felt that these collected pieces would make a worthwhile book; and, of course, of my wife, Donna, to whom this book is dedicated, and of my daughter and son, Kelly and Kevin, both of whom ended up in the news business despite the intimate look offered them into the frenzied family life of somebody who chases hard after news for a living.

In acknowledging further help in producing this book, I need also to thank New York, at once the most amazing and frustrating state in the union. It's huge—sprawling over 50,000 square miles and home to some 19 million souls. Two-thirds of those souls live in the five boroughs or their suburbs. So, when most people around the country think of New York, they think of skyscrapers, Broadway, Times Square and Ground Zero. They seldom think of upstate, which is larger than most European countries and home to more people than most states can boast in their entire populations. For most upstaters, you should understand, New York City might as well be Mars—which probably explains why no New York City mayor has ever made it to the governor's mansion.

Despite Manhattan's population density of 50,000 people per square mile, the whole of New York state really is a microcosm of America. We have it all here in the Empire State—from the deafening deluge of Niagara Falls, to the pine-studded slopes of the Adirondacks, to the gleaming Gotham spires, to the glittering sand beaches of Long Island. Sorry, but I'm an unabashed New York chauvinist. Really, in most ways it just doesn't get any better than this.

Acknowledgments

I was born in upstate New York, spent my childhood here and then went to Philadelphia and Long Island for college and career reasons. I moved back upstate just before Ronald Reagan moved into the White House. I've spent the years since observing and chronicling New York life and commenting on it. I've done that as a newspaper editor and columnist, as a broadcast personality, as a candidate for public office and as a scribbler of books, both truthful and imaginary. Several of my novels are either set in upstate New York or feature characters with roots here.

The pieces that make up this book all appeared in pretty much this form in the Albany *Times Union*, my professional home for 21 years. For much of that time, I kept sort of a public diary for the *TU*'s readers and for readers of the New York Times News Service, which distributed the column to about 660 newspapers nationally. My column first appeared once a week on the *Times Union* Op-Ed page and then grew to four times weekly on the newspaper's Local Front. In it, I shared with *Times Union* readers what I saw and heard and what I thought and felt about those things. My goal was to create for them a portrait of their place and time. I tried also to tell those stories through their eyes and not through the eyes of the people who were running things.

As I learned from firmly principled editors early on, journalism's greatest sin is its tendency to focus mainly on the pronouncements of the powerful and the pompous—on the reliance of reporters on "official sources" and on the reluctance of craven editors and publishers to take a chance on offending anybody—especially anybody with power over the flow of revenue or social influence at the country club. As a result, reporters too seldom deal with ordinary people and the way the powerful affect them in the course of their daily lives. Too many reporters practice top-down journalism—gleefully rubbing elbows with the powerful and bowing and scraping before those well-placed sources in exchange for some crumb of news brushed casually off the table of the mighty.

Too many reporters and editors view incompetence,

venality, deception and corruption on the part of the powerful as some unavoidable force of nature to be taken for granted, like gravity. Their cynicism robs them of any real capacity for outrage. Consequently, they're disinclined to examine the performance of important institutions and the people who run them and the often devastating impact of that shoddy performance on the lives of ordinary people.

To the greatest extent possible, it was my goal as a daily newspaper columnist to do bottom-up reporting—to illuminate and explain the time and place I was writing about not from the perspective of those who made the rules but, instead, through the eyes of those forced to abide by those rules or suffer the consequences. And, as you'll see as you go through this book, too many ordinary people end up suffering consequences.

Even when they broke no rules to begin with.

—Dan Lynch
Clifton Park, N. Y.
May 2002

Introduction

Writing a newspaper column four times a week, which is how Dan Lynch earned his bread for years, is a seldom emulated attainment. Even the most active of his peers nationally do three at best; many write fewer.

Turning out these tight and neat essays that have a narrative coherence—beginning, middle and end—and, moreover, make a point that has eluded other observers, is heavy lifting. Only the most skilled can bring it off.

When quality considerations are factored in—penetrating insight, the breadth of the knowledge and the vigor of expression—the reader can appreciate the magnitude of Dan Lynch's achievement.

For years, I couldn't go anywhere in town without two things happening. Most often I was told that I was speaking with a constant Lynch reader. Or, I was first asked if I actually knew Dan Lynch before hearing that his columns were a treat.

The fact is that I've known Dan Lynch for more than 20 years and have been from the first encounter his colleague—I hired him—and soon thereafter became and still remain his friend. We worked closely together, he as managing editor of the Albany *Times Union* and I as editor, for most of those years. In the course of this association, I got to hear Dan's opinions a lot more frequently than four times in seven days. Try four times a day, six days a week, and that would more accurately reflect reality.

Then and now, Dan Lynch was a smart man who had a

well-grounded instinct for where the news was and the know-how to get it into the paper. His journalistic values reflected his work as a columnist as they earlier had reflected his editing.

Dan knows why newspapers exist. They exist to tell the truth. They exist to champion the underdogs. They give voice to the voiceless, and they keep an eye on those amongst us who are inclined to take short cuts at the public's expense.

His work helped form the bulwark against those abiding tendencies in the media to improve market share by pandering to readers and skipping lightly over the sort of responsibilities for which the Founders invented the First Amendment to the Constitution. Purveying happy news like happy hours, in a panic to hold on to readerships (and viewerships, and listenerships) is not helping informed readers understand issues important to their lives.

Keeping the faith and flying the flag four times each week is not doable sitting back and thinking deeply. That helps, but it also requires shoe-leather reporting that takes you, the reader, out into the byways of our communities to talk to all manner of people. It takes knowing how the connections are made in our institutional structures. And when you are able to do all that, and also to have the ear to hear distressed people when they call out for help, then you understand how Dan Lynch did his job, week in and week out.

This collection of Dan Lynch columns provides the opportunity to assess them as a whole, rather than as periodic installments. Reading this book, you will see what I'm talking about.

And that I was very shrewd to have hired him in the first place.

—Harry M. Rosenfeld
Editor-at-Large
Albany *Times Union*

Everyday Heroes

Semper Fidelis

The party in the back room of Jackson's restaurant in Old Chatham—the one to celebrate Roger Machado's life—started at 7 Friday night, right after the wake. It lasted until 4 yesterday morning.

Then, just before they buried Roger Machado on a glorious, gilded October day—with sunlight streaming down like a shower of golden coins—somebody went up on the hillside behind the gravesite and erected a full-color, life-sized cardboard cutout of John Wayne, who'd starred in "The Sands of Iwo Jima."

Roger Machado had been there for real, in the second wave to hit the beach. He'd left a finger on Iwo. He'd been at Guadalcanal, too. He'd been at a lot of other places during his 21 years in the Marines, but none quite as mean as those two.

Yesterday, as John Wayne gazed down on that country graveyard, a full-color, life-sized cardboard cutout of Roger Machado in his dress blues—the uniform he could still fit into at 74 and wore proudly every Independence Day—stood a few miles away in the center of town, right outside the post office he'd lived over for some years.

I'd never met the man, but the cutout showed me what he'd looked like—dark-haired with gray sideburns. Not too tall, but square-jawed and trim and wiry.

"One tough little son-of-a-bitch," Bill Powers assured me.

And well-liked, too, it would seem. About 100 people showed up at graveside yesterday. They followed Roger Machado's flag-draped casket into the cemetery to sing the Marine Hymn over his grave, to hear bagpipes wail "Amazing Grace" and to feel shivers dance along their spines as a Marine honor guard fired him a salute and "Taps" rang out in the crisp autumn air.

So, why go to the funeral of a man you've never met? Well, for this reason:

Before I was born, American men like Roger Machado—kids, then, really—performed a reasonably important task. They saved the world. In the defining moments of this century, they were willing to risk everything and endure anything to rescue the planet from the greatest horror since Genghis Khan.

Nearly a half million of them died doing it—as opposed to the 37,000 or so who were killed in Korea and the nearly 60,000 who died in Vietnam. And when they were through, they came back home, rolled up their sleeves and proceeded to build the brawniest economy the world had ever known.

Now, at century's end, those who survive are gray and bent and worn down by the years. One by one, they're fading away, as Roger Machado faded away Monday. Every day, more and more of them begin their eternal slumber beneath carved granite monuments. In another decade or two, all but a few of them will be memories.

So, that was reason enough to go—to display some small measure of the enormous respect that my generation and our children owe these old men. But I went, too, because Bill Powers, the Republican chairman of this huge state and a veteran of five years active duty in the Marines, was going to speak at Roger Machado's graveside ceremony.

"I used to drive him in the Fourth of July parade," Powers told me the other day. "A great guy, and he dies. Totally unexpected. He walked five miles a day—200 situps, 200 pushups every day...."

"I'm going to have a tough time dealing with it.... My dad died from World War II-related illnesses. He was in the Marine Corps, spent a lot of time in the Pacific. I never saw him until I was 5 years old. I never really got to know him. He worked two jobs and died when I was 20.

"I was thinking about it when I was driving home the other night. It's got to be a generational thing. You look at people like that, Roger and my dad, they were children of the Depression. They didn't have a thing. The country went to war, and they were happy to go, to do what they had to do, and to come back—those that did come back. I lost an uncle on Iwo....

"That generation knew what sacrifice was when they were growing up.... My dad was one of seven, and they had to live with, 'What are we going to eat?' The generations that followed, our generation, they made it a little bit easier for us....

"I think of that whole era," Powers told me, "that Depression generation, and I don't think we're ever going to see people as tough as that again. And there aren't many of those guys left."

From what I was told about him, Roger Machado would have loved this funeral. He would have loved the five mounted, red-coated fox hunters who led his casket into the cemetery. He would have loved the gravesite beneath a towering evergreen. He would have loved the readings —some lofty poetry about every man's link to his fellow humans.

Roger Machado also probably would have loved Bill Powers' brief history of the Marines. Powers told the group, "The United States Marine Corps was founded in 1775—fittingly, for Roger—in a tavern in Philadelphia."

Roger Machado surely would have been pleased to be laid to rest near other members of his generation who died as the millennium approaches—but who, like Pvt. John A. Scherer, listed their World War II military rank on their gravestones.

The world turns, and yet another generation moves from its surface into its soil.

But this is one generation we should never, ever permit to be forgotten.

—October 18, 1998

An Attack of Honesty

About once a year somewhere in this country, a big bag of money falls off some armored truck somewhere. Everybody in the street scoops it up and runs like hell. Generally, about half the money is returned after people think it over.

A moment like that is when you have to decide who you really are. If you're rich, then you can afford conscience. If you're not . . . well. . . .

Joe Giuliano isn't rich. He's 21, a former Spa Catholic basketball star. He lives with his girlfriend, Chrissy Poirer, in an apartment house in Saratoga Springs.

The other night, Joe Giuliano was coming home from working one of his two jobs when he spotted something sitting in the hallway. It was a large duffel-style woman's handbag.

"This thing was open," he told me yesterday, "so I looked in. And there was a $50 bill hanging out. I went, 'Oh, My God! A fifty!'"

Joe Giuliano could tell that this bag was jammed with money. He called Chrissy out into the hall. They both stared at it. The world being what it is, they wondered if this wasn't a setup, some kind of scam. How often do you find bags full of money sitting in the hallway outside your apartment?

The bag was near the door of the apartment across the hall. Joe banged on the door for 20 minutes, no answer. He took the bag inside his own place.

"I opened it," he said later, "to look for I.D. and stuff, and I noticed that there were rolls of hundred dollar bills—16 of them."

Also in the bag was a cashier's check made out to his neighbor across the hall—a check for a hundred grand. He took it all out and spread it out atop his table, in awe at so much cash in one place. And, he couldn't help but realize, in *his* place.

Joe works at his father's restaurant in Wilton, north of Albany. He also works at Staples office supply in nearby Queensbury. He works a lot. He and Chrissy have a baby coming next month. There's also this house they're having built, even though they're seven grand short of closing cash at the moment.

Joe knew he could grab the money, which turned out later to total twice what he needs to get into the new house. He could do that and put the bag with its cashier's check back in the hallway. And who would ever know?

And, frankly, Joe could have taken the cashier's check, too. His father, Sal, is a retired Troy cop. Joe knows there are ways you can score with somebody else's cashier's check.

He called his father. Sal said he should come right over.

"I said, 'No, Dad, I don't want to.' But my better nature got the best of me, and I went there. We called the Saratoga police. They met us at our restaurant. They counted all the money and gave me a receipt."

The cops went to the apartment across the hall from Joe's and Chrissy's. They pounded on the door for a long time until the woman who occupies it finally opened up. She's an elderly lady who'd sold her house in Queensbury. She gave Joe 50 bucks as a reward.

Maybe enough for a few boxes of Pampers for the baby

when it comes. Not quite enough for the new house closing.

Joe is OK with all this, though. And his old man, Sal, couldn't be prouder of him. This was, after all, everything this woman would ever have.

"I guess I can always make money," Joe Giuliano told me yesterday. "She can't any more. In the end, that's what got the better of me."

—December 10, 1997

Fighting the Red Devil

Dan Marciniac was in Station Two on State Street, doing paperwork, when the call came in around 9:30 Sunday night. It was a 99.

Schenectady firefighters see maybe half a hundred 99s a year. When a 99 comes in, it means the fire is big and mean and fully capable of killing you when you do battle with it.

That has happened to 11 Schenectady firefighters in this century. Most went down from what the professionals refer to as fire heart attacks. You're fighting this thing—the Red Devil, they call it—and all your body's systems are operating at full-tilt boogie.

Sometimes your heart can't take it. You don't know that until it happens.

It was a fire heart attack that killed Donny Collins three years ago. Dan Marciniac still misses him. These professional firefighters are tight. They live together in the station. Many of them are related. As with police work, fighting fires is often a family calling.

Dan Marciniac's father was a fire department lieutenant, just as Dan is, and he went out on disability after a fire heart attack. A 22-year veteran as of this week, Dan Marciniac is 47, which is heart attack territory even if you don't fight fires for a living.

As his rig rolled to the blaze on Chestnut Street, Dan Marciniac wasn't thinking about that. He also wasn't thinking consciously about the six firefighters who'd died just two days earlier in a blazing warehouse in Worcester, Mass., only 150 miles east. After all, there are so many ways to die when you fight fires, why sweat it when you have business to attend to?

This fire was in an old house that had been chopped into four apartments. Schenectady is crammed with these tinderboxes. They're aged structures of dry wood, erected before flame resistant materials were available. They go up like paper.

Tim Farry, a guy of 40 who's in his 12th year as a Schenectady firefighter, had responded from Station Three in Mont Pleasant. He was on the back stairs, wrestling with a hose, when something came down on him. He's still not sure what it was. All he knows is that it knocked him off his feet, and he went down the stairs face first, slamming his head into something.

"The next thing I know," he said yesterday, "I was lying out in the yard and people were standing over me yelling at me to move and not to move and all kinds of stuff. They said I went as limp as a noodle when I hit."

Dan Marciniac was coming up the stairs when Tim Farry went down. Dan Marciniac went on to the attic, where guys already on the scene were running out of air. The air tanks are supposed to be good for a half hour, but you suck up a ton of oxygen when the Red Devil is raging around you. You're lucky if you get 15 minutes before your warning bell goes off.

After a while, amid the smoke and the flames, Dan Marciniac's bell sounded. He bent down to take off his mask. That's when some chunk of fire debris came down on him and slammed him to the floor. Three other guys were there. One took off his breathing gear and put it on Dan Marciniac. They loaded him onto an orange plastic stretcher. Six guys carried him down the stairs and got him the hell out.

Dan Marciniac came out of Sunday's fire OK. Tim Farry has a concussion, but he knows he's fortunate that he didn't snap his neck when he hit. The Red Devil wasn't so lucky.

He was beaten to death by a group of gallant, gutsy guys who wouldn't dream of making a living any other way.

—December 8, 1999

Dominick's Day

Yesterday was a Renoir painting—a wondrous glory of a day adorned with golden spangles of sunlight and caressed by silken breezes.

It was Dominick Lizzi's day, his glittering personal property. He's a retired social studies teacher who understands that the shape of the world is the product of human character. For better or worse, the world is what it is because certain people were in certain places at certain times and behaved in certain ways. With somebody else in the same place at the same time, the world would wear a different face.

Slavery, for example. It festered as an open sore for generations until Abraham Lincoln became President. Hitler might have consumed the globe but for the unique resolve of titans like Winston Churchill and Franklin Delano Roosevelt.

And the Republic of Ireland might never have been born if not for Martin H. Glynn. He was the son of Irish immigrants. He was born 127 years ago yesterday in the Greene County Village of Valatie, where Dominick Lizzi serves as municipal historian.

Armed with a law degree, Glynn went to work for the *Times Union*. He ended up as publisher and, eventually, as the newspaper's owner. Finally, he sold the *Times Union* to the Hearst Corp., the current owner, and concentrated on politics.

Martin H. Glynn served as a member of Congress, as state comptroller and as lieutenant governor. In 1913, when Gov. William Sulzer was bounced out of office in a vicious war with Tammany Hall, Martin H. Glynn—not Al Smith—became the first Catholic to sit as New York's governor.

Glynn left business and politics as a wealthy and honored man. As a prominent Irish-American, he involved himself in the Irish rebellion. Serving as a liaison between British Prime Minister Lloyd George and IRA leaders Michael Collins and Eamon De Valera, he brokered the peace that led to the formation of the Irish Republic.

On Oct. 23, 1923, Lloyd George came to Albany and delivered a speech lauding Glynn for his critical role in the birth of the Irish republic. Dominick Lizzi documented all this in his book, "Martin H. Glynn, Forgotten Hero."

But, for decades now, the name of Martin H. Glynn has been mentioned only in hushed whispers among people in the know. That's because, 11 days before Christmas, 1924, at his home at 28 Willett St., he shot himself to death. Glynn had endured 40 years of excruciating back pain. Surgery had failed. Despair and prolonged, relentless agony finally had swallowed him whole.

For a Catholic, there's no graver sin than suicide. That's why, for decades in this heavily Catholic city, Martin H. Glynn rested, more or less anonymously, in St. Agnes Cemetery. Dominick Lizzi believed that this extraordinary man's life should be honored with a memorial, despite the despondency that had provoked Glynn's suicide.

One day earlier this year, Dominick Lizzi called me for help. I spoke to Mayor Jerry Jennings, who immediately recognized the need to acknowledge Glynn's accomplishments. Whatever his other failings, Jennings gets things done. He got this done quickly and elegantly.

Yesterday, in a dignified ceremony outside Glynn's former home on Washington Park, a plaque honoring this talented, tortured man was unveiled. I was among those asked to say a few words to the crowd gathered for the occasion, and so was Dominick Lizzi.

After 74 years, a significant human being was finally honored for a noble life that towered over the tragic circumstances of his death. Sure, it was Martin H. Glynn's plaque, and he had it coming.

But that lush, lavish day was the exclusive property of Dominick Lizzi, the persistent historian who'd rescued the memory of a memorable human being.

—*September 18, 1998*

Citizen Kermani

This morning, Rod Kermani—a retired, 76-year-old rug merchant—will attend a YMCA breakfast at the Desmond to be honored as the Y's citizen of the year. This is worth noting here for several reasons:

• This is a distinguished award. Prior recipients include the late Erastus Corning 2nd, Albany's mayor for 41 years, and the late Lew Swyer, builder and philanthropist—men who left enduring marks on this town.

- The devoted work of service organizations like the Y and the Lions, of which Rod Kermani is also a member, are too seldom noted in the press except in the smallest of towns. We cover government, politics, sports, the arts and business. We tell you too little, though, about the activities of private, volunteer organizations.
- Rod Kermani is not a household name in his town. One of his sons is active in media and lobbying circles in state government, and his nephew is a conspicuous patron of the Albany Symphony. Both are better known to the Albany public than he is.

Rod Kermani is simply one of those unsung people who make such a positive difference in a community's life. He and others like him unselfishly devote time, effort and energy to service and charity work—raising money, donating money, helping thousands on a daily basis. To a large extent, that quiet network of service organizations makes up the backbone of this town.

All this is especially notable because the man known in Albany for 63 years as Rod Kermani was born Khodamorad Soroushian in Kerman, Iran. He came to this country in 1933 for a two-week visit to see his older brother, Rustam. At Rustam's urging, he stayed to work in Rustam's rug shop.

Rustam, 20 years Rod's senior, rented an apartment on Lancaster Street from Alexander and Viola McKown, people of substance for whose family an Albany suburb is named. Viola McKown became a special person in Rod Kermani's life—his "American mother."

"They had lost their only son," he told me the other day. "Sleeping sickness, they called it in those days. He'd just graduated from Yale University, so you can imagine what they were going through. So she was lonesome for her son, and I was lonesome for my mother and father and sisters and brothers. I filled up her empty spot. And she filled my empty spot."

Viola McKown cared for Rod and nurtured him and, in

1935, convinced Rustam to send his younger brother to YMCA camp. The boy from a crowded Mideast city saw the glory of his first forest sunset glowing fiery red over an Adirondack Lake. He has been devoted to the Y ever since. He and his wife, Ruth, pay for poor children to attend Y camps.

He volunteered for service in World War II, expecting to go to the Mideast as an interpreter. Instead, he received his citizenship papers on a blood-soaked spit of sand called Guadalcanal. He came home to marry, build a family and a business. And to give, whenever he could.

Several years ago, Lions International honored him with the Melvin Jones award, named for the organization's founder. The award has been given out precisely three times in 60 years.

So, today is the Y breakfast and this new award. And life goes on for this smallish, soft-spoken man whose name is known to so few in a town where attention goes disproportionately to politicians and media figures who, ultimately, make less positive difference in their communities than the Rod Kermanis of this world.

But wouldn't Viola McKown be proud, though?

—June 5, 1996

A Trial by Fire

It started, apparently, when somebody sneaking a smoke heard some footsteps and ditched the butt.

Larry O'Shea wasn't born yesterday. He'd suspected that some employees would interpret the no-smoking signs as reading, "Don't let the boss catch you smoking." That worried him.

Justifiably, as it turned out. The fire started small and got big fast. It was Feb. 12 and cold outside, but Larry O'Shea and his 55 employees left the warehouse without their coats, confident that firefighters could drown this thing in a hurry. They couldn't, though.

Instead, in just a few hours, the Adirondack Tire Corp.'s 45,000-foot warehouse was reduced to charred, smoking rubble. Twenty-two thousand tires, virtually the entire inventory, gone, poof, just like that. Two decades earlier, Larry O'Shea had moved up from New Jersey to set up this business in Colonie. When the enormity of this disaster sank in on him, he threw up.

Well, now what? You struggle for 20 years to build a business with seven outlets that moves maybe 900 tires a day, and a stray cigarette destroys the heart of the whole operation in just a few hours. So, do you take your insurance money and go off to play golf for the rest of your life? And, if you do, who could fault you for it?

But, as an entrepreneur, Larry O'Shea had come to realize that owning a business is not like holding down a job. A job you can walk away from, if you've socked away enough money. If you own a business, though, other people count on you. You're responsible for them and to them.

"When you own a business," Larry O'Shea says, "it's like, 'Hey, I don't have a boss.' Well, no. Fifty-five employees are your bosses, and 800 customers are your bosses. There's a ton of bosses. There's a ton of obligation. And you have an obligation to those employees to preserve their jobs, no question."

If he'd been 75, then maybe Larry O'Shea could have justified taking a hike. At 43, though, with the ashes of a viable enterprise at his feet, he felt a powerful duty to rebuild. He had to do it quickly, too, before his competitors in the low-margin tire distribution business rushed in to eat his lunch. The rubble was still warm when competitors started calling his customers, informing them through crocodile tears that Larry O'Shea and his company were history.

"Basically," he says, "the thing that I focused on immediately was that this is a problem. What can we do? How can we move along from this? What do I have to do to get up and running tomorrow?"

Within hours, he'd conferred with his insurance guy, with the telephone company people, with his computer people, with his suppliers. With smoke still rising from the ruins of his warehouse seven miles away, Larry O'Shea was renting warehouse space on a month-to-month basis on Fuller Road.

Most important, he was assuring his employees that they still had jobs. Everybody was about to bust his buns on 15-hour days for a long while, but nobody would miss a paycheck. Nobody's kid would miss a meal.

Today, Larry O'Shea's new warehouse is up and running on the site of the old one on Morris Road. The new building is better than the old one. The old warehouse was dark. Sunlight pours through skylights in this one.

Larry O'Shea is a proud, hard-nosed capitalist. He appreciates profits. But at a time when too many businesses are gleefully lopping off employees' heads to squeeze out an extra ounce of profit, Larry O'Shea also understands that capitalists have obligations to the communities they serve.

And to the workers who count on them.

—November 30, 1999

Happy Campers

Down the hill, across the road and on the beach where kids were playing, pinpoints of sunlight danced a summer jig on the rolling waves of Keuka Lake—like diamond dust drifting down from the sky.

Debbie Gilham watched from the porch of the mess hall. She wore shorts and a T-shirt, Camp Iroquois formal wear. At the camp in Penn Yan, she never wears her uniform until the last night, at the weekly awards ceremony around the bonfire. That's when the kids find out that she's a cop.

Until then, Albany County Deputy Sheriff Debbie Gilham is just one of the nice grownups here in a pristine, pretty place where all the grownups can be trusted—which, for many of these kids, is a rather dramatic change of pace.

"You talk to some of these children," she told me, "and their home life is unbelievable. . . . They come here tough, some of them. And some of them start out homesick. But by the end of the week, even the biggest and baddest of them don't want to go home."

Camp Iroquois is a collection of ragged red buildings sprawled across 29 acres of open hillside and forest and 1,100 feet of prime frontage on the prettiest of New York's Finger Lakes. For years, this was the Chemung County YMCA camp. As a kid growing up in nearby Elmira, I went to Camp Iroquois for two summers.

Then the camp business got tough. People with the money to send their kids off to camp sent them to specialty operations to learn to play soccer or basketball and, maybe, to eventually earn a college scholarship. Summer camp became just one more chance for a payoff down the road, and the Chemung County Y couldn't maintain the camp.

The New York State Sheriff's Association wanted to operate a summer camp for disadvantaged and at-risk kids. Other sheriff's associations in other states take a special interest in such matters. In Florida, for example, the sheriffs operate an extensive program for poor kids.

While most other police organizations seem to focus largely on labor-management issues, the sheriffs organizations nationally operate from a broader perspective. The New York sheriffs took over Camp Iroquois. In the course of a typical summer, it sends as many as 500 kids here, free of charge, from all over New York, from Brooklyn to Buffalo.

The campers are boys and girls aged 9 to 12 selected largely by each department's D.A.R.E. officer—kids deemed likely to derive some benefit from a relationship with cops that does not involve handcuffs.

Headquartered in Troy, the New York sheriff's association has 40,000 members, the vast bulk of them outside law enforcement. It has money, too. After leasing the camp for nine years, the association bought the place outright in 1994.

That 1,100 feet of Keuka frontage would support about 15 summer homes, each of which would sell for about a quarter million. But neither the Chemung County Y nor the sheriff's association wanted to see the place go for real estate development.

The sheriffs got it for about $650,000. There's no mortgage.

The camp is run by an Elmira gym teacher named David Sherman. The counselors are high school and college kids. But, during any given summer week, the place is alive with sheriff's deputies from all over New York.

They work around the camp, doing construction and hanging with the kids, trying to show them that cops are just like real people. So in a few years, when you're 16 or 17 and out in the streets, remember the nice deputies you met during your week at camp, OK?

Will this work? There's no guarantee. But maybe if you look after the molehills the mountains will look after themselves. If your job is preventing crime, then something like this is worth a shot.

Debbie Gilham regularly makes the four-and-a-half hour drive here from Albany on her days off—to spend time with other people's kids, to try to make a positive difference in their lives. She does this because she knows that, like it or not, these kids are going to do to the world precisely what her own kid did to her. He's 23 now.

He went and grew up.

—July 28, 1996

There's No Business Like Show Business

A Hell of a Life

In medieval times, people probably would have said that Maureen Stapleton was possessed by demons—some good demons and some bad ones, too.

The good demons gave her the towering talent that established her as one of the great stage and screen actresses of her generation. They helped her create the role of Serafina in "The Rose Tattoo," which won her a Tony. They helped her bring Emma Goldman so vividly to life in "Reds," which earned her an Oscar. They gave her the engaging warmth and earthy wit that makes her such good company.

The bad ones, though, they've made her crazy over the years. She'll be the first to tell you that.

And, in fact, she does tell you in a feisty, entertaining, utterly candid autobiography to be released this month. She spent a year, off and on, talking into a tape recorder for a writer, Jane Scovell. She wanted to call the book "Back on First," after First Street in Troy, N. Y., where she grew up. Simon and Schuster re-titled it "A Hell of a Life."

Yes, it has been that.

The other day, Maureen Stapleton—in a house dress and with the ever-present cigarette clutched between her fingers—sat at the kitchen table of her modest condominium unit in Lenox, Massachusetts and looked back over her 70 remarkable years.

"I just lived in the movies as a kid," she was saying in that distinctive, gravel road of a voice. "I had this terrific crush on Robert Taylor. I said, 'I gotta be in the same line of work.'

That's what really prodded me. I had a goal—a very strong goal—and it was Robert Taylor. Acting came later."

She met her share of leading men. She met Burt Lancaster at a Hollywood party. She was drunk at the time, a not uncommon condition for her in those days. She tried to punch him in the nose for reasons she can't entirely recall. It took Humphrey Bogart to lead her away from a puzzled and bemused Lancaster and care for her.

She met Lawrence Olivier, too, whom she addressed as "Sir God." She was close with Marilyn Monroe, Montgomery Clift, Lillian Hellman, Colleen Dewhurst and Tennessee Williams, to name just a few. She remains close with Ann Jackson and Eli Wallach and Julie Harris and just about every other major figure of her time in American stage and film. They're all in her book.

But this author won't be doing the usual publicity tour—appearing on Jay Leno and Regis and Kathie Lee or the other talk shows. She doesn't drive, and she gets the willies riding over high bridges. She can't take long trips on a train; they make her nervous. She won't go to California; earthquakes. She has a bum knee, so climbing stairs is out. So are elevators. She lives in mortal terror of them. Planes, too.

"I've never forgiven the Wright brothers," she said. "I want the whole world to travel in golf carts, or by horse and buggy. What's the big rush?"

Fourteen years in analysis didn't solve much for Maureen Stapleton. She has had to learn to wrestle with the demons by herself—or to live with them. They were born in her on First Street, in a house where Jack and Irene Stapleton were joined in a stormy union doomed by Jack's relentless boozing and evil disposition. It was a house to escape from, and Maureen did—into Troy's five movie theaters, almost every day.

By age 10 or so, she knew precisely what she wanted to be, which was somebody else. She told the family that she'd be an actress when she grew up. They patted her on the head and said, "That's nice." It was a huge, pie-in-the-sky dream for an Irish girl from First Street in the Depression years.

Then she went and did it.

A year out of high school, having socked away a hundred bucks working at the Watervliet Arsenal, and Maureen Stapleton was off for New York. She went to acting school and paid for it with work in department stores and modeling nude for art students. She did what it took. She was going to meet Robert Taylor.

Then the stage work began to come. For much of her life she has carried some extra weight, so she got roles in her 20s as mothers. She always played older. That's where the work was. And once she got started, the talent—that enormous gift the demons gave her—carried her up and up.

But the demons demanded their due. Demons are like that.

They cost her two husbands. They led her to booze and pills and a brush with death that scared the hell out of her. The demons gave her marvelous, fascinating years of breathtaking highs and heart-rending lows—a surging, roller coaster ride of a life that, for the last eight years, has centered on Lenox and her nearby grandchildren. She would work again, but it would have to be work close to home.

"I can't travel any more," she told me, smiling slightly beneath her crown of white hair. "I could go to Toronto or New York, I suppose. If they'd shoot it around here—in Albany or Troy—then I'd be in Heaven. But otherwise? No, I don't think I can."

She spends her days grappling with crossword puzzles, entertaining her grandchildren and watching "Jeopardy" and "Wheel of Fortune." She watches Angela Lansbury, too, and old movies. She never watches films in which she appeared.

"I can't learn anything," she said. "All I can see is my fat ass and my fat nose, so I can't evaluate."

Her younger brother, her aunt and her oldest and dearest friends are in and around Troy, and she sees them.

They tell her that the old neighborhood has gone bad. She can't see it.

"I was there on First Street about a year ago," she told me, "and it looked exactly the same, and it seemed exactly the same. I don't get back to Troy as often as I'd like. I really feel great over there. When I was young, I couldn't wait to get out."

She never got to meet Robert Taylor, though. He was dead by the time she was big enough in the movies to move in those circles.

"Nor Clark Gable," she said, puffing on her cigarette. "Joel McCrea I met. He was the third one. Then it became a job, a profession. But you have to be blind to do it."

Maureen Stapleton gazed at the ashtray for a long moment, remembering.

Then she said, "I don't know if I could have done anything else."

—*August 30, 1995*

Capra's Town

Fran Caraccilo saw the movie—really paid attention to it, that is—maybe 25 years ago. We're talking about Frank Capra's "It's a Wonderful Life."

If you've never seen this film, rent it. By modern standards, it's hopelessly sappy. But the story and the characters still work, five full decades later.

It's about George Bailey, who operates a small savings and loan association. George yearns to experience the world. But obligation to his family and to the savings and loan tie him firmly to Bedford Falls—a tiny, upstate New York mill town with a river running through it.

Bedford Falls is populated by Irish and Italian immigrants who work the mills. They're kept in tenements by Henry Potter, an evil banker played with masterful malice by Lionel Barrymore. He and George clash when George builds Bailey Park, a low-cost housing development for working people.

Potter gets even. Find out how when you rent the movie. One snowy night near Christmas, a dejected George Bailey is ready to commit suicide by jumping off a bridge. Then his guardian angel appears and shows him how horrible life would have been for all the people in town if George had never lived.

The moral: you don't have to travel the world to change it. Even small lives have enormous value when they're lived with courage and compassion.

Today, Fran Caraccilo is 42 and the village planner in Seneca Falls, about 185 miles west of Albany on Route 20. He's the town's leading local history buff. He's convinced that Bedford Falls was modeled on Seneca Falls. Me, too.

You have the Seneca River and the bridge—that's the Bridge Street bridge, visible from Fall Street in this pretty town of 8,000 or so. And you have the history.

Caraccilo is certain that George Bailey was modeled after John Rumsey, a 19th century Seneca Falls factory owner who built low-cost housing for his Irish and Italian immigrant employees. He even advanced them the money for down payments on houses in what was then called Rumseyville.

"Who was Henry Potter modeled after?" I asked Fran Caraccilo the other day.

"That's a tough one," he said. "That's dangerous to get into."

Which means that Henry Potter's descendants still live in town and, presumably, still enjoy some clout all these years later. Such are the joys of small town living.

The parallels between Bedford Falls and Seneca Falls

are positively uncanny. There's no evidence that the script writers, Frances Goodrich and Albert Hackett, ever heard of the place. That's apparently true also of Philip Van Doren Stern, a noted writer of Civil War books whose story, "The Greatest Gift," was the source of the movie. But director Frank Capra had an aunt who lived nearby, and he got his hair cut occasionally in a shop on Seneca Falls' main street. Odds are that he heard the stories about Rumsey and his battle with the local power brokers.

Certainly the set constructed for the movie bears an uncanny resemblance to real-life Seneca Falls, but was that by design or merely a coincidence? Did Capra recognize Seneca Falls in the story he encountered in later life? Was that one of the factors that led him to make the movie? Unfortunately, Capra and the writers are all dead now, so there's nobody to ask.

The fact is, too, that Seneca Falls doesn't really need recognition as Bedford Falls. As the home of Elizabeth Cady Stanton and the site of the first women's rights convention in 1848—not to mention an entire national park devoted to feminism—Seneca Falls attracts 30,000 tourists a year.

Last month, though, Denison, Iowa—the hometown of Donna Reed, who played George's wife—threw a big party to celebrate the movie's 50th anniversary. Donna Reed was the biggest thing ever to come out of that town. And Chamber of Commerce people believe firmly that every time a cash register rings, another angel gets his wings.

But Denison isn't Bedford Falls. Seneca Falls is.

Even if none of it ever really happened.

—*July 31, 1996*

A Wonderful Life

In early 1941, my father's younger brother, Jim, was stationed with the U.S. Army Air Corps at Moffett Field on San Francisco Bay.

One day, a new soldier showed up on base. He was a 32-year-old corporal named Jimmy Stewart. The year before, he'd won an Oscar for his performance in a movie called "The Philadelphia Story."

My uncle was a 22-year-old airplane mechanic. Stewart was a drill instructor fighting to get into flight training. My Uncle Jim couldn't believe he was serving with a movie star.

"He was a very lean, slender fellow," Jim Lynch told me yesterday when I called him in Elmira, where he lives. "He didn't weigh 200 pounds, and he was about six foot three or four. But he was tall and lean and long-waisted. He looked entirely different than he did on the screen. . . .

"I asked him why the hell he went and joined the army like I did. In 1941, the war was on in Europe and everything, but I was just looking to my future. And he told me he was doing the same thing."

Stewart was a bachelor at the time and a devoted private pilot. He'd decided that flying was more important to him than making movies. His studio contract wouldn't permit him to fly as a civilian. It was apparently silent on him flying as a soldier.

"They were still paying him," my uncle told me yesterday, the day Jimmy Stewart died in Hollywood at age 89. "He was getting twenty five hundred bucks a week. And he would donate it each week to something different—like, you know, the USO or this or that. He wouldn't accept the checks. . . .

"He made sergeant while I was there. What I admired about him was that he'd get right in the payroll line the first day of the month. He was making all of about 80 bucks a month as a sergeant.

"And he'd get in that line and sweat it out just like all the rest of us to pick up that 80 dollars. Meanwhile, he was turning down 2,500 bucks a week that they were sending him....

"We used to kid him because he had a thing for Lana Turner at the time. Whenever one of her movies came to the post, he'd go to see the movie. And we'd sneak in behind him and make raw remarks about Lana Turner.

"He was a regular fella. He drove an old car, and he'd let you take it if you wanted....

"I remember the day he came down to qualify as a pilot. I handed him his parachute. In order to fly in a military plane, you had to draw a parachute. And, of course, you had to sign for it. So I grabbed that and said, 'That's my autograph.' He qualified and went off to multi-engine school to fly the big bombers....

"Stewart went on to become a flight commander. He flew about 40 or 50 combat missions.... He was a leader, and he was a great, great guy."

Jimmy Stewart stayed in the reserves after the war. He ended up a brigadier general. He also resumed a glorious career in films. His great gift was his ability to portray himself on screen as an essentially decent man whose only concern was figuring out the right thing to do.

Then simply doing it.

And, according to my Uncle Jim, who knew him long ago, Jimmy Stewart was never really acting.

—July 3, 1997

A Mother's Wrath

I was maybe 6 years old—7, tops.

The President was an old bald guy named Eisenhower, who'd been a soldier once. The heavyweight champion of the world was Rocky Marciano, from up around Boston.

The biggest movie star in the world was John Wayne. The hottest singer around was somebody named Patti Page, who sang about doggies in windows. And there was this boring guy on our 12-inch, black-and-white Emerson television set at least a couple of nights a week. His name was Arthur Godfrey. He played a ukulele.

That was what the world was like the day that Gene Autry knocked me out cold. And—it scares me to think about it—but I remember it like it was yesterday.

Those were the thoughts that hit me the other night. I was listening to the radio when the news came on. Gene Autry was dead at 91.

I thought to myself, "He was how old? Good God!"

The wanton hours fly past. Mark Twain said that. Or, maybe I just think it was him who said it because I grew up in the town where he spent much of his life. You think of Mark Twain, and you think of the Mississippi. But he was a struggling writer with a terrific line of bullfeathers who'd married the richest woman in Elmira, N.Y.

Twain lived out his warm weather days in my home town, sucking up bourbon and scribbling, largely on the old lady's dime. When I was a kid, the downtown hotel was named after him. That's where Gene Autry knocked me cold.

I suppose I ought to explain that.

Gene Autry came to town to put on a few shows at the Colonial Theater, only a block from where Twain's wife's family's house had stood. The city fathers, in their wisdom, had long before permitted the house to be torn down and a shopping plaza to be erected on its site. But Autry's only interest in anything remotely connected to Mark Twain was the hotel bar, the Connecticut Yankee Lounge, to which he retreated between shows.

My mother had taken me to one of those shows. Afterwards, she'd dragged me across the street to the hotel restaurant for ice cream. Then Gene Autry himself had entered, with his cowboy hat and his camel hair overcoat. He retreated to the bar for sustenance before cruising back across the street for the next show.

When Autry came in, I was so excited that I spit ice cream clear across the table. My mother ordered me to settle down, but I couldn't. I kept slipping away from the table to peek through the swinging doors to the bar and watch Gene Autry slug down manhattans. He never did that in the movies.

Finally, Gene Autry got up, threw some bills on the bar and hit those swinging doors, catching me right between the eyes. I went out like a light. First graders have glass jaws.

I awakened to see Gene Autry against a wall, wide-eyed, with my mother about to rip him into shreds while a frantic waiter pleaded with her to, "Please, lady, calm down." Finally, she did, and Gene Autry hustled out of the place like it was on fire.

For the rest of her life, my mother never had a good word to say about Gene Autry. I always liked the guy, although not as much as I liked Roy Rogers, my very first hero, who died in July.

I met Roy Rogers once, too, in 1974, in one of his fast-food restaurants on Long Island. I was surprised to discover that Roy Rogers was sort of a little guy—very gracious and polite, but short. My mother wasn't very big, either.

But she probably could have kicked his butt, too.

—*October 4, 1998*

Dad's Kind of Guy

Al Lewis was my old man's hero.

When I was in high school, there was this top-rated television show called, "Car 54, Where Are You?" It was a comedy about two New York City cops.

Al Lewis had a supporting role. His character had a wife named Rose, who could talk a blue streak. Every time Rose would launch into one of her machine-gun monologues, Al Lewis would sit there on our black-and-white TV screen, utterly silent and scowling darkly.

After a while, he would get fed up and snap, "That's all, Rose!" And, instantly—in mid-word—Rose would clamp her mouth shut, like she'd broken her jaw.

At which point the old man would turn to my mother and say, "Why don't you ever do that for me, dammit?"

And the war would be on—every Sunday night, religiously.

So, I remember Al Lewis from "Car 54" much more vividly than I recall him from "The Munsters." In that show, he played Grandpa, who was a vampire. He had gray streaks in his hair and this terrific flowing cape. Grandpa was a vampire with a marvelously guttural New York accent, which you didn't see much in those days.

But when Grandpa told somebody, "That's all," it never was. Nobody ever did anything Grandpa wanted done. That's because, given the fact that he was a vampire, Grandpa was a bit of a wuss.

Al Lewis had this terrific career as one of the best character actors of his time. Now, after starting a public affairs talk radio show in New York City, he's probably going to run for governor. I wish the old man was alive to see this.

He would be out banging on doors for Al Lewis. He would have Al Lewis signs on his lawn. He would have an Al Lewis bumper sticker next to his American flag decal—right where he placed bumper stickers for other lefties like Gene McCarthy and George McGovern.

There's No Business Like Show Business

The old man never met a leftie he didn't like. And, the other day when I talked to Al Lewis, I found myself liking him, too. How do you not like a guy who says he's 16 the hard way—two eights?

If you don't know what's going on here, I'll explain:

In New York, a political party can be legally recognized only if its candidate for governor gets 50,000 votes. If that happens, the party is automatically on the ballot for the next four years. If a party isn't on the ballot, its candidate has to obtain 15,000 signatures on petitions to get on the ballot in any statewide election, which is a serious pain.

The Green Party, which is about as far left as you can get without coming out and fessing up to being a commie, is thinking about running Al Lewis for governor. The Greens figure that a good many people remember and feel deep affection for Al Lewis, and he just might get 50,000 votes for the party this fall.

That could happen, too. When the Greens got Ralph Nader on the New York ballot for President in 1996, he pulled about 75,000 votes. And Ralph Nader is nowhere as funny as Al Lewis.

He may also not be as bright, either. Sixty-seven years ago, Al Lewis got a doctorate from Columbia in child psychology. He figures that'll help him in dealing with reporters.

Al Lewis doesn't expect to win this election, and he shouldn't. If he does, though, he says he'll be nice to the journalists who cover the governor.

Which would be a pleasant change of pace, actually.

—*May 18, 1998*

Ah, Yes, I Remember It Well

"You'd better call me," the guy said into my voice mail last Friday. "Clearly, you have a medical problem."

I called right back. "So, what's this medical problem I have?"

"You apparently suffer from a severe memory disorder," he said. "In today's paper, you wrote about Al Lewis, the old actor who might run for governor for the Green Party. You said he played a character on 'Car 54, Where are You?' You said that in the show he had a wife named Rose who babbled on and on until Al Lewis said, 'That's all, Rose.' And she would shut her mouth like a bear trap."

"Right," I said. "That Al Lewis character was my father's greatest hero. He liked Al Lewis even better than he'd liked Roosevelt."

"Well, the actor in that show whose character was married to Rose was Carl Ballantine, not Al Lewis."

"Carl Ballantine? I remember him. He was in 'McHale's Navy.' Also, didn't he also have some kind of comedy magic act he did on TV?"

"Same guy. And on 'Car 54,' he was the guy married to Rose with the big mouth."

"Then who was the Al Lewis character?" I demanded.

"He played a guy named Schnauzer. Schnauzer had a wife named Sylvia. She wouldn't shut up either—especially not if Schnauzer told her to."

"Wait a minute," I said. "The whole premise of that column was that if my father were alive he'd have been voting for Al Lewis for governor this year because he loved that character so much. And you're telling me that I had Al Lewis playing the the wrong character?"

"Trust me," he said.

"How do you know this?" I demanded. "That show was on TV years ago."

"I used to watch 'Car 54' all the time. And from your picture in the paper, I figure that I'm a few years older than you

There's No Business Like Show Business

are. You were just a kid then, right?"

"Yeah," I said, "but I remember all kinds of stuff from those years. That show came on when Malcolm Rockefeller was governor."

"Nelson Rockefeller," he told me, "It was Malcolm Wilson."

"Are you sure? I thought it was Nelson Harriman."

"No, that was Averill Harriman. Good God, didn't you check that stuff on Al Lewis?"

"Sure, I checked. The clippings said that Al Lewis was in the show. I even talked to the guy about what a great show it was. And I remember minute details from when I was a kid. For example, I vividly remember Roy Rogers and Dale Evans. And I remember Roy's palomino horse, Champion."

"Roy's horse was Trigger. Gene Autry's horse was Champion."

"No, it wasn't. Gene Autry's horse was Topper."

"That was Hopalong Cassidy's horse, you dope!" he bellowed into the phone.

"Oh, yeah?" I yelled back. "Well, for your information, smart guy, I know for a fact that Hoppy rode a snow white stallion named Silver."

He slammed down the phone, and I did some more research. The guy was right on everything—Carl Ballantine, Al Lewis, Trigger, Champion, Topper, all of it. And I've heard from several other people since.

One guy even sang me the show's theme song—"There's a scout troop short a child, Khrushchev's due at Idlewild, Car 54 where are you?"

So, Al Lewis is on deck to run for governor and not Carl Ballantine, which means that the old man probably wouldn't be as thrilled as I first thought.

Milton Caesar, though. The old man would vote for him in a heartbeat.

—May 22, 1998

Old Blue Eyes

I wasn't much of a fan. I thought that Perry Como and Vic Damone had better voices—not to mention Sammy Davis, Jr. I thought that Steve Lawrence and Mel Torme had smoother technique.

And, from what I'd read, Sinatra hadn't struck me as anybody I would like on a personal level. Here was this rich, immensely successful guy who'd thrust himself in the public eye well before I'd been born. And he was punching out news photographers—or having one of his knuckle-dragging goons do it for him.

Or he was calling female reporters vile names. Sinatra had an extensive vocabulary for women, apparently.

I wasn't wild about the mob ties thing, either. In my line of work, I'd come across a few of those guys. They weren't my favorite people. Ring-a-ding-ding didn't do it for me; neither did scoobie-doobie-doo.

But Sinatra was into his 60s at the time, and some friends were urging my wife and me to join them in seeing him at Carnegie Hall before he pulled an Elvis—which, in fact, he finally did the other day. So, we went.

He sat on the stage in a tux, fronting a huge orchestra, smoking as he sang and sipping liquor between numbers, speaking only rarely. And, though the voice had begun to falter even then from age and booze and tobacco, I was a fan when he finished.

You have to reach a certain age to appreciate Sinatra. You have to know what love is all about once the dew has dripped off the roses. You have to let life elbow you in the gut a few times. And you have to grasp instinctively that your only choice is to keep on going, making the best of everything, staying intensely alert for the moments that make living a worthwhile activity.

That's what Sinatra sang about so beautifully. And I'm talking here about the mature Sinatra, the guy with the receding hairline and the lines in his cheeks—not the skinny kid in the bow tie who's only a silky voice on a record for somebody my age. And certainly not the ancient, bloated Sinatra with the Marc Antony rug who barked out lyrics with which he'd once made magic.

The mature Sinatra had matchless musical taste. He sang about adversity and defiance and loss and the determined management of grief. He sang about rolling with the punches as they rain down relentlessly. And he did it gently, without cynicism—with just a sad, worldly resignation.

He sang "The Wee Small Hours of the Morning" that night at Carnegie Hall. He sang "Quarter to Three." He sang "All The Way." We sat well back in the theater, listening to that smoky, boozy voice caress the lyrics. And, since that night, I've often found myself in the car hitting the seek button in a quest for some easy listening station, hoping they'd play a little Sinatra as I cruised the highway.

We don't really know entertainers, even though some of us delude ourselves that we do. The Sinatra of film was not a real person. But whatever his thuggish tendencies in real life, the Sinatra of the tuxedo and cigarette resonated with anybody who has lived long enough to have loved and lost—or to have taken one or two of life's thumbs squarely in the eye.

Sinatra the man was apparently a study in contrasts—alternately vicious and generous, a wretched husband but a doting father, a friend to some who didn't deserve friendship but capable of instilling enormous affection in countless worthwhile people who knew him intimately.

Like Picasso and Mozart, a profoundly flawed human being.

But, also like them, an artist of towering powers.

—May 17, 1998

The Fading Lights

At the Broadway ticket kiosk in Times Square, panhandlers circle the line of tourists like sharks in feeding frenzy. They display an uncanny ability to zero in on out-of-towners.

"Spare change?" I'm asked by a guy who looks disturbingly like Charles Manson.

Politely, I explain that I can't imagine a circumstance—including my winning the Irish Sweepstakes and the New York Lottery on the same day—that could conceivably result in my possession of "spare" money. Manson shrugs and moves on to a Japanese guy festooned with cameras.

"Spare yen?" Charlie asks.

A block or two away, on Eighth Avenue, another facet of the city's face reveals itself in the form of young women who seem to find me dazzlingly attractive. I'm repeatedly asked if I want to go out. I decline politely. I'm extremely married.

Plus, I'm not eager to spend the next decade or two on antibiotics.

Life around Times Square—beggars and hookers and Broadway. This city has everything.

Broadway has changed, though. Neil Simon refused to open his new comedy here. The costs were too high. He took it off-off Broadway and figured his name would carry it. Musicals are doing well here, but they tend to be musicals launched abroad first—"Miss Saigon," "Phantom of the Opera." Both opened in London and came to Broadway after they'd made names for themselves.

More and more, it appears that the original American musical—a show like "Camelot" or "Oklahoma"—is a thing of the past. Tommy Tune will open soon in "Busker Alley," but economics threaten the show's success.

At $70 a ticket, audiences no longer see musicals without reputations, whether those reputations are first established elsewhere or were established in years past. That explains the explosion of revivals on Broadway. Moreover, with the cost of mounting a Broadway musical in the 1990s approaching $8 million, investors won't take chances on unproven productions—except, perhaps, a review featuring music the audience will recognize, something like "Crazy for You" or "Smokey Joe's Cafe."

In the glory days of the American musical, ticket sales were only part of the business. Broadway songs became hit records and brought in bucks long after the show closed. Hollywood made lavish movies of Broadway musicals.

Today, though, hit records are made by hip-hop groups, and the movies haven't adapted a musical since "Grease" nearly two decades ago. "Evita" is still under option, but the movie might never be made. If the Broadway costs are outrageous, musical production costs in Hollywood are bloodcurdling.

Even the revivals and foreign-mounted musicals are hardly sure things. To lure audiences, Broadway has stooped in recent years to hiring movie and TV performers with no stage credentials.

Jerry Lewis reportedly negotiated $40,000 a week plus a percentage of the profits to star in "Damn Yankees," which made him the highest paid Broadway performer ever. Glenn Close pulled down a reported 30 grand a week in "Sunset Boulevard."

But "Damn Yankees" was foundering before Lewis came aboard. So was the revival of "Grease" before Brooke Shields joined up. And so was "Kiss of the Spider Woman" before Vanessa Williams was hired.

What's sad about all this is that we Americans have invented only two major forms of musical art—jazz and the classic American musical. Jazz remains a functioning creative form, but the original American musical seems to be running out its string.

Unless you're willing to cough up $70 bucks to see Burt Reynolds as King Arthur, that is.

—September 22, 1995

POLITICIANS, PERVERSE PRIORITIES AND PUZZLED PEOPLE

The Madman's Big Day

It was a gray, grim, bitter downer of a day. The wind whipped wickedly across the Saratoga National Battlefield in Stillwater, bending trees and slicing through clothing.

Like a fool, I hadn't worn a coat. But the wind's bite helped me understand the surge of desperation that must have swept over a shivering Gentleman Johnny Burgoyne 221 years ago this month.

Burgoyne was 54—tall, handsome, an ambitious member of Parliament, a prominent member of England's soldier-politician class. Yes, the rebel army before him was larger than his. And, no, the reinforcements he'd been expecting from New York City weren't coming. And, yes, he knew that his plan to crush the colonials in a bold strike from Quebec had failed.

But it was too late for Gen. Burgoyne and his hired German troops to flee back to Canada. It had taken him many months to fight his way this far south. Now, he couldn't make safe haven in Quebec before the brutal northern winter enveloped him. Fighting was Burgoyne's best chance, his only chance. Despite the odds, he might even have pulled off a victory.

If not for the madman.

I was at the battleground that day to seek out the madman's monument. I found it amid a stand of trees. It's a small statue of a cavalryman's high boot. It rises inside a black steel fence. The monument honors the battle's boldest hero. But it never mentions his name.

Politicians, Perverse Priorities and Puzzled People   43

That's because the great hero of that momentous battle at Saratoga—the military confrontation that convinced the French king that the rebels could win and that he should finance the American Revolution—was a surly, hot-headed, hard-drinking lunatic named Benedict Arnold.

He'd been a druggist in Connecticut. When war broke out, he left his wife and children to fight. By 36, he was a general—and a widower. After the loss of his wife, Arnold seemed not to care if he lived or died. His mindless bravery inspired his troops. He was, by most accounts, the finest battlefield commander of the war.

At Saratoga, after an initial engagement with the British, Arnold clashed with his boss, a stodgy bureaucrat named Horatio Gates. Gates fretted that Arnold was too rash. Arnold was relieved of his command and confined to his tent.

When the forests rang with the sound of Burgoyne's second attack, however, Arnold roared out of that tent. He mounted a horse, galloped wildly around the camp, then used his sword hilt to smash open a cask of whiskey. He grabbed a dipper and shot down jolt after jolt of liquid courage.

Soldiers surrounded the general, curious and amused. Then he wiped his mouth with the back of his hand and threw the dipper to the ground. He pointed his sword skyward and urged the men to follow him toward the sound of the guns. When he galloped off, they did just that.

Arnold and his force hit the middle of the British line, breaking it. He took a slug through the leg. His horse went down, crushing the wounded leg. Benedict Arnold was carried from the field by cheering soldiers, his agony deadened by glory.

The following year, he was given command of Philadelphia. There he met a pretty woman, Peggy Shippen, a royalist. Arnold married her. Soon, he was a royalist, too. Then he became a traitor, almost managing to deliver the fort at West Point to the British.

He fled to England. At 60, gravely ill, he asked to be

dressed in his Continental Army uniform. Then the madman died.

But his leg is memorialized at Saratoga, inside that steel fence.

On a monument to the only honorable part of Benedict Arnold's body.

—October 13, 1998

A Giant's Disappointment

I have a friend whose father labored in the service of Nelson Rockefeller. It was interesting duty, I'm told.

My friend's father was in New York's executive mansion on Eagle Street in Albany the morning the architects brought in their model of the Empire State Plaza—the huge government complex that Rockefeller dreamed of building in downtown Albany. The model portrayed a collection of tall, sleek, modernistic towers looming up over a vast mall.

Rockefeller, eating breakfast, studied the model closely through his black-rimmed glasses. Then, my friend's father told him, Rockefeller removed one of the towers and replaced it with his soft-boiled egg in its cup.

"That's what I want," he rasped out.

That's what he got, too—a performing arts center known today throughout upstate New York as "The Egg" because it looks like one. Is this story true? Nelson Rockefeller is dead nearly two decades. I can't ask him. My friend's father is also gone.

But if it isn't true, it could be. Rockefeller always knew

what he wanted. He got it, too—with one conspicuous exception.

It was a raw day when I thought of Rocky and went out to study his creation—that huge governmental complex that people in state government sometimes refer to as "Rockefeller's erection." A white winter sun sprinkled diamond dust on the Hudson as a bitter, bone-chilling wind rampaged down Albany's State Street hill. At the edge of the vast mall that sprawls to the south of New York's red-roofed Capitol building, a lone state worker sat on a bench, shivering in her coat, eating lunch out of a brown paper bag.

Anything to be outdoors in the rare glare of the sun during the upstate winter. Anything to breathe in the sheer space the Empire State Plaza offers in an old, gray city of attached buildings huddled tightly on a hill above a river.

That, I think, was part of what Nelson Rockefeller had in mind when he conceived of the plaza. He wanted that stark, naked plain of concrete as the center of his monument to himself. He might have wanted to afford his state's public servants a chance to experience a few moments of freedom during draining days of office drudgery.

Rockefeller hit Albany like a hurricane nearly 40 years ago—a dynamo of drive, desire and energy. He radiated the boundless self-confidence you get when somebody hands you 200 million bucks at age 21.

Not quite one of the folks, that Rocky. I knew a reporter, the late Pat Brasley of *Newsday*, who had to explain to Nelson Rockefeller the meaning of the phrase "take-home pay."

Rockefeller wrested the office of governor from Averill Harriman, who'd also earned his money the old-fashioned way—by inheriting it. Rockefeller then bent New York to the shape he'd envisioned in his fertile mind. He created an enormous governmental machine that his latest successor, George Pataki, seems bent on dismantling today. He imagined the plaza, his own private Brasilia.

When balky legislators threatened to stand in his way, he went completely around them. He bonded the thing through Albany County and gave the mayor, Erastus Corning 2nd, the non-bid insurance contract on the project as a reward.

Rockefeller was a visionary, a schemer and a doer. He was a larger-than-life figure who towered like a colossus over New York's political landscape—and the nation's, too. He was also a spirited womanizer who checked out in the company of a lady young enough to be his granddaughter—precisely the way he'd have wanted to go.

He was a man of huge flaws and huge accomplishments—a giant of his time who's worth remembering in a more modest era of smaller dreams and conspicuously smaller politicians. For all his victories, one prize forever eluded his relentless grasp. Nelson Rockefeller never got to be President.

Even giants suffer their disappointments.

—*January 26, 1996*

Bashing the Kennedys

The death of John F. Kennedy, Jr., seems to pose a perplexing problem for Kennedy-haters—or, at least, for the ones who called me yesterday.

They can't criticize JFK, Jr. for romancing mobster molls, like his old man. They can't fault him for an unseemly thirst for booze and broads, like his Uncle Teddy. They can't even accuse him of political naivete. Young JFK never really expressed a partisan sentiment.

They can't accuse him of laziness or stupidity or greed. He went through an Ivy League university and a tough law school. He finally passed what's probably the roughest bar

Politicians, Perverse Priorities and Puzzled People 47

exam in the country. Instead of hooking up with some ritzy Wall Street firm, he used his education to prosecute purse-snatchers before starting up a fairly classy national magazine.

JFK, Jr. did all this, by the way, when he could have used his inherited wealth and movie-star looks to loll on the beach in Cannes with a blonde on each arm—and who would have blamed him for it?

So, they're stuck with assailing him for hubris—for letting his courage as a fledgling pilot outweigh his skills. And they do that when nobody knows yet just what really happened over the sea off Martha's Vineyard. No experienced pilot I've heard is ready yet to level those criticisms. I'm hearing them, though, from people whose most intimate experience with aviation is watching Sky King reruns on TV Land.

The Kennedy-haters are stuck with wailing about the excessive media coverage of the death of somebody whose bloodlines they dislike. They also complain bitterly about all the taxpayer resources devoted to finding the plane's wreckage and the bodies. Several people who called me yesterday moaned that nobody paid this much attention last October when a 49-year-old Albany lawyer named Ronald H. Sinzheimer died in the crash of a private plane he was piloting in the same general area.

They're right about that, too. Sinzheimer's death was Metro Page news in this newspaper, not front-page news all around the world. And the Coast Guard used a single helicopter to search for the wreckage of Sinzheimer's plane while this search involves a flotilla of air and sea vessels that rivals the D-Day invasion.

But this is a scandal?

Ronald H. Sinzheimer, I'm told, was a fine man of substance and accomplishment. He was not, however, the son of a President and the nephew of two U.S. senators. He was not somebody whose daily life was of intense interest to millions.

Get real, Kennedy-haters. This is the best you can do? The fact is that JFK, Jr. was a significant man from a significant family.

You might not understand what the first JFK's election 39 years ago meant to the one in six Americans of Irish extraction. His entry into the White House signified, quite simply, that we finally were full-fledged Americans.

In retrospect, his 1,000-day presidency wasn't momentous in terms of substance. But his style and personal grace made us proud. JFK's son, as a public man in his own right, demonstrated those qualities in wide-screen technicolor. In a tabloid era that would have made his philandering father a figure of derision, young JFK relentlessly exuded class, quality and character.

From all reports, this was a thoughtful, responsible guy who understood that millions he never knew had expectations of him—not that he become President, but that he live life in a way that reflected credit on both himself and on those who recall what his father represented. Until that plane crash Saturday night, that's precisely what JFK, Jr. did.

So, Kennedy-haters, give it a rest, OK? Wait until Teddy checks out.

Then you can live it up.

—*July 20, 1999*

The Ordinary Folks

The man who might have been President was sitting behind a microphone on the second floor of a city building at 200 Henry Johnson Blvd.

It's time to move on, Al Gore was telling the crowd of Albany politicians, media people and community activists.

Politicians, Perverse Priorities and Puzzled People

The U.S. Senate just voted against throwing Bill Clinton out of office. Now, let's put this thing behind us.

This was Friday. About 100 onlookers were gathered across the street. Two cops sat astride horses between the people and the building in which the vice president was speaking. They'd caught only a glimpse of Al Gore as he'd gone in.

One onlooker was a white guy who stood out in a mostly black crowd. He waved a sign. It read, "Al Gore is Clinton's whore."

The sign caught my eye as I came out of the city building. Then I saw a scuffle erupt around the guy. I hustled across the pavement, between the two mounted cops, losing sight of the fool with the sign behind one of the police horses.

What a suicidal move, waving that sign on that day in the most dependably Democratic ward of this dependably Democratic city. When I got there, I glanced around, looking for the demonstrator.

"What happened to the guy with the sign?" I asked somebody in the crowd, who said that his name was Dennis and that he teaches school.

"He's over there," Dennis told me. "Somebody grabbed his sign."

"Oh, then he's not dead."

Dennis laughed. "No, he's not dead. Hey, this is America. Everybody has a right to an opinion."

Then I spotted the guy who'd waved the sign. His sign was dead, but he was OK. He was standing there, noticeably subdued. He didn't strike me as particularly happy at the moment. Then again, nobody in that crowd seemed particularly happy.

They'd come to see Al Gore, the guy who'll probably be the Democratic party's presidential nominee next year. But Al Gore was across the street, inside that building, hanging out with Albany's big shots. And the ordinary folks who'd gathered to see him were huddled on Henry Johnson Boulevard under skies of battleship gray with a couple of mounted cops between them and the auditorium where Al Gore was calling for unity in a deeply divided country.

"He ought to come out here," one guy told me.

"Security," I said. "Ever since Reagan got shot, the Secret Service goes nuts when these guys go into crowds. Clinton does it once in a while. He must give the Secret Service heart attacks."

The guy was a fairly big man of early middle age, bearded, clutching a rose in his hand. He told me that his name was Rainbo Star—no "W."

"Any relation to Ken Starr?" I asked him.

"No. I've been here for two months. I was homeless when I got here. I came in from Santa Cruz, California. I'm here today for the homeless veterans. They ought to bring welfare back."

I said, "You left California to come to Albany in December? Good plan."

Rainbo Star said he'd been here once before, a few years ago. He'd come back to Albany because he figured he could get an apartment. They're cheaper here.

Somebody asked if he was a veteran. Rainbo Star said he doesn't like to answer questions. Nobody thought it was a good idea to ask him any more.

So, we stood there on the sidewalk—me and Dennis the teacher and Rainbo Star and the dopey guy who'd waved the sign. And, inside the building across the street, the man who might have been President talked about the need for us all to get along after this impeachment nightmare.

And, somehow, we will.

—February 14, 1999

The Old Warrior

Bob Dole of Russell, Kansas, and Washington, D.C. is finally hitting his stride in his Ahab-like quest for the White House. Yesterday evening, as he stood before a surging, cheering mob of party regulars in a hangar at Albany Airport, you could sense the scent of his party's nomination strengthening in his 72-year-old nostrils.

"America wants and demands leadership," he told the crowd. "This is a fight for the heart and soul of the Republican Party."

Bob Dole enjoyed a big win in South Carolina Saturday, and there's a boxcar full of delegates at stake in primaries around the nation today. And, two days from now, Dole goes into the New York primary with most polls favoring him and the party elite waging war on his behalf.

He desperately needs New York. Dole has burned nearly every dollar the law will permit him to spend on winning this nomination. And still Buchanan and Forbes and Alexander and the others snap relentlessly at his heels.

Between today and March 28, when Republicans in the nation-state of California cast their ballots, 70 per cent of the Republican party's convention delegates will be chosen in a swirling blizzard of primary elections.

If Dole does not have his party's nomination nailed down by then, his dream of two decades may well evaporate. Agree or disagree with this man, but recognize that, from a human perspective, this would be a tragedy beyond calculation.

I saw this once before. In 1972, Hubert Humphrey of Minnesota was 64 years old and chasing after the prize on which he'd fixed his eyes 35 years earlier. I was a young reporter, standing a few feet away as he announced his candidacy for the Democratic nomination.

"The great shame of 1968," Humphrey said, clutching his wife's hand, "was that Muriel didn't get to be first lady."

That summer, after he'd conceded the nomination to

George McGovern in Miami, I spoke briefly to Humphrey, asking him how he felt. I'd been a college kid when he'd lost to Nixon. I'd figured him then for a babbling fool. But I'd gotten to know him during the 1972 campaign—eating chicken sandwiches and drinking milk with him in his hotel room late at night.

The man was no fool—hardly that. The Oval Office was simply not in his destiny.

"It's not that important," he told me that day in Miami. "It's only a matter of who's elected President. There's more to life."

But not much more—not if you're a Hubert Humphrey or a Bob Dole in the twilight of a distinguished career and "Hail to the Chief" rings in your ears. If you have this virus—this lust to rule the world, as Mario Cuomo demonstrably did not—then you can go to your grave with a broken heart despite all your other triumphs.

Bob Dole stood at the microphone yesterday with the ever-present ballpoint pen clutched in his withered right hand—a daily reminder of the horrible war wound that forged this taciturn man's sturdy spirit five decades ago.

"America is a great place," he said, "the greatest place on the face of the Earth."

A campaign phrase—one of thousands that have fallen from his lips. But Bob Dole, his cheeks lined and the silver in his hair buried beneath dye, is in his last campaign now. The others were important—steps up the stairs toward this last, all-consuming battle. They had their meanings.

But for Bob Dole of Russell, Kansas, and Washington, D.C., this is the only campaign that has ever really mattered.

—March 4, 1996

Yeah, But Which Park?

Hillary Clinton has been warned repeatedly that a U.S. Senate run in New York would be no walk in the park.

That's why, I suppose, the First Lady has been calling Democratic party leaders around the state. So far, she supposedly has talked to roughly 200 of them. She has been asking about New York parks, presumably so she can take a walk in one. Recently, she got hold of an upstate party boss I know.

"Well," the boss told her, "we have many parks in New York. There's Washington Park, for example. That's in Albany, a few blocks west of the Capitol."

"Where, precisely, is Central Park?" Mrs. Clinton asked.

"That's in Schenectady," said the upstate boss.

"Really? I thought it was somewhere in Manhattan."

"They have one there, too, actually. It's east of Riverside Park."

"There's a river in Manhattan?" Hillary Clinton asked.

"Several. There's the Hudson River to the west, just east of New Jersey. Then there's the East River—to the east of Manhattan, naturally. The Harlem River is on the north, and New York Harbor is to the south."

"Then Manhattan is an island? I thought Staten Island was the island."

"They're both islands, Mrs. Clinton. Each is a borough of the City of New York. The city has three other boroughs as well."

"I know that. There's Brooklyn, Queens and Bronxville."

"Well, actually, it's Brooklyn, Queens and the Bronx. Bronxville is a community in Westchester. That's located just north of the Bronx."

"Really? And is there an Eastchester located south of the Bronx? Or a Southchester to the west? Or a Northchester to the east?"

"Uh, no."

"And Bronxville is part of Westchester?"

"Yes."

"That's a little confusing."

"If you think that's confusing, the City of Rensselaer is in Rensselaer County, but Rensselaerville is in Albany County, just west of the Hudson."

"Wait a minute. You just told me that the Hudson is west of Manhattan, and that New Jersey is west of the Hudson. How can The Hudson be just west of Rensselaer County and just east of Albany County? What happened to New Jersey?"

"Don't worry about it, Mrs. Clinton. You won't be campaigning there."

"Why not? I thought that's where the Giants and the Bills play."

"No, it's the Giants and the Jets who play there. The Bills play in Rich Stadium."

"And where's that?"

"Buffalo."

"I repeat, where's that?"

"It's near Ohio, Mrs. Clinton."

"Ohio? I don't want to campaign there. I'd rather campaign in New Jersey. Everything seems simpler there. For example, they named their high point High Point. What's New York's high point?"

"Uh, Mount Marcy, I guess."

"See what I mean? New York makes my head hurt."

"We can have that effect on outsiders, Mrs. Clinton. But you'll love it here. Wait until you see how pretty Columbia County is."

"I thought that Columbia was a university."

"It's a county, too, Mrs. Clinton. It's east of the Hudson."

"I thought that Manhattan and Rensselaer County were east of the Hudson."

"Well, it's quite a long river, Mrs. Clinton."

—*March 23, 1999*

Big Guys, a Big Deal

From a distance of 25 feet or so, the first thing you notice about Bill Clinton is that he's roughly the size of a Buick Park Avenue. The White House says he weighs 220 pounds.

In seventh grade, maybe. We're talking linebacker here. Huge dude, this guy.

Under a luminous fall sky of perfect blue, the President was clutching yesterday at Boris Yeltsin, whose dimensions more approximate those of a Lincoln Town Car. "Big presidents," Yeltsin called them, a couple of beefy bruisers.

Yeltsin and Clinton were wearing identical charcoal-gray business suits—purchased, apparently, off the same rack at the Head of State Boutique at Macy's. The President of the United States and the President of the Russian Federation were joined in a fierce hug on the steps of Franklin Delano Roosevelt's mansion.

As these behemoths embraced and pounded vigorously on one another's backs, you could almost hear bones crunch. If your brain worked like mine, an image of wrestling bears would pop unbidden into your head.

Welcome to yesterday's summit conference at the FDR home and library in Hyde Park. The mansion was decorated with red, white and blue bunting, and both American and Russian flags fluttered over the door. The weather cooperated for the occasion, but the bright sunlight highlighted how badly the big old house needs painting. Have no doubt that Clinton blamed those cheapskate Republicans in Congress.

Clinton and Yeltsin were in New York for the 50th anniversary of the United Nations. They needed to talk about Bosnia, and they wanted to do it someplace where they wouldn't have to say, "Hey, Fidel, pipe down," every five minutes.

So, here they were—two presidents; hundreds of cops and Secret Service Agents; another few hundred preppies in navy-blue, pin-striped political aide regulation outfits; enough satellite trucks to render half the males in Dutchess County sterile; about four million journalists, one metal detector and precisely six portable toilets.

The lines here yesterday were longer than the lines of people back in Russia forming up to shoot Boris Yeltsin.

"This is a great outing for the White House press corps," a Washington reporter told me as we sat in the sun waiting for something to happen. "Yesterday, we were all stuck in New York in the press center. This is wonderful."

The White House press corps, it would seem, is easily amused.

I'd never been to a summit conference, so I drove down from Albany in my 16-year-old Cadillac to witness this one. Clinton, as it turns out, brought three Cadillacs of his own—all shiny new limos.

Then he didn't use them. Instead, he and his minions arrived in an armada of deafening Marine helicopters, scattering leaves in all directions in the large field that separates Route 9 from Roosevelt's home, grave and library.

The President, in all his gray-clad hugeness, strolled along the tree-shaded path from the field to the house, waving at cameras and smiling broadly. He emerged when Yeltsin's two helicopters touched down 15 minutes or so later. Then the routine was walk back to the field, meet Boris in the field, walk with Boris to the house, hug Boris on the steps, pose with Boris for the cameras.

Then go inside and fight like hell with Boris over Bosnia.

At one point, the two of them went out back of the house for a glimpse of the fine Hudson River view the mansion offers, prompting a frenzy of excitement among camera people poised like starving vultures on the wooden platform erected outside the house.

A bee buzzed about Yeltsin's face. Clinton swatted at it.

For a second, it looked like he was taking a poke at Boris—which had 200 utterly delighted camera people clicking furiously. Then the presidents retreated inside, leaving reporters and camera people outside to swat at bees and munch cole slaw from White House box lunches.

After a while, I got bored and wandered out to Route 9, where I'd been told I could find anti-Yelstin protesters. Instead, I found a giant squad of cops lined up along the highway—national park police, state troopers, blue-clad Hyde Park patrolmen.

"Where're the protesters?" I asked.

"There was this one guy in a red beret," a national park cop told me. "He had a sign. It read, 'Yeltsin Sins Against Socialism.' He left, though."

There was an era in which the demonstrators outnumbered the cops—or, at least, the presidents—but we live in tamer times now. I went back to the house to resume waiting for anything that might resemble news.

The local TV people had already filed for the noon news and were sitting around hoping for an announcement, an assassination attempt—anything to break the boredom. Some radio guy called his office on a cellular phone.

"What do you mean how's it going?" he said. "I'm getting comatose."

Ah, the glamour of journalism.

About 1:30, the presidents emerged from the huge house to stroll over to the Roosevelt Library a few hundred yards away. Journalists swarmed along their roped-off route, snapping pictures and watching the two men stop and marvel over this bust of Roosevelt and that bust of Roosevelt—photo op stuff.

Secret Service agents with wires sticking out of their ears glared at the crowd of running reporters and photographers with undisguised suspicion, clearly eager for an excuse to shoot at least a few of them. Russian journalists shouted questions at Yeltsin. He waved at them in response. The Russian journalists scribbled hurried notes at each wave.

After a while, the routine was repeated when the presidents returned to the house, journalists scurrying along the rope corral after them. At 3:30 or so, Clinton and Yeltsin came out. They said they had a deal, details to be worked out later. Apparently, booze had been served with lunch.

You said this meeting would be a disaster, Yeltsin chided the reporters; you are a disaster. Clinton laughed so hard that his knees buckled and his face turned the color of cabernet.

Two big guys with at least that sentiment in common.

—October 24, 1995

Lubricating the Peace Process

You might recall that when Bill Clinton and Boris Yeltsin got together last week at Hyde Park, Clinton broke into an uncharacteristic fit of laughter at a remark Yelstin made during the joint press conference that followed the summit conference.

The President almost split a gut. Clinton turned bright red. His knees buckled. His eyes teared. He guffawed for a solid minute. White House press reporters said they'd never before seen the President break up like that. And he cracked up over a remark that turns out to have been mistranslated.

Yeltsin was chewing out the press corps for earlier stories expressing doubt that the summit would lead to anything substantial. Both Yeltsin and Clinton were there on the steps of the Roosevelt mansion proclaiming the summit a rousing success, although they would provide no real details.

Yeltsin spoke for a long time, forcefully and waving his arms. He paused only rarely for his translator to catch up with him. At one point, the harried translator quoted the Russian president as saying to the press, "You're a disaster."

That was when Clinton was hit with his attack of the giggles.

Only that's not precisely what Yeltsin said. According to several Russian speakers I know—including Dr. Sophie Lubensky, a Russian expert at UAlbany—Yeltsin's statement, *Vy provalilis,* translates roughly into "You failed" or "You made a mess of it" or "You botched things."

The Inuits supposedly have 15 distinct words for snow. The Russians have about 97 words or phrases for, "you blew it." Until just recently, those were usually the last words you heard just before being dragged off to the Gulag.

OK, so Yeltsin wasn't handing out roses to the press, but he wasn't slinging insults either. So why did Clinton find this so hilarious? I was on hand for this momentous occasion, and my theory at the time was that the president might have . . . well, had a drink or two.

After all, he was with Yeltsin, one of the more prodigious boozers ever to lurch unsteadily across the world stage. Plus, they had lunch together, and wine was served. A very good wine. And lots of it.

The Friday before the summit, the phone rang at Vinifera Wine Cellars in Hammondsport in the Finger Lakes. A wine consultant working for the White House wanted some bottles of Dr. Konstantin Frank's 1994 Dry Johannisburg Reisling for the two presidents to consume at lunch.

This reisling recently took two gold medals at state competitions. Dr. Frank's stuff enjoys a well-deserved reputation for quality. He was a Ukrainian viticulturist and vintner who perfected the technique of growing fine European grapes in general inhospitable North American soil. He's now dead, but his son and grandson run the winery, and they were thrilled at the chance to supply wine for the summit.

A phone call was made from Hammondsport to Larry

Reiter, wine manager for the Albany office of Eber Brothers, a wine and liquor distributorship. Reiter dispatched a salesman, John Smith, who lives in Kingston, with a supply of this fine wine. He delivered the stuff to Hyde Park just before the summit.

"How many bottles did you send down?" I asked Larry Reiter.

"A case," he told me. "That's 12."

"Did you get any of it back?"

"Well, no. We didn't expect to."

No, not with Yeltsin on hand. And, as an American, I'm proud to report that our President held his own in whatever went on inside that mansion during the talks.

He seemed to come out of the meeting in better shape than Yeltsin's interpreter, anyway.

—*November 1, 1995*

The Bounce

SAN DIEGO—Bob Dole told the New York delegation a revealing story the other day. He said that when he arrived here last week for the Republican convention that would nominate him for President, he told his wife he was getting excited.

"It's about time," Elizabeth Dole said.

This convention has done its job. It energized the party faithful and gave Bob Dole the 10-point bounce in the polls that usually goes to the challenger after his party's convention.

In a carefully scripted presentation—an informercial, Ted Koppel called it as he stormed out of town to find more compelling news—the Republicans have managed to avoid an unseemly public brawl over abortion. Sighs of relief were breathed all through the convention hall.

Wedge issues failed the Republicans four years ago. They've learned this much from that experience: Why have a venomous row over an issue that appears to lure more Democrats to the polls than Republicans?

But Bill Clinton certainly will emerge from his own convention in Chicago later this month with his own bounce. Traditionally, conventions give incumbents six points in the polls. So, after both conventions, Dole will still trail by 15 points-plus. The next big event on the campaign agenda will be the debate, which most professionals in the New York delegation dread like death.

"Dole ought to call for the debate right away," one New Yorker told me at convention hall the other night. "Let's just get it the hell out of the way."

George Pataki is more optimistic. On a blazing hot day yesterday, he sat in shorts and a sport shirt at a table on the seaside promenade of the elegant Hotel Del Coronado, wolfing down a burger. This is Pataki's first national convention. He said he's amazed at the electricity the event and Jack Kemp's nomination for vice president have generated in his party.

Now comes the hard part—winning.

"Dole has to do two things," the governor told me. "He has to let people know him as a person. They have to know that he's a very decent man, a patriotic man and a man of character. And you don't even have to draw the contrast to the president. You just have to establish what Bob Dole is really like. . . .

"The second is to have a very clear policy as to where he and Jack Kemp would lead the country. And I think that policy should be towards less spending, less government, lower taxes, more jobs, more growth and economic opportunity. And I think that if he can do those two things, he can clearly win this election."

There is, of course, a huge difference between "can" and

"will." For his entire Washington career, which began when Clinton was in the eighth grade, Bob Dole has been an expediter, a doer, a genius at making Washington's wheels turn. He's a professional lawmaker—excellent at intimate, persuasive conversations with colleagues designed to hammer ideas into statutes, weak on showmanship and oratory.

The bubbling Kemp is supposed to counterbalance that shortcoming. But the reality is that the Republicans go this election with a candidate who can't really talk and a running mate who can't really shut up. And they're going up against the smoothest Democratic campaigner in 36 years.

"Bill Clinton is a very good politician," Pataki conceded. "But there's a big difference between a candidate and a President. I think that's what the American people are beginning to see."

Nobody wants to talk about this—Pataki wouldn't, certainly—but the biggest campaign news of the week has not been Dole's nomination, which was a foregone conclusion, or Kemp's either. No running mate has ever saved a weak campaign.

Since Wednesday, the big buzz in San Diego has concerned Jim McDougal, the Clinton buddy in Arkansas convicted in the Whitewater scandal. McDougal is dealing with prosecutors. Every Republican politician in San Diego knows what that might mean—not necessarily in this election, but in 1998.

If McDougal's testimony results in indictments against either or both Clintons—let alone convictions—then the Republicans envision in 1998 the sort of tidal wave of victories across the country that Democrats enjoyed in 1974, when Richard Nixon had his little problem with Watergate.

New York Republicans know that, despite the presence of Al D'Amato in the U.S. Senate and Pataki on the second floor of the Capitol, New York remains a Democratic state. With Dole down this far at this point in the campaign, and even with Kemp on the ticket, the Republicans will need immense luck to win New York.

But two years from now, if McDougal has anything

worthwhile to say to prosecutors, it could be an entirely different story for New York Republicans.

And, by the sheerest of coincidences, that happens to be when both Pataki and D'Amato come up for reelection.

—August 16, 1996

Party On, Dudes

SAN DIEGO—God, the shrimp. You just wouldn't have believed those shrimp.

Large, succulent morsels of firm flesh, curving gently, pink and white. They were nestled on an alp of shaved ice amid glass bowls of fiery red cocktail sauce. Next to that was a platter overflowing with cajun shrimp in a zesty, flavorful dressing so potent it could cure your sinus problem.

Then there were raw clams reclining invitingly on the half shell. And the cold crab claws glistening under the lights.

This was the other night, after Colin Powell's speech to the Republican National Convention. The New York delegates cheered wildly.

Then they piled into their chartered buses. A few minutes later, inside a corral of yellow earth movers that Turner Construction had arrayed in a well-lit, tree-lined meadow in Balboa Park, the delegates, friends and families were gleefully ripping into the shrimp, cold cuts, three kinds of pasta, salmon, roast beef, sliced turkey and Virginia ham.

All washed down with cold beer, fine wine and a bottomless well of booze from four open bars.

Welcome to convention social life. It should not surprise you that many delegates to this Republican convention are elected officials with the power to dispense public funds. Consequently, all over this town this week, companies like Turner, which erects public facilities like Albany Airport, are throwing lavish parties for delegates from their states.

Sure, this sort of gustatory bribery by grasping corporate interests is vile, unprincipled and appalling—except, of course, for the press lounge paid for by Southern Bell in the hotel next to convention hall. You know, the one where reporters always eager to expose political corruption are swilling down rivers of free beer day and night.

And, when we tire of Southern Bell's selfless service to the First Amendment, reporters are partying right alongside the delegates, too. As they taught me in journalism school, no sacrifice is too great in the quest of source-building.

So it was purely out of a sense of duty that I found myself at the Turner Construction party the other night in the velvet evening air of Balboa Park. I figured it beat sitting in my hotel room, banging out a column on party unity while ravaging the mini-bar.

I was sipping a scotch on the rocks, listening to the terrific doo-wop group up on the outdoor stage. I was also watching delegates pose for pictures with the drop-dead gorgeous Marilyn Monroe imitator who'd just wowed everybody with her breathful rendition of, "Diamonds Are a Girl's Best Friend."

I was wondering two things: One, how much did this shindig cost? Two, how unethical would it be to go back for a third plate of that shrimp?

All of Turner's big wheels were there, but I didn't ask them about the money. That would have been intolerably impolite—like inquiring of Susan Molinari, who'd admitted lying to a TV reporter a few years ago about smoking grass in college, if she'd ever mainlined or free-based.

This party must have cost Turner a bundle, though. On the other hand, people in business understand that if you take care of customers they'll take care of you. During the 1995-

1996 fiscal year, New York state paid Turner $6.5 million. This fiscal year is still young, but Turner has already collected another $2 million in state fees.

Nickels and dimes, though, compared to the $30 million AT&T was paid by the state last year—or even to the $10 million in tax dollars that AT&T had collected so far this year. And I was looking forward with ever-increasing anticipation to the beach party that AT&T and its sister firm, Lucent Technologies, were throwing for the delegation the next night.

The fact is that this convention, like the Olympics last month in Atlanta, provides an opportunity for companies to achieve some visibility and to engage in some expensive honing of the old corporate image. Corporate honchos are willing to spend big bucks to accomplish both. It's tax-deductible, after all.

General Motors paid a pretty penny to provide the "Official Vehicles of the Republican National Convention." United Airlines, the "official air carrier" of the convention, gave party workers free rides and supplied little cloth necklaces bearing the company logo from which each delegate dangles his or her state delegation credentials.

Other companies, like AFLAC, Inc., a life insurance firm, and Entergy Corp., an energy firm, are spending many thousands to subsidize expensive skybox suites in which Republican bigwigs entertain party contributors. Georgia delegates were welcomed with a reception paid for by Atlanta-based Coca-Cola. Michigan-based Amway rented an 83-foot yacht to entertain delegates from that state.

A phone call to the press office of New York State Assembly Speaker Shelly Silver, a Democrat, failed to produce any measurable expression of outrage over this shameless exhibition of corporate largesse for the benefit of Republican politicians. Not a big deal, Silver's flack said; nothing we're going to get worked up about.

There's a reason for that. The Democrats, the Party of the People, are holding their own convention week after next. All their delegates are intensely curious about what the corporate shrimp will be like in Chicago. I'll let you know about that after I've spent a few days there.

Yeah, sure, journalism can be dirty work.

But somebody has to do it.

—August 14, 1996

Conventional Wisdom

CHICAGO—Democrats, being Democrats, seldom agree on much of anything. New York Democrats, being New Yorkers, agree on even less than that.

But, if the revelers at several receptions thrown yesterday for New York delegates are any indication, then New York Democrats are in accord on this much:

They can beat Bob Dole like a gong this November. Then they can use this presidential election as a stinger missile to blow away the spine of the New York Republican Party. And then, two years later, a newly energized New York Democratic Party can come back to knock off Al D'Amato and George Pataki.

Well . . . maybe, anyway.

That's more or less the official party line on national conventions these days—that these affairs work to strengthen state and local campaign organizations. But in New York, history renders this logic highly suspect.

In New York's last presidential race, for example, Bill Clinton whipped George Bush by 50 per cent to 34 per cent, with Ross Perot pulling up the rear with 16 per cent. Just two years later, the Republicans neatly picked off Mario Cuomo on their way to winning their first majority in the House of Representatives in 40 years.

But Democrats have to have some reason for being here in Chicago. For them, national political conventions haven't been about nominating presidential candidates for 30-some years. For the Republicans, the last time a convention really meant much was when Ronald Reagan came close to toppling Gerald Ford. That was 20 years ago.

So, if national conventions aren't about selecting candidates, then they can be about building party unity—about firing up the party faithful and setting the stage for a thumping victory back home.

Or something like that. Meanwhile, would you like another beer?

"It's become a social thing," said Tony Bifaro, an alternate delegate who works for a teachers union. "The reason we have so many receptions is that this is the time we used to spend fighting over party platforms and stuff ."

Rep. Mike McNulty, who represents Albany and its immediate suburbs, is automatically a delegate because of his status as a member of Congress. He more or less agreed.

"I think this is the last four-day convention we'll see," he told me yesterday. "A few days is all that's called for, given what we actually do at events like this."

Danny Donohue, president of New York's Civil Service Employees Association and a delegate, said that for some candidates further down the ticket, the margin of a President's victory or loss can have impact. But Donohue and the other New Yorkers staying here in Chicago's venerable Palmer House hotel fully understand that they're on hand mainly as extras in a televised show—namely, the nomination of a President so certain of his reelection victory that he hasn't even bothered to announce his candidacy for a second term.

Chicago has been the scene of 25 political conventions, but none lately. The last time the Democrats gathered in this city for presidential purposes, in 1968, they managed to shoot themselves in the foot—and with a howitzer. Both Chicago and the candidate are trying desperately to look good this time. That's what this show is really all about.

Bob Dole managed to disappoint a good many Democrats two weeks ago by refusing to bungle his own convention. While Dole is hardly a fireball on the stump, the polls showed that he managed to convey to voters that he's a decent, solid guy in the Henry Fonda/James Stewart middle-American mode. He thus came out of his convention with the 10-point bounce that an artfully run television production traditionally lends a challenger.

Now it's time for the Sultan of Slick to do his stuff. If real news emerges from a party convention, then you've done it wrong. That's why the show the Democrats will put on probably will be even smoother than what the Republicans did in San Diego. Look for four full days of snappy patter, glittering television images and the ghosts of Kennedys past called forth repeatedly to bless the effort.

If this convention goes off that flawlessly, then Bill Clinton can expect to get the five-to-10 point bounce in the polls that normally follows the incumbent party's gathering. That'll put him better than 15 points ahead of Dole—a cushy position for a sitting President on Labor Day weekend.

Tony Bifaro, Mike McNulty, Danny Donohue, et al, are delighted to help. They're eager to be herded in and out of convention hall like sheep at a dipping station. They're thrilled to cheer and wave banners on television to try to provide that first distant, rumble of a groundswell for Bill Clinton's reelection.

And to go to parties.

After all, there's no other reason for them to be here in the first place.

—*August 26, 1996*

Munchies, Big-Time

CHICAGO—Hog Butcher to the World. That's what they call this town.

That probably explains the barbecue.

It comes on a thick, crusty roll—a tender, tempting mound of sliced lean meat seethed in a tart, tangy sauce that crackles along the edges of your tongue.

And the lobster tails. Dozens of them roasted in their red-black shells over glowing coals on Navy Pier the other night. Smoke rising past the lobster from the charcoal grill sent a subtle, salty perfume into the evening air along Lake Michigan.

Party time.

That's what this Democratic National Convention is—one long party, with enough free booze to float the Titanic and enough free food to keep Jenny Craig in business until the turn of the century.

This week, The City of Broad Shoulders has been transformed into The City of Bulging Bellies. Anybody who mentions Chicago as The Windy City refers only to the flatulent byproduct of overindulgence.

The Republicans ate and drank their fill at their convention in San Diego, courtesy of corporations eager to curry the favor of government officials with power to make favorable laws and spend public funds.

Big Business is on hand here, too, to woo favors and contracts from Democratic politicians from around the country. But the Democrats also are being wined and dined by their old friends, Big Labor.

The other night, at a party thrown for the New York delegation at the Palmer House Hilton by the AFL-CIO, the union shrimp compared quite favorably to the corporate shrimp scarfed down two weeks ago by New York Republicans at an outdoor gala in a San Diego park.

Rochester-based Kodak threw a party for the Republicans two weeks ago. The other night, the company threw an equally lavish affair for New York Democrats here at the Palmer House. As I filed in the door, a sweet young thing tried to hand me a disposable Kodak camera. No thanks, I told her. I have my ethics. If you're a journalist covering events like this, your ethics boil down more or less to this:

If you can eat it or drink it within an hour, then it's research. If you can take it out the door with you, it's graft.

Various companies and unions have been throwing parties all week for the New York delegation, most of them honoring specific politicians. Seagrams threw a nice bash for Assembly Ways and Means Chairman Denny Farrell, for example. The AFL-CIO affair honored Assembly Speaker Sheldon Silver.

NYNEX also threw a pleasant little gathering for several hundred delegates, friends, family members and assorted hangers-on. So did the National Education Association and the American Federation of Teachers, both of which have rather specific legislative agendas in Albany and Washington.

The entertainment lavished on New York politicians, however, is all rather small time compared to what the national party has ground out of public-spirited companies and unions. Corporations like Chrysler and United Airlines have kicked in a hundred grand each to finance the convention. So has Philip Morris Co., Inc., which threw a party for New York Republicans at their convention.

Dow Chemical is throwing parties. So is Phillips Petroleum and a number of Washington law firms engaged in lobbying activities. Anheuser-Busch, which threw a big party for Newt Gingrich in San Diego, is also a co-sponsor—for $25,000—of a Democratic National Committee skybox at the United Center, where convention sessions are held.

Meanwhile, Chicago Mayor Rich Daley used his charm to persuade many dozens of local firms to kick in big bucks to form the city's host committee, Chicago '96, which just happens to be headed up by Rich Daley's little brother, Bill. The idea was to make the city presentable and hospitable for the

35,000 or so politicians and newspeople on hand for Bill Clinton's latest coronation.

Daley used a compelling argument to convince the local firms to contribute generously to the host committee. It's good for Chicago, he told them, and that's good for everybody. Conversely, what's bad for Chicago ...

. . . well, Chicago business people can recite that tune by heart.

—August 29, 1996

A Fashionable Rebel

Gerry Adams had just flown in from Pittsburgh on a plane about the size of a Honda Civic. It was late afternoon. He hadn't slept much, and he hadn't eaten since the day before.

And there he was, sitting in the seat just in front of me yesterday in a van roaring into downtown Albany from the airport, and I was bugging him about guns and bombs. I wanted to know what it would take for him to agree to a mechanism and a timetable to dispose of the Irish Republican Army's weapons. It was not a question he cared for.

I was saying, "The weapons were not among the details worked out in the agreement."

Gerry Adams glared at me through his wire-rimmed glasses. "No, that's not part of the agreement. I negotiated it. I do know what's in the agreement."

"OK, so you negotiated it. But what about the weapons?"

Gerry Adams danced for a while, but he finally

answered. Look, he said, the weapons aren't being used now, are they? And you can give up your weapons on a Thursday and buy new ones on a Friday, so what does it matter?

The Unionists, he insisted, are just using this business with the weapons as an excuse to avoid further negotiation. Other items demand to be addressed—the question of who'll police Northern Ireland, and how, and getting all the prisoners out from behind bars.

It was, from all reports, a rare touch of testiness from a politician famous for his controlled restraint. He has been shot and imprisoned. His home has been the target of rocket attacks. Until just the past year or so, he slept in a different safe house every night.

Through it all, Gerry Adams has been the cool, patient negotiator—an ex-bartender with the look and manner of a professor of the classics, tall and thin and bearded and bespectacled. And, three centuries-plus after the British conquered Ireland at the Battle of the Boyne, ready to do whatever it takes to ride history's wave.

He was in this town once before—a bit more than three years ago, before that wave had begun to crest. The United States government had let him in on a 48-hour visa, reluctantly and over British protests that America was welcoming a terrorist. In Albany, Adams was warmly greeted by politicians who knew that their metro area, the nation's 52nd in size, was contributing more money to Adams' cause than anyplace in the country except New York and Boston.

Then came the deal in April—the Good Friday Agreement, it's called. It was arrived at under pressure on the Unionists from Bill Clinton and Tony Blair, the new British prime minister. Amazingly, after three-quarters of a century of bloodshed over anti-Catholic discrimination and the partition of Ireland's six northern counties, lasting peace might actually be at hand.

And now dour, thoughtful Gerry Adams has been transformed into the Irish Huey Newton, the fashionable rebel of the 1990s—just as Newton and Eldridge Cleaver and their leather-clad Black Panthers were the radical chic heroes of the 1960s.

Hollywood stars crowd around Adams at fund-raisers. Donald Trump greets him lavishly. And yesterday, Albany politicians were more gracious to him than ever.

Jerry Jennings, Albany's mayor, greeted Adams at the airport and stuck to him like flypaper all through his visit. Gov. George Pataki descended from his fortress on the second floor of the Capitol to greet Adams at the Omni Hotel—and to remind the crowd at a $100-a-head Sinn Fein fund-raiser that he had an Irish-born grandmother named Agnes Lynch, who'd experienced the anti-Catholic discrimination that Adams has fought against for so long and with such resolve.

Adams did television interviews and thanked both the "murr" and the "gahv-ner." And collected the check, of course. That was the main purpose of this trip. In Ireland, as in America, it takes money to run a political organization—not to mention an army.

And, pound for pound, nobody in this country has raised money for the cause like the local Sinn Fein fund-raiser, a Colonie insurance man named Paul Murray, who was telling me 15 years ago that some of it probably went for guns, and that was awful, but it was necessary, too.

Speaking of those guns, Gerry Adams hemmed and hawed all through that ride into town. But he seems likely, eventually, to make a deal about them—if, that is, the Unionists will embrace a schedule for unloading their own weaponry.

After the Good Friday agreement, Adams' opposite number on the Unionist side, David Trimble, needs a deal to stay in power. Except for the inconvenience of the relentless IRA murders and bombings, the Unionists liked things pretty much as they were before Trimble made that deal to share power with the Catholics.

If Trimble goes, he could be replaced by a foaming loon like the Rev. Ian K. Paisley, who refers to the Pope as "an impostor and a blasphemer and a liar." And, in his more subdued moments, as "the anti-Christ."

A Paisley would never deal with any man who accepts Catholic dogma. He would do everything in his power to reduce the Good Friday agreement to confetti. So, Adams will deal, all right, but he'll squeeze Trimble a bit more before he gives in.

Sure, Trimble has a constituency that needs pleasing, but so does Adams. And, for Adams and his republicans, the weapons and the willingness to use them have always been the hole card. Without them, Adams has said repeatedly, Northern Ireland's Catholics would still be on their knees.

Also, just as David Trimble has his crazies, so does Adams. They must be placated while the dealing goes on. And each side still feels the need to rattle their crazies like sabers as they negotiate.

Ultimately, each side's crazies will have to be dealt with, or there'll be no lasting deal, no peace, no end to the killing, no united Ireland. Everybody knows that, and the crazies will be handled—as gently or as violently as the circumstance requires.

But not now. Not just yet. Not at the moment.

That's because, for each side, the crazies and their guns and their bombs and their blood lust are still too useful.

—October 14, 1998

Hero Worship

There were three of them, these shivering little kids, and they were standing outside Albany's Armory Center in 28-degree darkness watching grownups in fancy clothes cruise in to see Hillary Clinton.

Melshilia White, who's 12 and in the sixth grade at School 26, spotted me as I came out of the place into the evening chill.

"Mister," she said, "Can we go inside to see Hillary?"

"We" turned out to be Melshilia and her brother Sylvester, 10, and their little sister Shaniqua, 8. I asked them, "What're you guys doing out here at night? Why aren't you home watching TV like sane kids?"

"Hillary is my idol," Melshilia White explained. "Can you take us in to see her?"

Well, not really. I'd just gotten thrown out. I'd heard about this fundraising soiree for Hillary Clinton. You paid $125 to see her in a big group, downstairs in Armory Center near Bumpers Cafe, and you paid a cool grand to shake her hand upstairs in Yono's. So, I dropped by last night—amateur night, it turned out to be—to see just who was coming up with all this cash.

It's a reporter thing. We like to know who's giving money to politicians.

I went through the door, past the table where some of Mrs. Clinton's campaign staffers were collecting contributions. I said hello to a few Albany Democrats I know. Then I climbed the stairs to Yono's to see who was kicking in the really big bucks.

Mrs. Clinton was in the room, shaking hands, smiling. I was cruising around, checking out faces and finally settling into a conversation with Mike Breslin, the Albany County executive. Then this young guy in a black suit came over. He said he was Ramon Martinez, the Clinton campaign's political director, and this was a closed event. No other reporters were there, after all.

I pointed out to Ramon Martinez, political director, that I often show up in places where other reporters don't, but somehow that didn't impress him. I was about to tell this guy that I've been thrown out of better places, but I didn't because I haven't. Yono's is the best place I've ever been bounced out of, actually.

So, I went downstairs and started schmoozing with the players in the $125 cheap seats until Ramon Martinez came down after me and threw me out of there, too. Before I left, I insisted that somebody go upstairs and get my coat. If this guy was going to toss me without my coat, I was going to beg the cops to run him in.

So, I found myself outside listening to Albany Democrats complain that they'd gotten three separate invitations to this event and wondering where these Clinton people got their *meshuggeneh* mailing list. I was hearing people moan that the Clinton campaign wouldn't take checks, but that nobody had told them that until they got there and were embarassed for their trouble. And here were these three little kids begging me to let them see Hillary.

"See that table inside the door?" I said to Melshilia White. "Go ask that man to get Mr. Martinez. Mr. Martinez is a very nice man. I'm sure he'll let you see Hillary."

A few minutes later, the kids came out, crestfallen. They'd been bounced, too. The last I saw of them, they were crossing Colvin Avenue on their way home in the winter gloom—a truly masterful move on the part of these exceedingly brilliant Hillary Clinton campaign people.

If they'd let the local party people run this affair, their candidate would have left this town with the same money, at least.

And maybe even with a few friends.

—February 11, 2000

The Big Lie

Thomas Edmund Dewey died on March 16, 1971, just eight days short of his 69th birthday. He'd lived a remarkable life.

He'd been born in Owosso, Mich., the son of the local newspaper publisher. He graduated from the University of Michigan. He received a law degree in 1925 from Columbia. After graduation, he stayed in New York.

As a United States attorney, as the governor's special rackets prosecutor and as Manhattan district attorney, he earned an impeccable reputation. Tom Dewey was the original crime-busting prosecutor. He was a man of unimpeachable integrity in a time of widespread public corruption.

His personal honesty earned him three terms as governor of New York. During his time in Albany, he built fine highways. He pushed through New York's first law against racial or religious discrimination in employment. He revamped primitive rules governing unemployment and disability benefits.

The late Harry O'Donnell served as press secretary to five New York governors and one New York City mayor. He told me once that Thomas E. Dewey was the best governor he'd seen in his decades in politics. O'Donnell told me also that Tom Dewey was the finest man he'd ever known.

Twice, Tom Dewey ran for President. He lost big in 1944 to Franklin Delano Roosevelt. He lost narrowly four years later to Harry Truman. He spent his last years practicing law in New York City, revered and respected by both the public and by politicians of both parties.

Now there's a new movie out that portrays him as a sleazy crook and bribe-taker. For the benefit of anybody unfamiliar with who and what this man was and the thoroughly admirable life he led, I thought I would mention that the movie "Hoodlum" from MGM/UA perpetrates a blood libel against the memory of an honorable public servant.

Thomas E. Dewey, Jr., just turned 65. He's an investment banker in New York City. He bears his name with immense pride. I spoke to him the other day. He saw the movie. He's wounded beyond words.

"It's so bloody and so awful," Tom Dewey, Jr., said to me. "My son, the lawyer, made me go see it before I wrote a letter to the studio, which they had their lawyers answer saying that I had no 'cognizable legal rights' because it was a work of fiction."

Lies from Hollywood are nothing new. Hollywood routinely portrays heroic, forward-thinking Theodore Roosevelt as a childish buffoon. It portrays sober, thoughtful Thomas Jefferson as an oppressive womanizer. It falsely tells us that William Wallace fathered a king of England. Oliver Stone's "JFK" was a stunning compendium of simplistic lies.

"This is worse," Tom Dewey, Jr., told me. "With 'JFK' it was twisting. This is 180 degrees. . . . What makes the hypocrisy so much worse is that they have a web site up for this movie. And on the web site there is quite a bit of historical data on every one of the named characters.

"With one exception. And guess who that is? Then they tell me it's a work of fiction."

Under the laws of slander and libel, the Deweys are without recourse. The law holds that once a man dies he's beyond worldly harm. He no longer can be wounded by false charges that tarnish his reputation.

This is a good thing, not a bad one. Historians couldn't function without this protection. Neither could creators of fiction who weave tales for artistic purposes.

But, for the record, the real Tom Dewey who served New York state and this country with such distinction was not a crook. Understand that what appears on the screen in this movie is only make-believe.

And whatever you do, don't believe it.

—*October 5, 1997*

Battered and Bullied by the Brusque, Brutal Bureaucracy

Government Time

In part, at least, government exists to help people through periods of hard luck. Sometimes it works, and sometimes it doesn't.

And sometimes government just takes its own sweet time.

Jimmy Thompson knows all about that time thing. He began to learn about it when he was working as a transmission mechanic. He asked for a raise. Sometime later, he got into a disagreement with a boss and ended up fired.

Jimmy Thompson did the sensible thing. He applied for unemployment benefits. The employer challenged his application. Pretty soon, Jimmy Thompson found himself in front of a hearing officer at State Labor Department headquarters on the Harriman Campus in Albany.

He described his firing. The employer testified that Jimmy Thompson really had quit. Ultimately, the hearing officer found for the employer. I've read the transcript of that hearing. This hearing officer must have been from Mars.

Naturally, Jimmy Thompson appealed his case. He figured he'd gotten stiffed, and he had. He didn't know it at the time, but he was only one of many New Yorkers the system was supposed to protect who'd systematically been denied due process and a fair shot at benefits by this state's woefully inept unemployment system.

After Jimmy Thompson's case was decided, the state settled a lawsuit filed by a coalition of labor groups. The state admitted that it had failed to protect the rights of hard-luck

Battered and Bullied by the Brusque, Brutal Bureaucracy

claimants like Jimmy Thompson. In a consent decree, the state promised that it wouldn't do that any more. It also promised it would reopen 50,000 unemployment cases, review them and rectify its earlier mistakes.

That consent decree was signed in 1983, two years after the system had worked over Jimmy Thompson. The other day, Jimmy Thompson's lawyer, Richard Silber, got a thing in the mail. Jimmy Thompson had been denied his unemployment benefits on Dec. 3, 1981. The state finally had gotten around to reversing its decision.

On Aug. 11, 1999.

"So, he'll get this," Richard Silber told me, "but at what pay rate? His 1981 pay? I don't know. I've never seen anything like this."

For the record, the State Labor Department says it's now down to only 2,000 open cases, and it's trying hard to find the people it shafted so long ago. The Pataki administration also points out that this mess is one it inherited, that what went wrong had gone wrong under the Democrats between 1977 and 1983.

None of this, though, is much consolation to Jimmy Thompson. He lives on First Street in Albany. He was a man in his 40s when this thing happened to him. He had an eighth grade education. He went into the hearing without a lawyer because he couldn't afford one. And the system screwed him royally, as it was screwing so many others at the time.

He went through a long period of unemployment. He finally got into construction work and ended up injured. Then he fought a long, bitter battle with Workers Comp to get disability. Jimmy Thompson is now 63, banged up, and his working life is over.

He'll be happy to take whatever money the system might give him, although I did tell him that he ought to sue the system for some hefty interest, if he can manage it. But he really could have used those unemployment payments back then. The protection that government is supposed to offer working people who fall on hard times would have come in mighty handy for Jimmy Thompson.

"If you was a worker," Jimmy Thompson told me, "you couldn't say nothing. . . . But, you know, there's been a lot of times in life where I didn't get no justice. This is only one. There you go."

—August 20, 1999

The Agent

If his kid hadn't been such a whiz on the accordian, Vic Speciale never would have been mugged by the bureaucrats.

"I used to get him all the jobs," Vic Speciale told me one day as we sat in the office he maintains in his small, well-kept house on a pleasant street in South Troy. "So, I got two, three jobs at one time for him. And he said, 'Hey Dad, why don't you call another band and tell them to give you 10 or 20 dollars if you get them a job?'"

Which is how Vic Speciale, 77, came to quit the delivery business he'd operated in his working-class city of 52,000 and began booking bands fulltime.

He wasn't exactly Michael Ovitz. Vic Speciale was only a guy making a buck by matching up musicians with people who wanted to have fun. He did it for years. Then, out of the blue, New York State decided that Vic Speciale wasn't an agent after all. No, he was an employer. That meant that he owed the state thousands of dollars in unemployment insurance premiums.

This sort of ruling is not uncommon in New York, where state regulatory agencies possess so much power and exert such enormous influence over the daily lives of the state's

Battered and Bullied by the Brusque, Brutal Bureaucracy

19 million citizens. Every year, thousands of people hire independent contractors only to discover, somewhere down the road, that the state considers them employers, subject to all sorts of rules, regulations and expenses.

Hire somebody to mow your lawn. Hire somebody to clean your house. Hire somebody to watch your kids. Do that, and chances are that New York will consider you an employer.

But Vic Speciale hadn't hired anybody for anything. He'd only found work for people and collected a percentage of their earnings. And he hadn't even been active as an agent for a while because he was caring for an invalid wife confined to a wheelchair after a car crash. Vic lavished care on her. He hadn't been able for some time to get out to the clubs and hear the bands.

In short, he didn't have the money. He fought the order.

Initially, a hearing officer ruled in his favor. Then the case went to the New York State Unemployment Insurance Appeal Board. This is a panel of bureaucrats in Brooklyn who apparently arrived in New York aboard flying saucers.

The board ruled that Vic Speciale found work for the bands, told them what sort of music the client liked and asked them to let him know if the band was actually going to show up. Therefore, he exerted sufficient control over their work to qualify as an employer.

"I never paid nobody in my life," he told me. "They paid me. I lived on 10 per cent."

Peter Rubie, a New York literary agent I know, was astounded when I told him this story. Like all literary and theatrical agents, he survives on commissions.

"He's not an employer," Peter Rubie told me. "He's a facilitator. Have they done the same thing to William Morris?"

No, they haven't. William Morris, the biggest literary, talent and theatrical agency in the world, would hire a regiment of lawyers and fight the New York State Labor Department into the dirt. John Sweeney, the state labor commissioner in the first-term administration of Republican Gov.

George Pataki, was told about this case. I called him to ask how any state agency could do anything like this.

Well, said Sweeney—and I actually could hear him sighing—the system in New York has been a nightmare for decades. Historically, it has been used as a collector of hidden taxes. After I spoke to him, Sweeney went and asked his lawyers whether he had any legal standing to intercede.

While all this was going on, Vic Speciale had no choice but to cash in his wife's insurance policies and pay John Sweeney's department what he could scrape together. His Legal Aid lawyer, Peter Henner, told me that Victor Speciale couldn't even get a court to review this spectacular mugging until he paid every nickel—which Vic couldn't do.

The state was charging him interest at the rate of almost a buck a day. That's the sort of vigorish you get hit with down on the docks. Even with his payment, Vic couldn't get the debt down below $3,000.

Ultimately, Sweeney asked the appeals board to reconsider. He mentioned something about the whole crowd coming across like a pack of heartless jackasses. And, finally, the board reversed itself and decided that Vic Speciale hadn't been anybody's employer after all.

I'd heard a wealth of horror stories about the cruel, mindless tyranny of New York's unemployment system—the one that has employers putting down skid marks as they flee the state. But to take an old guy who's clearly not anybody's employer and hold him up for his sick wife's insurance money?

The Empire State's bureaucrats really outdid themselves with this one.

—August 7, 1996

By Any Other Name

Bob Allen and his son, Bob Allen, Jr., ran a paving business in Colonie. The business consisted of a big dump truck and a lot of hard work. The elder Bob Allen had a commercial driver's license and operated the truck.

Then, in April, Bob Allen, Sr., died. His son inherited the truck and needed a commercial license to drive it. Bob Allen, Jr. paid 40 bucks to take the test. He got a certificate to cover him for 10 days. But he had to get his license properly recorded in the DMV computer.

That's when Bob Allen bumped into the mindless, maddening bureaucracy that so often passes for New York state government. A clerk in the Schenectady DMV office discovered that the computer wouldn't issue him a commercial license.

Why not? Some totally different guy was in trouble with the DMV in another state.

Bob Allen told me, "This guy, his name is Robert James Allen. Mine is Robert Joseph Allen. I was born on Jan. 1, 1968. He was born on Jan. 1, 1960. He has his license suspended in Rhode Island. And they're trying to say that it's me."

Think about this. Here's a guy with a clean, valid New York driver's license that he has had for years. He and the Rhode Island guy have different middle names and different years of birth. And the DMV people tell the New York Bob Allen that this is his problem and not theirs.

He called Rhode Island DMV, spent hours in voice mail hell, and finally found somebody who told him: Hey, pal, you're on your own.

"They said, 'Well, Albany should know that it's not you.'"

Bob Allen then went to the DMV office on South Pearl Street. He was not exactly bowled over by a surging wave of sympathy.

"The supervisor in Albany," he told me, "she hands me a piece of paper with the number of Rhode Island DMV and then points to the pay phone in the corner of the room. She says, 'Here, you go call. It's your responsibility. We can't do nothing about it here.'"

DMV has made a big deal out of reinventing itself and placing customer service atop its concerns. And it is better, really. But anybody who works in government comes to understand quickly that internal consistency is valued far more than common sense.

Hence the phrase: "Sorry, Sir. But we have rules."

What bothered Bob Allen was that nobody seemed to care about his problem—not even Richard Jackson, the DMV commissioner, to whom he wrote. He never heard even a peep in response.

After I heard this horror story, I called George Filieau, a DMV spokesman. He told me, "The offices are instructed that if they believe that a person is applying for a license who's suspended in another state, based on a computer check that would match up the month and day of birth—even though the year of birth is eight years apart . . . and, if in their judgment it's the same person, then they would refer the person to the state in which they're suspended to get it cleared. So, the procedures that were followed in this case were correct."

Bob Allen is getting his commercial license, by the way, now that this matter has been looked into.

But if there's some other Dan Lynch somewhere in Rhode Island, I just hope he never gets tanked up and has his license suspended.

And, come to think of it, he better hope that I don't, either.

—*August 20, 1996*

Sorry, Wrong Number

The reason nobody can predict the weather more than a few days ahead, a scientist once told me, is chaos. A butterfly flaps its wings in, say, Sierra Leone, and sends air molecules into motion. Pretty soon you have trillions of air molecules careening off one another, and not even computers the size of Taco Bell signs can predict if it'll rain in Albany next week.

The system is random—beyond control or logic. Which, somehow, makes me think of government. Which, in turn, brings me to Jerry Duckor, the owner of an 11-year-old maroon Chevrolet.

Or so he thought.

A year or so ago, Jerry Duckor got a notice from a court in New York City informing him that his car had been abandoned in the Bronx and that he'd better have a hell of a good story. Which, fortunately, he did.

His car was in his Loudonville driveway at the time. Neither he nor the Chevy had been anywhere near the Bronx. So, Jerry Duckor sent the City of New York a ton of paperwork attesting to his possession of the car at that very moment, 150 miles north of the New York City line. He even sent along a statement from a New York state trooper.

So, naturally, he was found guilty and fined $275. You were expecting justice, maybe? You dreamer, you.

Jerry Duckor then wrote letters to New York Mayor Rudy Giuliani and to Jerry Duckor's two New York state legislators, Sen. Mike Hoblock and Assemblyman Bob Prentiss. Which, miraculously enough, worked—and it wasn't even an election year. Jerry Duckor was delighted to receive not one but three separate notices from the City of New York—all issued on different dates—saying, essentially, fuggeddaboudit. (That's New Yorkese for "summons dismissed.")

You'd think that would have been it, right? You cock-eyed optimist, you. On Tuesday, Jerry Duckor went to the

New York State Department of Motor Vehicles operation near his house.

"I hopped down there a couple of days before my registration came due," he told me the other night. "I'm retired. I don't have much else to do. And when I tried to register it, they said, 'No, your car has been junked.' And I said, 'Really. It's sitting out in the parking lot.' And they said, 'No, it's been junked. It's in our computer.'

"I said, 'Can't somebody come out and look at it?' They said no. It was in the computer; that was it."

Somebody was kind enough to give Jerry Duckor a month's extension on his registration to get this straightened out. After he mentioned this little adventure to me, I called George Filieau, a spokesman at state DMV headquarters, to find out how a thing like this could happen.

Apparently, the New York City Sanitation Department had come across an abandoned car in the Bronx—another 1985 Chevy, although this one was a different color—and had taken down its Vehicle Identification Number. Then the city had gone after the vehicle's owner.

A VIN number is as long as a Bill Clinton speech. Whatever bonehead had copied down the number had screwed up at least one digit and mistakenly recorded the number of Jerry Duckor's car. When the abandoned car was junked, the City of New York had dutifully notified the state DMV.

So, next week Jerry Duckor plans to drive the maroon Chevy that doesn't exist to DMV central headquarters in Albany in an effort to get this fixed. I, for one, wish him a lot of luck.

Dealing with government—the original iron butterfly—he'll need it.

—*May 31, 1996*

A Philosophy of Politics

Everybody needs a philosophy of life. Here's mine:

Get over it. Stop whining. Tend to business. Just figure that if you're getting a raw deal, it probably won't be the last time. Raw deals are part of the human condition.

OK, so that's not complex thinking. It's not a reflective representation of any particular school of philosophical thought. It does have this virtue, however: You didn't have to pay me for it.

If Ruben Diaz's bill goes through, though, you'll have to pay a philosopher to give advice like that to somebody—to anybody, actually—who qualifies for taxpayer-funded third-party payment. And then, of course, the private health insurance companies would be pressured to offer the same payment.

Just as you and I now pay shrinks to help Medicaid recipients get their heads on straight, so, too, would we pay philosophers.

Assemb. Ruben Diaz, Jr. of the Bronx is 25, the youngest member of the Legislature. Twice now, he has introduced a bill to set up a state board to license philosophical practicioners. It would set minimum educational standards—a doctorate in philosophy. It also would regulate philosophical practicioners, or counselors, once they're licensed.

What's really important about this bill, though, is the third-party payment angle. That means that taxpayers would pay philosophers just as taxpayers now pay psychologists to offer advice on how people might get their acts to-gether.

This bill was introduced by Diaz at the request of the American Philosophical Practicioners Association. This is a group of three dozen people with advanced degrees in philosophy—mostly City University of New York professors—who figure that the advice they give is worth at least as much as the advice handed out by psychologists.

Psychiatrists, they concede, are physicians, but they mostly hand out drugs to people with emotional problems.

Paul Del Duca, Diaz's chief of staff, holds a degree in philosophy. Instead of treating a client's unhappiness with drugs or psychotherapy, he told me, "the philosophical therapist will ask, 'Well, what is happiness?'"

Lou Marinoff, the association's executive director, put it this way: "Most people have problems at one time or another.... You might have a problem in a relationship.... Your life might feel meaningless to you.... These are not, in and of themselves, mental illnesses. So a lot of people feel quite benefitted by speaking to philosophers about these subjects.... Call it therapy for the sane."

This is all fascinating, of course, but it raises an interesting question: Should this state limit third-party payment only to medical care? Or is it prepared to foot the bill for a wide variety of personal services that could help Medicaid recipients live their lives more enjoyably? And, if so, where does it stop?

If we clear the way for Medicaid payment to philosophers, for example, can personal trainers be far behind? Will Medicaid pay for gym memberships? How about art lessons, so depressed Medicaid recipients can unleash their creative energies?

How about fortune tellers? How about sex surrogates for the romantically dysfunctional? And don't tell me they don't provide a service that would be in heavy demand if taxpayers were footing the bill.

There's a word for a plan like this. That word is "nonsense." There's also a reason it's being proposed. For a dozen years now, American universities have overproduced Ph.Ds in the humanities. There are no fulltime teaching jobs for most of them—especially for highly educated philosophers. The Diaz bill would, in effect, create a taxpayer-funded market for therapy services that the philosophers can't peddle successfully in the free market.

"Medi" is in Medicaid for a reason. This bill will go nowhere. That'll probably upset the philosophers. My advice: Get over it.

Hey, no charge.

—May 31, 1999

Examining the Doctors

It was last week that Dr. Maynard Guest decided that he'd had it.

He's 78 years old. His wife is ill. After 40-some years of practicing internal medicine, he doesn't need the money the state has been paying him for the past dozen years or so as executive secretary of the Board for Professional Medical Conduct.

And now the Pataki administration is swinging a hatchet as it goes through the office that weeds out bad doctors in this state—and a dull hatchet at that.

So, on Tuesday, Maynard Guest turned in his retirement papers. A few hours later, I sat with him in his elegant old house in Slingerlands as he told me why he'd packed it in.

"What pushed me over the edge," he said, "was the fact that I'm spinning my wheels if I continue. We have 350 cases backed up. Maybe, within my projected lifetime, these cases might go to hearing. Meanwhile, the doctor continues to do his bad practices. So I'm wasting my time."

Nobody objects to the Pataki administration firing policy makers hired by the Democrats. That's what the Democrats did when they took over 20 years ago. Also, George Pataki was elected by a majority of New Yorkers to change the policy direction of state government. It's not only his right to do that, it's his duty.

And, yes, a change in administration always means dislocation and discomfort for much of the state work force. The state employee unions knew that when they decided to let Mario Cuomo sink or swim on his own, without much help from them.

This is the way the game is played. We're seeing democracy in action here.

But what's happening in the office charged with protecting the public from bad doctors is not politics as usual. This is not a political arm of state government. This is an office funded mostly by physicians' licensing fees, so there's no real savings to the taxpayer by reducing its horsepower. Moreover, the people in there, overwhelmingly, are not Democratic party operatives. They're physicians and lawyers engaged in a tough, dirty business to protect sick people from butchers.

"The critical people in administrative hearings, " said Maynard Guest, who just happens to be an enrolled Republican, "are the attorneys—the state's attorneys—who're comparable to prosecutors. . . . The Pataki administration has fired a significant number of attorneys with a caseload that keeps increasing all the time."

This state has never done a particularly good job at physician discipline. No state has. Because of tradition and the unavoidable involvement of physicians in the discipline process, the hearings are conducted in secret. It takes forever—years and years, generally—to lift the license of a bad doctor.

It takes forever, for example, to nail somebody like David Benjamin, the guy just sentenced to prison in New York for killing a woman during a botched abortion. Before that, while operating under a different name, he was doing horrible things to people out in Herkimer—chopping them up like so much sausage in his garage after the local hospital threw him out.

And, while this secretive process grinds along with the speed of a glacier, patients in a blissful state of ignorance about complaints against their physicians keep going to David Benjamins, lying on the table and filled with trust while he slices into them.

"There was this doctor," Maynard Guest was telling me. "He was a Japanese guy known in Tokyo as the 'Tokyo Torpedo.' He specialized in Jehovah's Witnesses, who don't take blood, so he did very rapid surgery—very, very sloppy, unbelievable, terrible.

"In one patient he left this huge retractor that filled the abdomen. He saw it on a post-operative X-ray. He told the patient that he'd have to go back in to correct the incision. I don't know how he did it, but he got that thing out, and nobody ever saw it—at least nobody ever admitted to seeing it, and it just disappeared."

They got that guy. They also got the ophthalmologist in Buffalo, Dr. John Park, who outfitted an RV as an operating room and went around performing cataract surgery on people who didn't have cataracts. They get 40 or 50 of them every year. It's never easy, though—never an easy case.

Yes, of course, most physicians are able, dedicated men and women who do fine work. I don't want to hear from doctors claiming that I'm smearing their profession when I point out that a disturbing number of the 50,000 or 60,000 people with medical licenses in New York are incompetents. It's simply true—just as it's true of a disturbing number of lawyers and teachers and cops and journalists and deli clerks.

But we're talking here about doctors, and we have some bad ones in New York despite the arduous training and certification process they undergo to get medical licenses.

We're talking, too, about politics and about public safety. The governor's office has fired able, dedicated, non-political prosecuting attorneys in this office for reasons that seem to defy logic.

Take Liz Hogan. She worked 12 years for Albany District Attorney Sol Greenberg, which is where she got her experience as a prosecutor. Greenberg is a Democrat. Liz Hogan is not. She's registered as an independent. On April 7, the acting counsel of the agency called her into his office.

"He said, 'A list has come over from the governor's office. Your name is on it. You're fired.' I said, 'Why?' And he said, 'I really don't know.' I was carrying 16 cases at the time. What really gets me is that I'd just had my final evaluation, where they told me how wonderful I am."

Take Catherine Cholakis, who's a registered Conservative and a member of a big Republican family in Rensselaer County. They bounced her, too. The office had 24 lawyer slots the day before George Pataki took office. Every one was filled. Now the office has 25 slots. Five are vacant.

The Lord High Executioner in all this is supposedly one James Natoli, a high-ranking aide to Pataki. I'm told that it's his handwritten list of names that's faxed to the office periodically—his own personal death list.

I tried to talk to him, to ask him what this is all about. But this Natoli doesn't talk to reporters. He collects a big salary that you and I pay. He fires capable, non-political people engaged in crucial work. He sits in an office on the second floor of the Capitol and spreads terror for a living. But James Natoli doesn't want to explain to you why he does what he does and why it's good for the people of New York.

It's not easy to get the license of a bad doctor. They fight like demons when they're caught up with. They hire high-priced legal talent to do battle against $50,000-a-year state lawyers. Watch the O. J. Simpson trial for a while and see what happens when public servants go up against lawyers who command millions.

Watch that and ask yourself, why are the Pataki people doing this to that office? Who benefits from this? And at what cost?

Whatever else New York wastes money on, and a lot of it is spent needlessly, we've never put enough resources into the task of policing physicians. The medical establishment gave George Pataki hundreds of thousands of dollars in this last election, and what's happening there may be no more complicated than that. It also may be a simple patronage exercise, clearing out non-political people and replacing them with party faithful. Who knows?

You should know, I've been around a bit. I've seen party transitions in government in two other states. By any standard, this one has been conspicuously mean. People like Liz Hogan are fired and told to be out by the end of the day.

It's one thing to tell Democratic policy-makers that they're history. Live by the sword, die by the sword. It's something else to do that to non-political people doing important work just so you can put party hacks in their jobs.

And here's what's worse:

To enjoy doing it.

—September 17, 1995

The Art of Assigning Blame

The 211 shameless hustlers, hopeless dopes and well-intentioned innocents who make up the New York Legislature have gathered together 222 times now. Generally, this rowdy annual spectacle provides more fetching entertainment than Bill Clinton greeting a giggling contingent of Miss America contestants.

Not this time, though.

The current legislative session has been the ugliest in the memory of any living New Yorker. It started off mean and got meaner by the day. Now, in what should be the session's dying days, we New Yorkers seem to have on our hands a nightmare that exceeds even the exacting standards of the usual disastrous legislative get-together.

It's June 17, and there's no state budget in place. The law says they have to have one adopted by April 1. Well, hey, tough.

In six long months, not a single piece of important legislation has passed. The governor and the lords of the Legislature seem unable to conduct a conversation of even moderate civility. And none of this state's 2,200 lobbyists yet dares to schedule a summer vacation. Who knows when some grasping committee chairman might decide to hold another campaign fundraiser?

Who's to blame for all this? My vote goes to George Pataki.

OK, sure, Assembly Speaker Shelly Silver has been truculent and warlike from the beginning of this horror show. And, OK, Senate Majority Leader Joe Bruno has from the start seemed more concerned with next year's elections, the last ones before new legislative districts are drawn, than with the actual governmental business at hand in 1999.

But each of these guys answers to limited constituencies—to the local voters in their districts who send them to Albany and to the members of their party in each house who confer leadership duties upon them. Only one of the three major political figures in state government has direct and unavoidable obligations to all 19 million citizens of this state. That's the governor.

And George Pataki seems to have focused most of his attention this year on sucking up to George W. Bush, hoping to nail down the second spot on next year's GOP presidential ticket, and on keeping Rudy Giuliani from landing the Republican party's senatorial nomination next year against the President's much-abused wife.

In other words, if anybody is to blame for this stupendous logjam in the Legislature, it's the guy whose job description is to serve as a catalyst between the leaders of the upper and lower houses. Instead, Pataki has been about as visible in this year's state lawmaking process as his shadowy political consultant, Arthur Finkelstein, who hides from public view the way John Dillinger hid from the FBI.

As things stand now, both houses will be in session today. The State Senate may come back for a day or two next week. The Assembly might come back in three weeks, if anybody is in the mood. At the moment, nobody in either house seems to know which way is up.

The dominant motif in all this is more or less unmitigated chaos. The mood is uniformly grim. All the pressure groups are grumbling. The lobbyists are gazing skyward, praying to a higher power. And the governor is. . . .

. . . actually, as I consider it, I don't know where our governor is. New Yorkers, do you know where your governor is today? And what he's doing? If anything? And how much are we paying this guy, anyway? Didn't he just get a big raise? Say, now that I think about it, didn't all these bumbling bozos just get a big raise?

OK, so pass a few laws. Adopt a budget. Then, everybody get lost, OK?

Really, this stuff just isn't any fun any more.

—*June 17, 1999*

The Vintners

Joyce Hunt was gazing south from the unfinished deck that her husband, Art, was erecting next to the tasting room of their winery in Branchport.

"That was a Delaware vineyard," she said, pointing out over the spectacular array of vines and trellises that stretched in lush, elegant grandeur to the forest beyond.

"We're ripping it out," Art Hunt explained. "You have to stay in touch with reality. If the world market doesn't want Delaware grapes, you get rid of them. We're operating in a global economy. There's no sense growing grapes for nostalgia purposes."

The fact is, though, that few wine lovers are nostalgic over Delaware grapes. They were one of the mainstays of New York's wine industry not long ago—the Delawares and the Niagaras and the other native American grapes that worked to make New York a very distant number two in the nation's wine industry to California's number one. Today, 90 per cent of the wines produced in America comes out of California. But New York is second among the 42 wine-producing states. And, thanks to thoughtful, creative vintners like Art and Joyce Hunt and other wine producers who appreciate the art in the product they produce, New York wines are no longer second rate.

During the past 25 years, New York wineries have moved away from Niagaras and Delawares and begun producing world-class wines from European grapes and specially cultured hybrids and varietals. Art and Joyce Hunt's small winery, which sells a relatively miniscule 6,000 to 8,000 cases annually, has won medals galore in national and international competitions. So have a number of the other 100 or so wineries that dot this state from Long Island to the Finger Lakes.

The reality is, however, that New York state has been far less supportive of its wine industry than have a number of other states. Many of the producers of fine wines in New York find themselves struggling along, scrambling for nickels and dimes and unable to price their wines competitively against government-subsidized wines from Chile and Spain and France—not to mention California. New York vintners lack the sales volume to compete in terms of price. And what is state government doing to help? Damn little, actually.

A total of 35 states across this country permit wine sales

Battered and Bullied by the Brusque, Brutal Bureaucracy

in grocery stores—some in drug stores as well. But not here. Not in New York. Not in a state where the wine industry employs 10,000 people, pays $30 million a year in state and federal excise taxes and attracts a million tourists every spring, summer and fall.

Why not? Because the liquor store operators oppose grocery stores selling wine. Because Mike Long, chairman of this state's Conservative Party, is a liquor store operator. Because the liquor store industry has friends in the Legislature. We're talking here about friends like Pat Casale, the assemblyman from Troy, who—when he's not collecting tax dollars in his paycheck—runs a liquor store.

There's another reason, too. Politics in New York has historically been a monumental clash of competing interests. Laws here, to a greater extent than in most states, derive from an intense competition between competing interests that manifests itself in political contributions to lawmakers. New York's wine industry, one of this state's finest and most sophisticated cultural resources, can afford no lobbyist of its own. It has no real money with which to influence lawmakers. And it has no executive branch champion in a Republican administration elected largely on a commitment to improving life for small businesses.

New York's wineries are most definitely small businesses. With the exception of the Canandaigua Wine Company, which produces 80 per cent of New York State wine—including Richards' Wild Irish Rose for skid row winos and cheap champagnes for weddings in American Legion halls—most of this state's wineries are tiny, struggling operations desperately in need of more outlets for their products. Art and Joyce Hunt have only 55 acres in grapes and employ no more than six people year-round. They sell one-third of their fine wines at the Green Market in Manhattan's Union Square, another third at their winery in a remote spot on Branchport's Italy Hill and one-third in liquor stores.

The state's wine industry tried, six or seven years ago, to convince the Legislature to permit wine sales in grocery stores. Mario Cuomo was for it; he told me so at the time. A move like that would have increased the wine industry's outlets in New York from no more than 4,000 to nearly five times that.

But the liquor store owners and the wine distributors who supply them fought bitterly against such a change in the law. Some vintners who openly argued for the expansion of outlets found their products taken off liquor store shelves entirely. The result today is that you will look long and hard for a New York vintner who will argue publicly for a change in the law that would permit wine sales in grocery stores. They bear too many scars from that clash a few years back.

So nothing happens, which is the way it tends to work here in New York. If something is bad, if it works badly, it tends to stay the same because to change it—to make it better—would offend powerful people whose political contributions drive the law-making process.

There is probably a compromise that could be had here—an accommodation that would both please and disappoint enough people to become a law, if somebody could be found to make it happen. The question is, who will orchestrate the discussion necessary to make this work for everybody involved?

It won't be the Legislature, which is too divided and fractionalized and too dependent on contributions from pressure groups to see beyond its nose. It might be the State Liquor Authority, which in recent years has become more responsive to the industry it regulates. It might also be the Second Floor— the governor's office in the Capitol—if George Pataki is really serious about the campaign promises he made in unseating Mario Cuomo.

Clearly, strong forces exist to oppose in New York what 35 other states have managed to put into effect without crisis. Clearly, too, concessions would have to be made to the liquor store owners—Sunday sales, the ability to sell party-related products along with their wines and liquors. Also, clearly, somebody would have to deal with the virulent anti-alcohol forces in this society who have struggled to develop in the public consciousness a mindless equality between alcohol consumption and drug abuse—as though the use of a legal product thousands of years old and whose production constitutes a legitimate art form can be realistically compared to some lowlife snorting coke or smoking crack in a glass pipe.

So, now that the budget battle is out of the way, we'll see if the Pataki administration really means business. Or was all that talk last year about leveling the playing field for small businesses just so much hot air?

—July 12, 1995

The River People

It was a day when sunlight poured down like pale, liquid gold on the Mohawk.

When birds made magic music in looming, leafy trees beside the river.

When a soft breeze danced in off the water and embraced you on the shore like a tender lover.

It was a day like that when Mike Schillaci led me to the spot on the river that he loved so desperately—and lost.

"That was my garden there," he told me, pointing to a field of knee-high grass. "I had my dock over there. I tell you, this was heaven on Earth."

Mike Schillaci is 46. Ten years ago, reeling from a divorce that cost him a summer place on Lake George, he coughed up five grand for a modest, pale green cottage on the Mohawk.

The land was owned by the state and administered by the state Canal Corporation. Mike Schillaci could occupy it if he paid $750 a year for a permit.

His was one of a few such camps in the Vischer Ferry Nature Preserve. Permits had first been issued when postage stamps cost a nickel—before anybody had ever heard of Chappaquiddick, disco, ATMs or the Internet.

Mike Schillaci's neighbor, a steelworker named Jack Dunbar, had found his river refuge in 1961. John Miller—Mickey, everybody called him—came in the next summer.

The River People drank some beer there, held barbecues, caught some walleyes, laughed a lot. The kids splashed in the water.

Kids build matchless memories in spots like that—images they can summon up as personal visions of paradise as they lie on their deathbeds in old age. Couples who elbow their way through life's ordeals find moments of placid proximity that remind them why they got together to begin with. Old people bask in the sun to savor a world they know they'll soon enough depart.

The River People were there for decades, renewing their spirits each summer. Then the Town of Clifton Park asked the state to throw them out. Camps didn't fit in with the town's new master plan for the preserve.

I don't know just what the problem was. Town parks and recreation chief Patricia Haffner wouldn't return my calls.

Besides, Clifton Park has trouble with municipal water—has had for decades, as $2 billion worth of upscale housing sprouted up on farmland. Now, with 35,000 people, Clifton Park was digging wells near the camps for a public water supply. And those River People had septic systems.

The River People begged. Grandfather us in. Let us stay until we die, then issue no more permits. We'll abandon our septic systems and install holding tanks, whatever you want.

No deal. The first of this year, the permits were revoked. The camp that Mike Schillaci was driven from suffered ice damage. It stood there in the sun the other day—abandoned, a gaping hole in its face, a mangled corpse amid the tall trees.

Mike Schillaci and his old neighbors hope to get permits for a tiny piece of state riverfront on the preserve's eastern edge, away from the wells. They would put a few trailers there. They would paint them dull, woodsy colors to blend in.

Anything. They'll do anything anybody demands if they can just get back to the river.

Mickey Miller won't be there, though. This spring, his first away from the river in 36 years, he died at age 69.

Mike Schillaci will assure you that Mickey died of a broken heart.

—June 8, 1997

LAW AND DISORDER

Justice Delayed

Here's a story about murder, justice and love.

And about a corpse that offered damning testimony against a killer three decades after it was lowered into the ground.

The story began 34 years ago last week in Jackson, Miss. Medgar Evers, 37, was his state's top NAACP official. As he arrived home from a meeting, a sniper's bullet ripped into his back. His wife and three small children ran outside to find him dying.

A .30-06 bolt-action rifle was found in a nearby clump of honeysuckle bushes. It bore the palm print of a white supremacist named Byron De La Beckwith. He told the cops that somebody had stolen his rifle.

Two all-white juries heard evidence against Beckwith. Neither would convict. Beckwith went free. Medgar Evers, a World War II veteran, was buried in Arlington National Cemetery.

Three decades later, the district attorney in Hinds County, Miss., came up with indications that Ross Barnett, the governor when Beckwith had been tried, had tampered with jurors.

D.A. Ed Peters went into the case file. The murder bullet was missing. So was the autopsy report.

So, Peters called Albany. He spoke to Dr. Michael Baden, the chief forensic pathologist for the New York State Police, whom he'd met some years earlier. Ed Peters wanted to nail Byron De La Beckwith for that long-ago assassination. Would Baden help?

Sure, Baden said.

Medgar Evers was dug up and shipped to Albany Medical Center. With the body came Bobby DeLaughter, the Hinds County assistant D.A. handling the case, and Van Evers, Medgar's youngest son.

Van was a photographer in his 30s. He'd been only three years old when his father had been murdered.

"He wanted to be present when the autopsy was done," Baden told me the other day. "He had no recollection of his father. . . . I told him, 'Look, we don't know what we're going to find. It may be very upsetting to see decomposed remains.' I suggested that he stay at a local hotel here until after I'd been able to work out some way of him seeing his dad. . . .

"But when we opened the casket, the most amazing thing was that the body was in excellent condition. It was as if he'd been embalmed the day before."

Medgar Evers had been buried in a metal casket in a deep grave on a high hill with good drainage. No water had invaded the casket to ravage the body. His corpse was intact to offer evidence against his murderer.

"So," Baden told me, "the young man came in to look at his dad. He looked just like his dad. They were both about the same age, he and his dad. You could see the strong resemblance. . . .

"He reacted very emotionally. He started to cry. And then, spontaneously, he, the black son, and Bobby DeLaughter, the white prosecutor, extended their arms toward one another and hugged each other over the exhumed body of Medgar Evers. . . .

"It was a white person and a black person hugging one another in a way that would not have been possible at the time his father was killed. . . . The two of them holding each other was the most marvelous thing."

Then Michael Baden performed the autopsy. Beckwith's defense had argued that Evers had been shot with a pistol, not Beckwith's rifle. Uh-uh, Baden testified. The bullet had hit bone. And it had come from a rifle.

Byron De La Beckwith was convicted of murdering Medgar Evers.

After 31 years, justice.

—*June 15, 1997*

Cus's Boys

Kevin Rooney was standing in the marble hallway of the federal courthouse on Broadway in Albany when the shy kid in the red sweatshirt came over. In a soft voice, the kid said that his uncle had met Rooney somewhere and had told the kid to say hello.

With a practiced eye, Kevin Rooney studied him. He has studied a lot of kids like this over the years. Rooney knew what was on this one's mind.

"You a welterweight?" Rooney asked.

"Lightweight," the kid responded. Eagerly.

"Yeah," Kevin Rooney said, "well, you can come on down to my gym if you want. You'll have to drive down to Catskill. But, yeah, you want to come on down, that's good. That's OK."

The kid said thanks and faded away just as Mike Tyson cruised by, heading back to the courtroom where he and Kevin Rooney were locked in mortal combat over a minor matter of 50 million bucks, give or take. Tyson's massive shoulders were encased in a burgundy suit jacket. He moved with slow deliberation, a relatively short guy with a neck the size of an ordinary human's thigh.

He passes by you up close, and you can sense the almost inhuman power in that thick body. You can believe that this is the Baddest Man on the Planet. With the exception of just one fighter—an also-ran named Buster Douglas, who had one great night in him—everybody Mike Tyson has ever stepped into the ring with has believed it, too.

Mike Tyson pretended not to notice Kevin Rooney, who glanced Tyson's way as the fighter passed by. Then Kevin Rooney resumed his conversation.

"He's not as good as he should be at this point," Rooney was saying. "Yeah, he's got some of the head movement back, the stuff Cus and I taught him. But he's not stepping to the side. He's not getting the right leverage on his punches. He's trying to do it all with speed and power."

Rooney shook his head. "You know, he should have made a billion dollars by now. He should have been the first billion-dollar fighter."

Then Kevin Rooney went back inside Courtroom Two for another installment in the great human tragedy that is the life of Mike Tyson.

It began on the streets of Brownsville, Brooklyn, with a mother with a weakness for smack. At 14, Mike Tyson was an accomplished thug, banging away mercilessly at older guys in a prison gym. Then somebody brought Cus D'Amato, the old fight manager, around to see him, to talk to him. And D'Amato saw something there.

A born fighter? Sure, Cus D'Amato saw that. But he also saw a complex human being with a sharp mind—an untrained, undisciplined mind, but fertile soil for the D'Amato Outlook.

And that was, quite simply, this:

Be the best person you can be. Live life with honor. Treasure your friends.

A fistic philosopher, that was Cus D'Amato. For years, he'd lived a spartan life over the Gramercy Gym in Manhattan, imparting metaphysical wisdom and physical advice, never taking a nickel that wasn't his—and giving up a good many that were. He stood up to the Mob, and he stood up for his boys.

Make fear your friend, he told his fighters. Overcome your weaknesses. Be a man. And throw combinations.

When he first saw Mike Tyson, Cus D'Amato was in semi-retirement in Catskill, living on memories. He'd had his share of champions. He'd even led one fighter to the heavyweight title. Another Brooklyn street tough named Floyd Patterson had done him proud, earning millions, growing into a fine, admirable man.

Now, in Cus's old age, somebody shoved this new kid in front of him. A kid bigger than Patterson had been—more powerful, more complicated, meaner.

Cus won Mike Tyson over by smothering him in love. He went to court and adopted the kid as his son. And when another D'Amato fighter named Kevin Rooney ran out his string in the ring, Cus D'Amato made Rooney Tyson's trainer—the daily, living link between the hulking, brooding, explosive kid and the wise old guru who'd seen so much, who so keenly grasped the essentials of the human condition.

Then Cus died. He was 77, and he didn't mind, really. The world had changed on him, grown strange and cold, and he'd set it all up before he went. Kevin would be with Mike. Cus's life would be over, but theirs would go on. Together.

Cus had figured everything but Robin Givens, the actress. The heavyweight title his, Tyson fell for Givens, married her and fell into the deepest pit of Hell with Robin and her mother. Kevin Rooney, nobody's diplomat, spoke against the women, and Tyson chose the TV goddess over Cus's chosen successor. Tyson fired Rooney and fell under the spell of Don King, con man supreme—the grinning, grasping Rasputin of professional boxing.

Then Robin left Tyson, complaining of beatings and brutality. After that came a late-night encounter with a beauty contestant in Indianapolis that led to a three-year prison term for rape. Then, after Tyson's release, came three fights for a total of eight rounds and $180 million in purses. And now, at

30, Mike Tyson sits in a courtroom on the fourth floor of a U.S. courthouse in Albany, pondering an upcoming fight with Evander Holyfield and doing battle with Kevin Rooney over money.

Was their agreement a career-long contract? Is Cus's appointed successor entitled to 10 per cent of everything Tyson will ever make? A jury of eight men and women sits in that courtroom prepared to render a judgment on that question.

And, meanwhile, a kid in a red sweatshirt comes up to Kevin Rooney in the hallway and radiates dreams the way Mike Tyson radiates menace. And you can see Kevin Rooney's sharp eyes as he gazes at the kid, wondering.

Could it be, he wonders?

Could this be another Mike Tyson?

—September 22, 1996

A Hard Luck Guy

We'll call him Vito.

It's not his real name, but the guy who told me this story did so only on the condition that I not mention Vito's real name. Vito is a sweet guy, I'm told, but he's also somebody who pushes his luck.

People like Vito suffer from what shrinks call a flawed capacity for risk assessment. Larry Walters was like that. He lived in the Los Angeles area. About 10 years ago, he bought 40 weather balloons and hooked them up to an aluminum lawn chair he'd tied to his truck bumper. He blew up the balloons, lashed himself into the chair with a pellet gun in his lap and untied the line to the truck.

The idea was that Larry Walters would rise gently, hovering in the breeze a few hundred feet above the ground. Instead, he shot up like the space shuttle to 13,000 feet.

He disrupted traffic patterns at Los Angeles International Airport. He also scared the hell out of himself.

So, he started shooting out the weather balloons. Unfortunately, all the balloons he shot out were on one side. He came down, all right, but hanging sideways in the lawn chair, clutching it for dear life. He smacked into some power lines. Electricity to a few thousand homes was cut off.

Larry Walters didn't get killed, but he sure got yelled at.

Vito pushed his luck on solid ground. He did it Wednesday as he delivered pizzas for a joint in North Troy. The cops had set up a road check on Schoolhouse Lane in Waterford. Vito came over the bridge from Troy in his car, a warm pizza in the seat beside him.

The cops say, where's your license? Hey, I forgot my wallet, Vito says. I'm just working, OK? I'm delivering this food. Whaddea say, gimme a break?

The cops give him a break. Go ahead, they say. So, Vito goes ahead.

Later in the day, Vito cruises into the checkpoint again. Where's your license? Left it home, sorry; won't do it again. I got this pepperoni and mushroom job here, all right? It's getting cold. OK, fine, go on through.

All of which is terrific until Vito comes through the police checkpoint a few more times and, finally, just happens to get the wrong cop. Where's your license? Hey, I forgot it. OK, says the cop, give me your full name, date of birth, middle initial. Then park over there and wait.

So, Vito does that. The cop gets on the horn to the computer center in Raybrook and runs Vito. The call comes back, and there's this thing the cops call a Signal 31. That means there's a bench warrant out. In this case the bench warrant is from Troy. And, by the way, Vito's license is suspended for the fourth time for failure to pay tickets and for no insurance.

Vito is very polite when all this is mentioned—and, wisely so, since the cops have all the guns. It's gotta be a mistake, Vito says, just let me go deliver my pizza. But, no, now the cops call Troy, and the Troy cops are going to meet everybody at the bridge, and Vito can explain all this to a judge.

Vito has one request. He wants to call the lady who ordered the pizza and tell her to come get it. So, the cops take him to a pay phone. The woman arrives at the scene for her pizza. She counts out the money, about $8.50. Then she gives Vito, who's in cuffs, a huge tip.

Take it, she says. You're going to need it, I think.

And let's all hope that Vito doesn't use the money to buy a lawn chair.

—February 19, 1999

Marketing and Murder

As a concession to the reality of theft, Rocky Roy doesn't have the CD on display. But he reached behind a counter and handed me one to look over.

There was Christopher G. Wallace in the cover photograph—all six-foot-three inches and 300 pounds of him. He was garbed in black and leaning against a hearse and glaring balefully at the camera. Just above his head was stuck an orange-glow price tag—$20.99.

Rocky Roy owns and operates the Music Shack on the north side of Albany's Central Avenue, just a few doors west of Henry Johnson Boulevard. He has another store in Troy.

Precisely a week ago, he got in 600 copies of Chris Wallace's new rap CD release, "Life After Death." He has sold hundreds of these things already. One shop in New York City, he told me, sold 1,700 copies of "Life After Death" the first day the CD hit the stores.

"I've never seen anything like it," Rocky Roy said. "Everybody knew this was going to be huge even before his death, but this is incredible. I have people come in here and say, 'Well, I know it's expensive, but I've got to pay my last respects.' And they buy it."

Chris Wallace was 24 years old when he was killed in a drive-by shooting in Los Angeles three weeks ago. Just a few years earlier, he'd been a smalltime Brooklyn drug dealer. Then, for amusement, he'd begun making rap recordings in somebody's basement.

He was a gifted writer and a moving storyteller. His despairing raps dealt with warm blood on cold city sidewalks and flying bullets and the desolate danger of his life. Some of his recordings made their way to Arista Records.

That's when the merchandising geniuses got hold of Chris Wallace. He was repackaged as The Notorious B.I.G., Biggie Smalls. His first release, "Ready to Die," sold millions of copies, and Biggie Smalls was soon engaged in a nasty rivalry with West Coast rapper Tupac Shakur.

Then Tupac Shakur was gunned down in Las Vegas six months ago, followed by Biggie Smalls' own assassination March 9. And whatever else you might think about all this, you have to give Chris Wallace credit for a brilliant career move in getting murdered. His newest release is the hottest item in the memory of anybody in the record business.

Clearly, Gangsta Rap strikes chords in millions of people. How could anybody justify any effort to suppress it? Not me, certainly.

But if you believe that art serves both as a mirror and shaper of cultural values, then what do you make of a mass-produced art form that glorifies street carnage?

This isn't just about poverty and the crime and violence

that accompany it. It's too easy to smugly dismiss this phenomenon that way.

A century and a half ago, two million Irish swept into New York. Within 15 years, 50,000 Irish immigrant women were plying the streets as hookers. The Irish were committing 60 per cent of the city's violent crime. A few decades later, the Italians got their turn.

But that all took place in an era before mass entertainment—before merchandisers so cynically romanticized the pathology of poverty. You have to wonder about the extent to which today's manipulative merchandising works to perpetuate rather than alleviate the agony that Chris Wallace wrote about.

When the history of this time is written, what judgment might be rendered on the marketing geniuses who turned the late Chris Wallace into the Notorious B.I.G.?

—April 1, 1997

A Stoned Society

It was the limp that attracted John Burke's attention.

Like a lot of middle-aged guys, including some who write newspaper columns, John Burke owns tender, delicate knees. He watched the woman limp awkwardly into the restroom at the Albany bus station, and he felt sorry for her.

When she came out, she wasn't limping any more. That's when John Burke's sympathy gave way to curiosity. Narcotics cops tend to be nosy people. And Inspector John Burke is the head narc in the Albany County sheriff's office.

The woman was a mule. She had drugs stashed beneath her skirt. She'd been limping into the restroom because the package was coming loose. After a search, she ended up as another drug bust.

That happens to somebody in this country every 20 seconds. As you read this, nearly 2 million Americans are behind bars. Four in five of them either violated drug or alcohol laws, were wasted at the time of their arrest, stole something for drug money or have histories of drug abuse and/or alcohol addiction.

We Americans are the most conspicuously stoned population in the industrialized world. This society has a drug problem because it has a demand problem—an apparently insatiable appetite for intoxication that lands roughly one American in 150 in the slammer at any given moment.

The New York State Department of Corrections estimates that at least three in four of its 71,000 inmates could benefit from drug treatment. Every year, it runs about 37 per cent of the population through such programs. Since the average inmate does 30 months, the state figures it pretty much exposes each inmate to treatment, but the recidivism rate for drug-related crime remains enormous.

That's because some people can't stay away from the stuff, and some just don't want to, not even after 30 months in the can. Also, there's huge money in the drug trade, and towering sums of money are spent fighting it. John J. DiIulio, Jr., a criminologist of serious repute at the University of Pennsylvania, frets that it now costs so much money to imprison drug offenders that policing itself is at risk. When you look at police force reductions in Albany and Rotterdam, as just two examples, you can't help but wonder if DiIulio doesn't have a point.

This wasn't a good week to snort nose candy on State Street. That's because about 800 narcs were at the Crowne Plaza hotel for the most recent meeting of the International Narcotic Enforcement Officers Association. The hotel was crawling with federal narcs, state narcs and local narcs. John

Burke was the official host. All these narcs spent the week studying techniques to more effectively nail druggies.

The drug trade pros are increasingly shrewd. The other day, a crew-cut guy named Sgt. Mike Lewis of the Maryland State Police ran a seminar on interdiction—on spotting mules on the highway and locating their stashes in their vehicles. Experienced dealers and mules aren't in Beemers or Mercedes any more, he was saying. But keep your eyes peeled for more modest vehicles with tinted windows. Mules still don't like people seeing what goes on inside their cars.

When the Legislature convenes in January, modifications in the Rockefeller drug laws probably will be on the table again. In recent years, the cost of imprisoning so many druggies has become a political issue. We now have more people in the slammer than any other democracy, mainly because of drugs. That's troubling stuff in a free society.

The real problem, though, is that demand thing. We Americans live in a drug and booze-soaked culture where use and even abuse is increasingly accepted. Slowly, it's bankrupting us.

And in more ways than one.

—*October 15, 1999*

Motherhood, Misery and Murder

A mustard-yellow school bus thumped gingerly over one of the enormous speed bumps at Apple Meadow Village apartments in Greenport the other day and came to a ragged stop. The door opened. A stream of children poured off.

I watched as a ruddy-faced girl of about 5, with a shimmering shock of blonde hair, bounced merrily past the doorway of unit G-5 and into the waiting arms of her mother, who hugged her.

G-5 is empty now. Anna Christina Santana and her six-month-old son had occupied that apartment until Nov. 20. On that day, according to the authorities, Anna Christina Santana murdered her baby.

I don't know if she really did that. A judge and jury will decide. But, having nearly finished raising two kids of my own—after living through every joy and sorrow of their journeys into adulthood—I felt a compelling need to know this:

What could motivate a mother to murder her child? What dark, soul-killing forces could be at work in a crime of such immense unnaturalness?

And I needed to know how social workers, supposedly aware that a mother had abused an older child, could permit that mother to leave a structured family environment and place her alone in a welfare apartment with a new baby?

Here are the answers:

If the authorities are correct, there was a cruel reality at work in that little apartment in Greenport, population 2,070, that plays itself out 600 or 700 times a year in this country. That's how many children are murdered annually by their mothers, in towns large and small, across the face of America.

Often, the mothers are poor, single and engulfed in a cloud of despair that others can only guess at. Barely more than children themselves, they are alone and profoundly unhappy.

Anna Christina Santana seems to fit that pattern. She's a dark, smallish woman of 20 with a mole on her right cheek. She has had two children by different men. She was on welfare, going nowhere in life and getting there in a hurry. She knew it, too.

Scholarly researchers at McMaster University in Hamilton, Ont., have studied this phenomenon. They found that biological parents who kill their children generally do it "more out of sorrow than rage." The parent apparently sees the killing as rescuing the child from the harshness of the human condition.

If the parent has a gun, the child is likely to be shot. If not, the child is smothered. The act is often followed by the parent's suicide.

No gun was found in Anna Christina Santana's apartment. Edward, authorities say, was smothered. After Anna was arrested, she was subjected to a psychiatric examination and moved from the Columbia County Jail to a state mental facility near Utica.

And, according to someone close to this case, Columbia County authorities didn't know that Anna Christina Santana had abused her older child and lost custody of her in Albany County. When faced with the decision as to whether to put the young woman in an apartment by herself, with just her new baby, Columbia County couldn't gain access to her Albany County history. Some judge had sealed the records in the interest of confidentiality.

So Columbia County authorities made the decision to let her go alone with her baby without information that, in a sane world, would have been available to them. The records finally were obtained through the Columbia County coroner's office—a day after Edward's death.

Ross Prinzo, Jr., Albany County's commissioner of social services, told me that he's forbidden by law to even acknowledge my questions on this. He checked with a lawyer. This is a law framed by lunatics. A mother can stand accused of murdering her child, and nobody can talk about how such a horror could come to be.

Apple Meadow Village is a neat, well-kept collection of two-story, vinyl-sided buildings erected about 20 years ago. It was built with federal money. Its tenants are low-income people, mostly young families struggling to climb into the middle class.

I spent the first five years of my life in a project like this, only not as nice. Nobody had a dime, but it was the

1950s—an era of optimism. Everybody believed fervently that a better life lay ahead.

Joyce Giordiano, who manages this complex, told me about the poetry, scribbled on scraps of paper, that she saw in G-5 after little Edward died. From what she saw, Anna Christina Santana felt no hope for tomorrow.

"I found a poem on the floor of her place," Joyce Giordiano said. "It read, 'Everybody knows I'm here, but no one really cares.' It said something about some man—'I loved him, and he hurt me.' Her family took it."

Her family consists of a sister, Lorenza DeJesus, 35, who lives in the county seat of Hudson, population 8,000, with her two teenagers and labors at a factory called Kaz, Inc. From conversations with her and others close to this case, it is possible to piece together enough of Anna Christina Santana's life to understand how nightmares like this can happen in the real world.

She was born in the Dominican Republic. The family went to Puerto Rico and then some of the family members came to New York. There's a mother in Puerto Rico, and a brother, William. There's a sister, Bonita, in Hempstead, Long Island.

Anna lived five years with Lorenza and attended high school in Hudson. She came to Albany and lived somewhere on Clinton Avenue, taking courses through the job corps. She got pregnant by a man known to her family only by a first name—Johnny. She gave birth to a daughter, whom she named Alicia.

Then, apparently, she began to abuse the baby.

I was told by a person close to this case that she would squeeze Alicia's nose, cutting off her air, until Alicia turned blue. Then she would take the child to the hospital, where doctors would fuss over the baby and the baby's mother. There is a long and complicated medical name for this practice. It is thought to be a bid for attention on the part of the mother.

While the Albany County Social Services Department is

forbidden by an archaic and senseless law to discuss any aspect of this case, I know that Alicia was taken from her mother and placed in Lorenza's custody in September, 1994.

Almost immediately afterward, Anna became pregnant again. She never mentioned the name of the father to her sister. She went to Puerto Rico to have the baby, whom she named Edward. Then she and Edward returned to Hudson to live with Lorenza.

If the baby cried or was troublesome, Anna had help from Lorenza and Lorenza's two teenagers. Much of the responsibility for motherhood was lifted from her shoulders by other members of the household.

Lorenza described her younger sister as, "a quiet person. She never said anything. If she was watching TV, she was happy. She wanted to get an apartment, to get her life in order. I have a job and two children of my own, and I have Alicia. I said OK."

A social worker from a firm that contracts with Columbia County got Anna Christina Santana the apartment, according to Joyce Giordiano. A social worker took her shopping on the day of Edward's death.

According to figures supplied by the U.S. Justice Department, Edward was, from the start, in more danger than Alicia had ever faced. A survey of murder in families in the nation's 75 largest counties reveals that mothers are more likely than fathers to kill their children. When fathers kill, the victim is equally likely to be a son or daughter. But mothers kill their sons twice as often as they kill their daughters.

Nobody knows why. Boy babies are sometimes more difficult than girls. Maybe that's why it happens. Edward cried a lot on the day he died.

This is what the state police say Anna told them:

Edward was crying. She tried to feed him. He still cried. Then, police say, she put a pillow over his face to quiet him. When she took away the pillow five or 10 minutes later, the child made no sound, but she thought he was breathing. Later, she realized that he was not. She called for help. A week later, after an autopsy, she was charged with murdering her baby.

"I wish I had known she was so sick," her sister, Lorenza, told me. "I would have helped her. But I'm not a doctor. I have her baby, Alicia, and that's all I could do."

Joyce Giordiano said that during their four days at Apple Meadow Village, Anna and Edward slept on the floor. They had no phone, furniture, no lamps, only overhead lights.

And, probably most crucial, state police say, the empty apartment in which Anna Christina Santana and her baby boy were placed by a county government that couldn't obtain her records lacked one other thing—a critical piece of equipment, it seems.

The apartment had no TV.

—*December 6, 1995*

In the Name of Mercy

On a typical day in America, about 6,000 people turn 65 and take on the status of senior citizens. From Portland, Maine, to Portland, Ore., about 6,000 people die every day, too, most of them elderly.

One of those senior citizens died Tuesday in Malta. Jack D. Hearn was 69. He suffered from acute, clinical depression and the aftereffects of a stroke. He was about to enter a nursing home.

At about 10 a.m., according to police, Hearn's wife, Jane, stuck a pistol in his mouth and pulled the trigger. She'd planned to do the same thing to herself, they say, but she didn't.

In the sunlight that gleamed down through yesterday's crisp, clean spring air, the Saratoga County jail could have been taken for some modernistic office building mysteriously erected off a rural road in Milton. This is a relatively new structure, built a decade ago at a cost of $9.8 million and containing 140 cells.

Yesterday it was home to 175 prisoners—one a 64-year-old retired school librarian who almost certainly never imagined herself in such a place.

If you're a cop, you arrest somebody who does this. If you're a prosecutor, you charge her with murder. If you're a judge, you look at a thing like this and you wonder what in God's name you're supposed to do with it.

The last such case in this state took place in New York City. A guy who'd spent eight years editing the World Almanac helped his sick wife kill herself with a drug overdose. He ended up serving four months. It wasn't until he'd served his time that he mentioned that he'd also put a plastic bag over her head to help the process along.

The law is not equipped to handle violent crime committed by old people—especially when those crimes are committed in the name of mercy. It is particularly ill-equipped to handle handgun murders by 64-year-old women.

Some 70,000 people live in prison cells in this state. Only 25 of them are women over 60. The eldest is Ruth Scott, a 74-year-old druggie from Buffalo. The likelihood is that she and Jane Hearn will never meet.

The law understands druggies and has decided how to deal with them. This sort of thing, nobody understands.

Is this the future? As this country's population ages, will we see a surging wave of retired school librarians jamming pistols into the mouths of their mates? Are we going to have Jack Kevorkian move into franchising—opening up "Suicide 'R' Us" parlors right next door to every McDonald's in America?

Was this nightmare in Malta only a preview of some large-scale horror show? Sure, it's a shame that you can't begin life at 90 and slowly work your way back to 19, but what sort of society have we created when people who've led decent, productive lives come in old age to view killing as an act of love?

Some of these people may always have taken Rodney Dangerfield's view of the human condition—that life is just a bowl of pits. But the true tragedy here is not merely death, which is a natural part of living. It's what seems to die inside some people as they encounter the hardships of aging.

You would hope that humans would better grasp the essence of life as they near its end—that they would realize that living is like licking honey from a thorn. I'm glad I'm not the judge here.

But I hope that the judge turns out to be somebody who views life, with all its warts, as a feast to be savored.

And not as a predicament.

—*April 11, 1997*

Big Steve

It's a shame they retired Old Sparky.

For a while there, the electric chair was toasting New York's bad guys at quite a snappy pace. Then the U.S. Supreme Court declared New York's death penalty statute unconstitutional. That cheered liberals but offered scant comfort to the 700 or so guys who'd already ridden Old Sparky into eternity.

Then George Pataki came along and restored the death

penalty, this time specifying the wimpy method of death by lethal injection. So far, though, nobody has been subjected to the needle. The way this law is written it's even possible that nobody ever will.

That does not, however, keep district attorneys running for election from asking for the death penalty every chance they get. Albany County D. A. Sol Greenberg, for example, is going for the needle in two murder cases. Now it looks like Ken Bruno will get his chance right next door in Rensselaer County.

Steven Williamson is a 6-foot-9-inch Guyana national charged with murdering his sister-in-law in her Griswold Heights apartment. He's also charged with the vicious beating of the dead woman's 3-year-old daughter.

This is a guy with a seriously nasty history. He pleaded guilty in Florida in the 1991 beating death of his roommate. He somehow managed to walk after serving only three years, apparently in a Florida effort to ease prison overcrowding. Now, according to police, Williamson has done his part to ease overcrowding in Troy's public housing, and nobody is happy about it.

By statute, Bruno has 120 days to decide whether to try to stick the needle into Williamson—who's certainly a prime candidate, if you go for that sort of thing. But Bruno says he'll make up his mind more quickly than that, and my guess is that he already has.

Bruno is filling out the unexpired term of the prior D.A., who became a judge. He could face a tough fight this year. He's the son of State Senate Majority Leader Joe Bruno, which means that he has at his disposal some canny and experienced political guidance. And, according to all the polls, four in five New Yorkers favor the death penalty.

From a political standpoint, Bruno would be demented not to go for the needle for Steven Williamson. The only mystery in any of this is where the prison system might find a gurney to fit a guy the size of an NBA power forward. Hey, big Steve's feet could get cold.

Old Sparky could prevent that. The good folks in Florida, which let Steven Williamson go, showed us how the other day. Florida authorities were cheerfully frying one Pedro Medina, another murderer, when the guy actually caught fire.

No kidding. When they poured the juice into Pedro Medina, flames started shooting out from his metal skullcap. According to witnesses, it was like a Fourth of July pyrotechnics display. Smoke filled the execution chamber.

You can do some amazing things with a 74-year-old contraption built to blast 2,000 volts into human flesh.

Bob Butterworth, Florida's attorney general, seemed thrilled with the way the execution went down. Not only was Pedro Medina effectively dispatched to Final Judgment, but Butterworth speculated that the flames and smoke might even serve as a stronger deterrent to violent crime than an electric chair that works properly.

The fact is that killing these guys deters nobody and costs taxpayers a fortune. Plus, the needle is boring. The show's star merely goes to sleep.

Old Sparky, at least, could provide death penalty fans with some fun fireworks.

—April 9, 1997

Compassion and Consequences

Keep your eyes open for Marc Plano.

He's a white guy, 36, five-foot-ten, about 175 pounds. He has sort of a wide-eyed stare and a full head of dark hair that he wears a bit long.

Two days after Christmas, 1996, Marc Plano was at the Delmar home of his ex-girlfriend's mother. The woman was 83 years old. Marc Plano walked into her bedroom. He ignored her requests to leave and spent hours beating her. He left the elderly woman with broken ribs.

Incidentally, he also raped her.

Even though he had a conviction for a violent felony in another state some years earlier and a string of less serious beefs with the law, he was sentenced about 13 months ago in Albany County Court as a first-time violent felon. He got two-and-a-half to five years. He also was given credit against his prison term for time served in jail before his conviction.

I suggest that you keep your eyes open for him simply because that sentence means that he'll be out of prison soon. The parole board can release him as early as August of next year. And the system absolutely has to let him go by July 2, 2000.

For the rape and beating of an 83-year-old woman, Marc Plano will serve no more than 38 months in state prison and possibly as few as 27 months. If you wonder why there's so much howling about this system and its shortcomings, Marc Plano is only one conspicuous example.

It's because of outrages like this that the Pataki administration has been fighting for sentencing reform. Under current law, violent felony offenders might receive a sentence that sounds tough—say, three to nine years. But they're eligible for parole after serving one-third of that sentence, three years, and must be paroled after serving two thirds, which would be only six years.

So, the top end of any such sentence basically constitutes consumer fraud. Nobody serves the full sentence.

Under Jenna's law—named for a young woman murdered in downtown Albany by a violent felon on parole—felons would be given fixed sentences. And, if that sentence is nine years, they'd have to serve 6/7ths of it. That would be seven years and nine months. Also, if they behaved badly in prison, they'd serve the full nine years.

The Democrats initially opposed changing the law—especially in an election year. They didn't want George Pataki running around bragging that he'd gotten done what needed to be done. Now Assembly Speaker Shelly Silver says he favors a change in sentencing laws, but he'll offer a proposal with his stamp on it, not the governor's.

Silver also wants to pump more money into prison drug and alcohol and education programs, which seems not to appeal very much to the Republicans.

So, at the moment, we have a stalemate. Meanwhile, bad guys like Marc Plano, who really do hurt people, are being sentenced all over this huge state to prison terms that sound far tougher than they really are, thanks to the Empire State's generous parole provisions.

It's intriguing to note that two New York City cops have been killed so far this year, each by a paroled violent felon, and that 28 states around the country don't even have parole. They simply keep their criminals locked up for their full terms and off the street for as long as possible.

Of course, those are states that treat violent criminals as though they've done something wrong.

In New York, we're far too kind, compassionate and enlightened to think that way. We're pussycats.

And we pay for it.

—*June 6, 1998*

Nothing Serious

Richard Geisel wants everybody to know that he's "very, very sorry" for killing Robert Rowe, III.

Which is only appropriate. A guy who gets behind the wheel blind drunk and runs down a 21-year-old kid certainly should be sorry.

But, the other day in Albany County Court, Richard Geisel got only two to six years in prison. That means that, sorry or not, he'll be back on the street in 40 months or so. Just think how sorry he would be if they'd given him six times that sentence.

Although, Geisel is only 42. He could serve 20 years and come out in time to collect early Social Security. He would still have his golden years ahead of him.

Robert Rowe, III won't have golden years. He never even lived to enjoy his 20s. Something is profoundly wrong with a body of criminal law—the one we have in this state, for instance—that says you can get 25 years for peddling a few ounces of crack. But if you get bombed and kill a kid on the highway, you walk in just a few years.

Take Deborah Moquin, for example. Ten years ago, she got a sentence of three to nine years for getting plastered, cranking her car up to 85 miles an hour and slamming into another vehicle, killing a 15-year-old girl.

Moquin blew a .25 that night. That's not quite as drunk as Geisel was. He blew .30—which, for most people, is legally dead.

But Geisel had a clean record. Moquin had a history of drunken driving. Well, no matter. She's out now. She served less than five years.

Oh, and the girl Deborah Moquin killed? She's still dead.

Then there's this case in Troy, the one everybody seems to be talking about. Last weekend, a 16-year-old girl named Allison Bodnar was standing in the street late at night with some friends. A station wagon came along and killed her.

And kept going.

The next day, a 27-year-old hairdresser named Michele Tracey went to the Troy cops. She said she'd been boozing it up at a party that night, hit something at that location and figured she ought to mention it to somebody.

She's charged with leaving the scene of a personal injury accident. The problem authorities have with putting her in jail for any length of time is the lack of a breathalizer or blood test. Nobody can prove that Michele Tracey was legally drunk at the time of the accident.

But even if it could be proven that she was as drunk as Deborah Moquin or Richard Geisel, it wouldn't make much difference. The likelihood that Michele Tracey would serve any serious time would still be remote.

That's because killing somebody while driving drunk in this state is treated by the penal law as nothing very serious. At the moment, the Legislature is engaged in a typical display of handwringing over lowering the limit for legal intoxication while behind the wheel from .10 to .08.

The reality is, however, that casual drinkers aren't killing people. The heavy duty drunks are doing that.

Maybe if those serious boozers understood that attending AA meetings is vastly preferable to a few decades in the slammer we might have less blood on our streets. But the New York Legislature—benevolent enablers to killers like Deborah Moquin and Richard Geisel—shows no inclination to approve stiffer sentences for drunken drivers who kill.

As things stand now, the safest way to murder somebody in New York is to get tanked up and run that person down.

Don't sweat it. You'll be out in no time.

—April 24, 1998

Delicate Sensibilities

Herbert Thomas says I've hurt his feelings. Gee, that's a bummer, Herbert.

This all stems from a column I did in July on the wealth of frivolous lawsuits filed every year by inmates of the New York state prison system. A guy in Riverview sued the state because, after he'd been returned to public accommodations following an escape, he discovered that some of his personal stuff was missing. Another guy in Riverview sued the state because he got a phone call and a guard took a sloppy message.

In all, according to a report issued the other day by State Sen. Michael Nozzolio (R-Someplace Rural), New York taxpayers spend about $7 million a year for publicly supported legal actions on the part of inmates in the state prison system—many of them valid, but many of them dopey suits like those. We New Yorkers, roughly seven per cent of the nation's population, pay more than one-fourth of all the inmate legal bills in the country.

In that column, I mentioned Herbert Thomas, who will be a guest of the public until at least Jan. 30, 2003, when he's up for parole. He sued the state because a guard confiscated an obscene photo of his wife.

I characterized Mr. Thomas in that column as "a serial killer," a designation provided to me by the attorney general's office. Mr. Thomas objected to that description.

So he's suing me. He wants two million bucks in damages.

He's also suing the attorney general for $27 million, and Fred Dicker of the *New York Post*. He's suing everybody he can think of. And Mr. Thomas has a great deal of time to think of whom he might sue. He's doing 25-to-life at Great Meadow.

Characterizing him as a serial killer, Mr. Thomas contends in his suit, has caused him great mental pain, anguish and emotional distress; held him up to public contempt, scorn, ridicule, disgrace and prejudice; caused irreparable injury to his name and reputation; has damaged "what little social standing defendant had"; and has caused him loss of self-esteem and the respect of his friends.

After all, Mr. Thomas points out, he has been convicted of only one lousy little murder.

That much is true, actually. He has only one murder conviction, in Brooklyn. However, he was charged with an earlier murder in the Bronx that was pleaded down to first-degree manslaughter. He did three years for that. He was on parole for manslaughter when he committed the murder that led to his current status as a guest of the state.

That, according to the attorney general, makes him a serial killer. The FBI, the attorney general's office maintains, classifies you as a serial killer if you kill at least two people in separate incidents, which Mr. Thomas definitely did.

The fact is that Mr. Thomas, 51, has a long and fruitful association with the criminal justice system, stretching back to 1960. He was busted for various indiscretions eight times in New Orleans and three times in Indianapolis. He first came to public attention in New York in 1971, in Manhattan, on charges of petit larceny and possession of stolen property.

He failed to show up in court for that one, and a month later was busted for first-degree robbery, assault and resisting arrest. He did seven months in Rikers Island. Then he got 60 days in the Westchester County Jail on a petit larceny beef in Mount Vernon and six months for drug possession in the Bronx. After that came the Bronx murder and the manslaughter plea. A first-degree robbery soon followed, accompanied by the Brooklyn murder.

Here, I'm told, is what happened in that incident:

Early in the morning following Christmas Day, 1977, a man named William Huhn went to a private club on Jamaica Avenue to meet a barmaid, one Doreen Mazzio. Mr. Thomas and another guy burst into the joint and demanded money from the cash register. Then, according to Ms. Mazzio's testimony, Mr. Thomas suggested killing both witnesses.

Mr. Thomas' business associate was not wild about this plan. He argued against it as both Mr. Huhn and Ms. Mazzio were ordered to lie face down on the floor. Ms. Mazzio heard two shots and braced herself for the bullet that would end her own life. It never came. The two men fled.

She then looked over at Mr. Huhn and saw that he'd been executed, shot to death like some sick dog—a Christmas present from Herbert Thomas, a Brooklyn jury decided later.

It's a shame that Mr. Thomas is so upset. Given his history, this is not a guy I'm eager to have sore at me, even though he's locked up for now. I meant only to point out that he, like many other inmates, seems to have way too much time on his hands and that the state should limit their capacity to file silly lawsuits like this one.

Even if he feels that somebody has tarnished his sterling reputation.

—*October 18, 1995*

Making Tracks

Everybody has one—every reporter, every cop, every prosecutor, every defense lawyer, every judge.

Everybody involved in any way with the criminal justice system has a favorite story about how dumb criminals can be.

My favorite involves a robbery a few years back somewhere in California. These two guys stuck up a bank, jumped into a getaway car and roared off. They ditched the car. When they were later arrested, they denied that they'd been the guys that a witness outside the bank had seen jumping into the car.

They were on trial, sitting together at the defense table, when the prosecutor got the witness on the stand.

"Now," the prosecutor said, "Were you outside the bank that day?"

"Yes, I was," the witness said.

"And did you see two men run out of the bank, jump into the car and speed off?"

"I did."

At which point the prosecutor, in his most dramatic tone of voice, asked, "And are those two men in this courtroom today?"

Before the witness could answer, though, the two defendants stood up.

I liked that story even better than the one about the junkie who went into a sporting goods store somewhere down south, pulled out a knife and announced that this was a stick-up and that he had a gun. The store clerk took a shotgun from the display case, pumped a shell into it and pointed it at the would-be crook.

"No, jerk," the clerk explained. "You've got a knife. I've got a gun."

But, as of yesterday, I have a new favorite story about crime and stupidity. According to a story in this newspaper, somebody ran wild in a nice Clifton Park neighborhood Saturday night. They torched mailboxes, slashed tires, kicked in windshields and stole money and tapes from the vandalized vehicles.

The damage ran into the thousands of dollars. The good news was that a Saratoga County sheriff's deputy named Anthony P. Timpanaro, employing an advanced law enforcement technique, was able to make quick arrests in the case. Three 16-year-olds were charged with a total of eight felonies and six misdemeanors.

And what was this advanced law enforcement technique employed by Deputy Timpanaro? Well, this crime was committed during the month of March in upstate New York. And, in this part of the world at this time of year, it sometimes snows.

In fact, it snowed Saturday night. It was, in fact, probably snowing even as the crime was being committed.

Nonetheless, according to the cops, it apparently didn't occur to the three boneheaded kids who committed this crime that they were leaving footprints in the snow. Deputy Timpanaro followed the tracks to the kids' houses and busted them.

Like, duh.

This little episode seems to rank right up there with the one in New York City involving the guy who stood in a long bank line waiting to rob the teller. When he finally got to the window and handed her the robbery note, the anxious expression on her face prompted the dozen other people in that bank line to pull out their service pistols.

It seems that the robber was trying to stick up a bank located across the street from New York City's FBI offices—on the FBI payday, yet.

Now, of course, thousands of dollars worth of vandalism damage is nothing to laugh about. And, yes, these arrests are genuine tragedies for the kids and for their families.

But I still like this story even better than the one about the burglars who hit a camera shop one night.

And, when they split, left a pile of Polaroid pictures they'd taken of each other.

—*March 25, 1998*

Different Strokes

Normally, when Alice Green starts her shtik, I roll my eyes and mutter to myself, "There she goes again."

Alice Green is a Ph.D. who runs a left-wing operation in Albany called the Center for Law & Justice. Currently, she's wound up over the case of one Eirshawn Donley, a black Albany High School student just sentenced for pointing a revolver at another kid on a school bus. Donley wanted the kid's seat.

Alice Green says it's not Donley's fault that he had the gun; it's society's fault. If society didn't want guns floating around then Eirshawn Donley wouldn't be in this fix.

Yeah, well, the fact is that Eirshawn Donley is precisely the sort of kid who should be separated from society by steel bars. At the time he pulled the gun, he was on probation for felony assault. Once, during one of his stints as a juvenile in Family Court, he bit a deputy.

Simply put, Eirshawn Donley is an out-of-control troublemaker who shouldn't be on the streets. Or in school. What high school needs gun-toting, 18-year-old sophomores with a tendency to chomp on people who annoy them?

Under new, tougher state sentencing laws, Judge Tom Breslin gave the kid 11 years in a plea bargain. Eirshawn Donley faced 20 years if he went to trial. He might not have been much of a student, but even Eirshawn Donley could figure out the difference between 20 and 11.

Alice Green objects vehemently to the tougher sentencing laws. She also objects to prisons. She thinks they only make bad kids worse when they get out. She also objects to a court system that sends three blacks to jail for every white.

She's about half-right. Prisons are grim places. Given the available world, though, where else do you put people you don't dare let run loose? And, while the courts are statistically tougher on African Americans than on whites with similar criminal histories who commit similar crimes, it's also statistically true that young black males are more likely to do bad things than young white males.

But let's go back a bit in time. Six years ago, a white Shenendehowa High School football player got tanked up and took a loaded shotgun to school in comfortable, suburban Clifton Park. He waved the gun around, scared the hell out of the whole town and ended up being designated a youthful offender. He got probation and went on to college.

Now, that kid had no prior record, and this incident unfolded before the tougher sentencing laws were passed. Still, won't it be interesting to see what happens to these eight white, middle-class Fonda-Fultonville football players just charged with planting homemade bombs around town for laughs? We'll see if anybody there ends up sharing a cell with Eirshawn Donley.

Don't hold your breath until that happens.

So, as loopy as Alice Green's comments sometimes are, she seems to have a point here. She wouldn't have objected if Eirshawn Donley had gotten two to three years with some serious, professional counseling to get his head on straight—assuming that's possible.

"I'm not totally unrealistic," she told me. "There are some people who can't function and pose a serious threat in a community.... I wouldn't go so far as to say that no person should ever be put inside a prison."

There, that's something, anyway. And, when you look at these three cases together, you can understand how Alice Green might conclude that the system can be just a teensy bit unfair now and then.

—*October 18, 1996*

An Affair of the Heart

It's a sunny winter day on Albany's Delaware Avenue. Paula Taylor is turning her head to the right and pushing back her meticulously cornrowed hair to display her scar.

It's paper thin—the sort of neat, surgical line a razor blade leaves. The scar runs from her left ear to her chin, just an inch or two above her jugular vein.

"Was he going for your throat?" I ask her.

"Oh, yeah," she tells me. "He was definitely trying to kill me."

Paula Taylor is a pleasant, well-spoken woman of 27 with rotten taste in men. The guy who slashed her, according to her and the Albany police, was King Tut. That's his street name, anyway. He also goes by Tony Wilson sometimes.

He's really Shaun Tutt, DOB 7/2/65, New York state criminal identification number 5909280H. Five-nine or so, maybe 190 pounds. King Tut has a lengthy history of bad behavior—including an 18-month stint in Downstate Correctional Facility and a misdemeanor assault beef involving another woman in North Carolina nine years ago.

Paula Taylor liked King Tut. She let him move into her place. It was not a placid relationship. After 18 months, Paula Taylor put him out. Protection orders were issued all around.

"I was home," Paula Taylor told me. "It was on a Friday. I was on my way to work. It was about 8:35 in the morning. I happened to be standing in the living room almost immediately by the door. He pushed the door open. . . .

"He touched my face area. I just immediately grabbed my face and dove to the ground. And he stood over the top of me, and he said, 'I'm going to kill you, you effin' B. I told you I was coming back.' He tried to turn me over. He slashed me on my arm. . . .

"On that day, there was someone who'd driven him to my place. And the person had no idea as to what was going on. And when he saw this guy standing over me, he immediately jumped out of the car and came in and pulled the guy off of me."

The cops busted King Tut, charging him with burglary and assault. His story was that he'd gone back to get his stuff and ended up forced to defend himself. Witnesses told varying versions.

King Tut got a first-class defense lawyer, a 50ish guy named Ray Kelly. The Albany County Assistant DA handling the case was one Bryan Rounds, a man with 20 years less experience.

Ray Kelly made routine defense motions. Rounds never responded. Months went by. And more months. No response from Rounds. Finally, County Court Judge Larry Rosen, after repeated warnings to Rounds, dismissed the case. King Tut's right to a speedy trial had been violated.

Now, Paula Taylor says, she's just waiting to die.

"I don't know where he is," she told me, "whether he's coming back, how he's coming back or whether he's going to send somebody else after me. . . . I'm petrified."

I tried to reach Rounds and failed. I asked DA Sol Greenberg how a thing like this could happen.

"We're dealing with thousands of cases a year here," he told me. "It's too bad it happened, but it happened."

This did not strike me as an adequate response—not in a case with so much blood involved. Yes, the DA's office contains some immensely talented people. Yes, it's woefully underfinanced. And, yes, everybody has a tough job.

None of this, however, is much consolation to Paula Taylor. King Tut is out on bail at the moment on an unrelated charge. She spotted him the other day on Morton Avenue.

King Tut, she says, blew her a kiss.

—February 2, 1999

The Final Sentence

Joe Franchi was tanked up.

He was out with friends, cruising the gin mills in the Lansingburgh section of Troy. Somewhere in the course of the evening, some guy started giving him some serious lip. Joe Franchi decided that this guy might have a gun.

So, in a burst of brilliance, he went home to get his shotgun.

A shotgun he wasn't even supposed to have. He was on parole for sticking up a cab driver on Staten Island. It was the latest in a string of indiscretions that stretched back years.

Joe Franchi did construction work and operated a car detailing business, but his career routinely had been interrupted by sojourns in jail. No Eagle Scout, this guy—not when he was doping or liquored up.

That night, he went back to the tavern and slammed the shotgun on the bar. It went off. Three people at the bar went down. As it turned out, nobody was killed, but Joe Franchi didn't know that.

He immediately had another brilliant idea—run like hell.

He ran for Texas, where he had a daughter. About 10 days later, the cops in Amarillo nailed him. He got shipped back to Troy, pleaded guilty to assault two and was sentenced to three-and-a-half to seven in state prison.

While serving his time, he got married. And he developed back problems—bad ones.

"They told him it was arthritis," his wife, Laurie, told me the other day. "It got so bad that he couldn't even stand in the food line. The other guys were stealing pieces of bread for him, so he could eat."

In April, he went before the parole board.

"Parole is denied for the following reasons," the board wrote in its decision. "After a careful review of your entire record and this interview, it is the determination of this panel that if released at this time there is a reasonable possibility that you would not live and remain at liberty without violating the law. . . . Your pattern of criminality is evident."

At the time, an eminently reasonable decision. In September, though, when his legs stopped working, the doctors told Joe Franchi what was really wrong with his back—cancer. It had eaten away his spine.

In October, the doctors told him that they couldn't do anything for him. Joe Franchi was going to die. The only questions were when and where.

Laurie tried to get him released, so he could come home to Troy and leave this life surrounded by friends and family. She got nowhere. Joe Franchi had a lengthy history as a minor league criminal, and he'd fled prosecution.

A week ago yesterday, Joe Franchi lay in a secure ward in Albany Med. He'd grown so weak, Laurie said, that, "He couldn't even raise his hand to scratch his nose." That day, the parole board denied him release once again.

Immediate family members were permitted to see him only two hours a day. Toward the end, the rules were relaxed. He died at 3:47 AM Friday morning at age 44.

Laurie Franchi knows that her husband was capable of acts of dazzling stupidity when he was drinking or doping. She loved him anyway. Yesterday, under gray skies, she buried him in St. Mary's Cemetery in Waterford. What she can't bury is her resentment at how he died.

"His sentence turned out to be life without parole," she told me. "They should have let him come home. In the shape he was in, who was he going to hurt?"

—January 14, 1997

A System With Defects

Bernie Kennedy can show you exactly where it happened. He can point out with precision the site of the incident that's prompting him to abandon the city.

It's Western and Partridge, two blocks from Albany High School. Bernie Kennedy's kid was leaving school on Sept. 6, the first day of the school year, when he saw these four kids giving him the eye. Daniel Kennedy knew instantly that he was in trouble.

"He crossed the street," Bernie Kennedy told me the other day. "They started following him, patting him down, saying, 'Give me a dollar.' They actually stalked him a block and a half. Finally, they took a stick of gum from him. Then one of them knocked him to the ground and hit him while he was on the ground. He went for stitches, the whole thing."

The kid who struck the blows, authorities say, was Jermaine Cox, 15, of 41 Osborne St. His three buddies were Clarence Edmonds of 75 Third Avenue, Brandon Inman of 279 Northern Boulevard and Lewis Kornegay of 656 Myrtle Ave., all also 15.

The Cox kid goes to trial Nov. 21 on robbery charges. The other kids ended up in juvenile court. They've been kept out of school for a while, but they'll come back soon. Bernie Kennedy's kid was asking his mother the other day when those three are likely to be back in school with him.

"I'm mad about this," Bernie Kennedy was saying. "They said it was anti-violence week in school. My kid went to the hospital. I got a $240 emergency room bill and a $650 plastic surgery bill. . . .

"The D.A. told me he didn't want to waste taxpayers' money pursuing these criminals because they're not going to get anything. . . . What I'd like to see is that each of these kids goes away to detention for three months or six months and that they're never allowed back in school with regular kids. They get probation, and they laugh at you, they laugh at me, they laugh at the principal. They laugh at us because probation is nothing, and they know it."

Larry Weist, the first assistant district attorney, knows about this case. He thinks it was handled properly.

"We always have difficulty in the real world in prosecuting 15-year-olds for things that don't rise to magnificently heinous crimes," he said. ". . . The system has defects when you're dealing with juveniles."

Bernie Kennedy doesn't want to hear from defects. He grew up in Brooklyn. He knows cities and what happens to them when people in authority decide to let things like this slide. He came to Albany in 1977 to do tax work and operate some rental property. He came here because Brooklyn had slid right into the sewer.

"So the deal is this," Bernie Kennedy was telling me. "Some of these kids are supposed to pay me what the medical insurance wouldn't cover. Well, if they're going to send me ten bucks a month, all that means to me is that they'll probably mug another two kids a month to get that ten bucks. . . .

"My wife and I, we've looked at houses in Clifton Park. I spoke before a PTA meeting, and a lot of people came up to me and said their kids had been beaten up and this and that. Well, I'm not going to take it.

"We'll leave this place to the people who want to stick, but we're out of here."

—November 14, 1995

Family Matters

He stands 6-foot-4 and weighs 215 pounds. He's an accomplished thug with a taste for burglary and a fancy for firearms.

He's 15 years old.

The kid wears baggy jeans, gang-style. On his black T-shirt is the sullen, suety image of the Notorious B.I.G. He was the rapper blown away on a Los Angeles street a few months back.

The kid wears one other item of adornment, too—leg shackles. The clink of steel bounces off the pale green walls of the little courtroom on Van Tromp Street.

Welcome to New York's juvenile justice system. For years, this has been a closed operation, with cases decided in privacy to protect the interests of the kids. But the state's chief judge, Judith Kaye, has ordered the system opened to the public in September.

Albany County Family Court Judge W. Dennis Duggan runs a more or less open courtroom anyway. I asked him to let me sit a day there, for a preview of what everybody can see in just a few months.

Up on the bench in his black robes, Duggan gives the paperwork one more quick pass. As one of only three judges in Albany County Family Court, he's a busy man. He dispensed justice in roughly 5,000 cases last year. Each averaged 15 minutes of court time.

Every night, after dinner, Dennis Duggan's dessert consists of lengthy reports from shrinks, social workers and probation officers. They're thick chronicles of human misery consumed after long days of dealing with people too frail, too stupid or too careless to look after themselves or their doomed children.

"I can tell by the way you're sitting there," Duggan tells the kid, "that you think you're a tough guy."

The kid gazes impassively at the judge. Damn right I'm

a tough guy, he says with his eyes; I'm the baddest mother you ever saw.

Duggan tells him, "I've got even money that when you're 20 you'll either be dead or in state prison. . . . Maybe you can prove me wrong."

Then Duggan sends the kid out of the room and turns to the boy's father. Dad is a trim, bald-pated man of 54. He has a long record of his own for drug dealing, pimping and other assorted indiscretions. He has been out of prison just a year.

"The apple doesn't fall far from the tree, does it?" Duggan says.

Don't blame me, Dad protests. My son has emotional problems. His mother died of AIDS three years ago. The boy needs help.

"I wasn't no prime good guy," Dad admits, "but I love my son. I want to see him get help. His mother was white; that's a problem for him. I cry every night. I beg God every night."

Well, nothing against God, but He's busy. Leave it up to Him to raise your child and you take a big chance. Duggan gives the kid a year in a youth detention center, if they keep him there that long.

Next year, the kid is an adult in the eyes of the criminal justice system. The next judge he's likely to see is Tom Breslin, over in County Court. Tom Breslin sends bad mothers away for a long, long time every chance he gets.

Dennis Duggan is a thoughtful, soft-spoken man of 47 who looks a bit like the actor who played the President in "Independence Day." A graduate of Notre Dame and Albany Law, he has two kids of his own. He came up through the Albany County Democratic political system.

This judgeship is his reward for years of party service. Some reward. Every day, he gets to see up close what happens when parents choose personal gratification over parental obligation.

Sure, some kids seem simply to have been born bad— or dragged into badness by peers, MTV or whatever other cultural forces you want to blame—and even the best of parents can't handle them. Those are the exceptions, though.

For the most part, the kids Dennis Duggan sees are quite clearly what their parents have made of them—lost, hopeless souls from their first plaintive wails in the delivery room. The parents never bothered to marry. Or they found marriage too much trouble to stick with. A disturbing percentage of Family Court parents tend to be drunks, druggies or criminals—or all three.

Their boys are neglected or raged at by role models they find laughable. Their girls share housing with half-brothers and half-sisters with different names and different fathers while they struggle to avoid rape by one of Mama's interchangeable boyfriends.

To function effectively in modern society, human beings require intense nurturing for their first two decades of life. The juvenile justice system was designed to provide that nurturing when parents can't or won't, and sometimes it manages to accomplish that. But, for the most part, the system merely battles valiantly to contain the chaos in society's soft, vulnerable underbelly.

Family Court exists in a world in which people have sex early, casually and carelessly. They expel babies from their bodies as though they were vomit and then pretend that nothing in life has changed. They let their kids grow wild, like weeds, or leave them like garbage on the streets.

Then the hormones kick in, and the kids turn into what they see around them. They sink like stones in foul, filthy water.

The girl who takes the big, bad kid's place in the courtroom has suffered the misfortune of sprouting the body of a Vegas showgirl at age 13. The mother comes from a family of dopers but has stayed straight all these years. The girl's father, however, has split. Mom now works double shifts to put food on the table. The daughter is insecure, rebellious, wildly promiscuous and—in the language of the law—"in need of supervision."

Stay away from the men, Duggan advises her.

"They're not going to love you and honor you and cherish you," the judge tells her. . . . "They're going to leave you with chlamydia or AIDS and abandon you with a baby. How do I know that? I see it all the time. . . .

"At 28, you'll have four kids and be on welfare and your life will be over. Don't do it. Respect yourself."

The girl buries her face in her hands. From the bench of his tiny courtroom, Dennis Duggan watches her weep. Maybe his words have sunk in.

Not likely, though.

—*July 20, 1997*

What It Takes

William James, psychologist and philosopher, once said that the purpose of a college education is to teach you to know a good man when you see one.

By that logic, Gary McCarthy's idea makes sense. McCarthy is a Schenectady city councilman. He wants all future cops in his city to have four-year college degrees.

But people who hold four-year degrees constitute only a quarter or so of the adult population, and you can make a good case that an academic credential doesn't necessarily make somebody a good cop. Temperament, personality, judgment and experience count more in work like that.

Where I really take issue with McCarthy, though, is with his insistence that all new Schenectady cops be able to type 35 words a minute. I write for a living, and I'm not sure I can type 35 words a minute. Moreover, you ought to listen to this story I heard from Anthony J. Schembri, a friend of mine who served as Rudy Giuiliani's corrections commissioner, as police commissioner in Rye and also as the model for the TV character, "The Commish."

As a kid, Schembri found himself in Brooklyn's 90th Precinct one day watching Detective Johnny Burke painfully typing a report. Schembri told the detective that he'd taken typing in school. Burke called the kid over and said, "Let me see how you can type."

"So," Schembri told me, "I sat down and typed. . . . I must have typed pretty well that day because Johnny Burke asked me to come back and do some more typing for him."

Pretty soon, the kid the cops called "Ant'ny" was the unofficial precinct typist. Schembri told me, "All these detectives, I soon realized, had tremendous investigative skills, but they couldn't compose a sentence on paper. Nobody in the place could write proper English, but you wouldn't want to be investigated by any of these guys. . . .

"One night, I was being driven home in a prowl car, and a call came over the radio. Some guy was drunk and had a gun to his wife's head. Detective Tommy Hughes was driving. Johnny Burke was with him. . . .

"Johnny said, 'Let's go over there, Tommy.'"

"When we got to the scene, the drunk had his wife in a headlock with the gun pointed directly at her head. . . . Johnny and Tommy were looking at this guy, and he was yelling, 'Don't come near me! I'm going to kill her!'

"'I don't give a (bad word here),' Tommy said pleasantly. 'She don't mean (same bad word here) to me. But you ought to know, after you shoot her, I'm going to shoot you. I'm probably going to get detective second grade out of this.'

"At that point, Johnny Burke reached out and shook Tommy Hughes' hand. 'Congratulations, Tommy,' he said.

"It was like they'd rehearsed it. The guy with the gun was totally nonplused. He began shouting, 'Who's going to get promoted? What are you guys talking about?'

"It was all an act," Schembri told me. "These guys were masters at distracting people from violence. They had no intention of shooting this guy. They had no intention of letting him shoot his wife either."

Schembri, huddling in the car, thought the cops were nuts until he saw the drunk drop his gun and surrender. Later, in his own police career, he remembered what he'd learned that day.

"Those old-time detectives knew people," Schembri told me. "That's what it took then. That's what it takes now."

But, Councilman McCarthy, they couldn't type for squat.

—September 20, 1996

Of Your Peers

There were 14 of them in all, 12 jurors and two alternates.

They sat solemnly the other day in Judge Tom Breslin's ancient courtroom in downtown Albany. Occasionally, you could see Nicholas Eugene Pryor glance furtively at them from his seat at the defense table.

Well, why not? These people will decide Pryor's guilt or innocence in the violent death of Jenna Grieshaber—a murder that led to the frenzied passage of a new law in this state, Jenna's Law, that severely limits parole for violent felons. Why shouldn't Nicholas Eugene Pryor glance at the faces of the people who hold his fate in their hands?

I counted six women in the jury box. Only one juror

was African American, like Pryor, although roughly one in four citizens of Albany is not white. The jurors ranged in age from 19 to 65.

This group was meticulously selected from more than 200 candidates. The jury pool was chosen from voter rolls, from Albany County's list of welfare recipients, from state tax records. It's designed to serve as a cross-section of this community.

Yet Pryor's lawyer had argued ferociously for a change of venue in this case—had argued, in effect, that Albany was unfit to render a fair and impartial judgment on Nicholas Eugene Pryor's guilt or innocence.

Why not? News coverage, that's why. According to the Court of Appeals, New York's highest court, jurors are not supposed to know that a defendant has a criminal record unless his defense lawyer brings it up. And heavy news coverage had surrounded the passage of Jenna's Law, including stories about Pryor's history of violence and the fact that he'd been on parole when Jenna was murdered.

It's a good thing, not a bad one, that the courts fret over jurors making decisions in a criminal case based on anything they might learn outside the courtroom. But it's also a good thing in a democracy for people to understand why certain bills become law while others do not.

This case has been billed as an example of rights in conflict—as a clash between the right to a fair trial pitted against the public's right to know. If Nicholas Eugene Pryor is found guilty in the murder of Jenna Grieshaber, the conduct of this trial in Tom Breslin's courtroom is a certain ground for appeal.

You should understand, though, that this is one of the great phony issues of our time—pure smoke blown vigorously by lawyers in the era of mass communications.

In the early days of this country, when the framers of the Constitution adopted the jury system, America was a land of a few cities and many tiny farming villages. In courtroom after courtroom in the original 13 colonies, jurors knew all there was to know about the defendant. He was, after all, their neighbor.

Jurors also knew all there was to know about the victim, about the judge, about the lawyers and about one another. And the framers, smart guys all, had known that they would.

All that was asked of jurors was that they set aside their prior knowledge of the people involved and render their judgments solely on the basis of what they heard in the courtroom. What was required of them was intellectual honesty and fairness, not ignorance of the community in which they lived or the people who shared it with them.

Now, however, news cameras in New York are banned from the public's courtrooms because of lobbying by defense lawyers. That happened because the lawyers view the public's courtrooms as their personal preserves. And they prefer as jurors citizens who are estranged from their communities, jurors who are uninformed, jurors whom neither you nor I would welcome as judges of our fates.

Dopes. That's what they want.

Somehow, I don't think that's what James Madison, et al., had in mind.

—*September 13, 1998*

Just Who Are We Protecting, Now?

In case you haven't noticed how screwed up the world is, listen to Danny Piazza.

He's a masonry contractor with a wife and three kids, one of them just 9. He lives in Colonie. He and his neighbors have a problem.

"It's a nice middle-class neighborhood," Danny Piazza was telling me the other day. "About two weeks ago, a neighbor, whom I didn't know, came walking by and handed me a piece of paper that said there's a pedophile that's been released and is living virtually across the street in the development.

"I asked her a couple of questions. She said there's not a lot of information available because the crime was committed prior to '96. The police can't tell you who the guy is. They can't give you a description—can't even acknowledge that he's there."

This was cause for concern to Danny Piazza, as it would be to most people with kids. He knows that these guys have stunningly high rates of recidivism. They tend to fall prey to what shrinks call "uncontrollable urges."

That's why it's nice to know when they get sprung into your neighborhood. You want to be able to warn your kids to stay away from certain people.

"I called the Town of Colonie," Danny Piazza told me. "I spoke to a detective over there. He was pretty helpful except that he couldn't talk about this. He told me to give a call to this guy at the New York State Parole Board."

So, Danny Piazza called the parole board guy, who confirmed to him that, yes, there was a paroled pedophile in his neighborhood, but his identity is confidential. This state has a neighborhood notification law regarding sex offenders, but it applies at the moment only to people convicted after the law was passed. Offenders convicted before that date have gotten an injunction to keep their names confidential—at least until this is fully hammered out in the courts.

Also, this state's version of Megan's Law—the catchall name for such laws derived from the name of a New Jersey victim—permits you to get information from the New York State Sex Offender Hotline at 900-288-3838, but only if you already have the sex offender's name and one other piece of information about him—like his address or social security number.

And, by the way, only if you're willing to cough up five bucks for what should be free, public information.

For all that, though, word of these releases still gets around sometimes, as this one did. Somebody hears just enough information to get everybody in the neighborhood frightened and furious at a system that's supposed to protect their kids and doesn't quite do that.

"Somebody tipped off the North Colonie schools, where my son goes," Danny Piazza told me. "They heard something from somebody off the record. They said their teachers know what this guy looks like. They have a description of him. But they can't tell the kids anything. They can't send a notice home because this guy has got rights.

"I said, 'Hey, that's great. Everybody knows about this guy except the people who should know—the children and the parents in the neighborhood.'"

Danny Piazza was told by the parole board guy that this pedophile is considered high-risk. The parole people suspect that this guy probably will do it again.

Danny Piazza said, "I've been trying to get a picture, a name, so I can plaster it around the neighborhood. Now I'm being told by people who know about this stuff to let it go.

"Well, I can't. My son's a prisoner in his own house when I'm not around. It's ridiculous."

—May 10, 1999

Off the Wall

I hope that Leonardo Turriago, drug dealer and murderer, dumps his next victim in the trunk of a car parked directly outside the home of Israel Rubin. A whiff of some real-world stink might do this judge some good.

Justice Rubin and three of his buddies in the Appellate Division of State Supreme Court issued a ruling last week illustrating that common sense is little more than a rumor in New York courts. The judiciary complains that George Pataki is trying to score political points by bashing judges. If that really bothers them, then why do so many judges make themselves such fat, tempting targets?

On a November night six years ago, Turriago was driving a U-Haul van on state Route 17 in Orange County. When he roared by Troopers John O'Leary and James Van Cura at about 70 miles per hour in a 55-mile-per-hour zone, the troopers pulled him over.

In the van with Turriago were Dennis Torres and Edwin Supulveda. The cops asked Turriago where he was going. Binghamton, he said. It was the second day of deer hunting season, and the woods around Monroe are a favorite spot for poachers with illegal guns—guys from New York City, mostly. The troopers asked if they could look in the back of the van. Sure, Turriago told them.

Turriago then opened the van's cargo area, where troopers found a trunk. As Turriago was unlocking the trunk, he suddenly bounded from the van and tried to split. One of the troopers ran him down while the other finished opening the trunk. Surprise, surprise—there was the corpse of Fernando Cuervo, who'd been dispatched by a bullet in the face to that big crack house in the sky.

Naturally, everybody was taken into custody. For starters, none of the three had a valid driver's license. Second, they confessed. The cops were told that Cuervo had been shot to death in a Manhattan apartment—and beaten on the head with a hammer to ensure a job well done.

Police divers later found the gun in the Hudson River at 125th Street in Manhattan. In the apartment, cops found 11 pounds of coke, three more loaded guns and Cuervo's blood.

Torres and Sepulveda pleaded. Turriago went to trial and was convicted of murder. He has, for some years now, been a guest of the public at Shawangunk state prison. Thanks to the Appellate Division ruling, though, his lawyers are expected to move successfully to have him sprung.

Rubin's position was that the cops should never have asked to look inside the van, since they had no reasonable suspicion that these guys were engaged in criminal activity. But what about the fact that these guys weren't going to drive away anyway? Nobody had a valid license. Therefore, the van would have been impounded and the corpse discovered when the van was inventoried.

Tough, the judge said. The cops should have run the license check before asking to search the van.

"The system has to make sense to people," a highly annoyed Attorney General Dennis Vacco told me yesterday. "This type of ruling defies common sense."

Under federal law, Turriago would stay at Shawangunk. The U. S. Supreme Court ruled Monday that any evidence cops find in a traffic stop is admissable as long as the stop was legitimate.

Pataki is pushing for a law that would more closely tie state court rulings to federal rulings. Let's hope he gets it.

Without it, New York's off-the-wall judges will continue to demonstrate that the Empire State just isn't part of America anymore.

—*June 12, 1996*

Scales of Justice

We live in a time when you can't trust anybody, so nobody does.

Which complicates matters when you lose a lizard. Or, for that matter, when you find one.

Tony Impellizzeri found one. He's a guy of 50 who works for the State Senate. He's also a big deal in his bowling league. He was throwing a party for everybody on Fourth of July weekend.

When he went into the backyard of his house in Colonie that Friday night to prepare for the party, he glanced at his apple tree. There was an iguana.

It was roughly four-and-a-half feet long, the George Foreman of iguanas, with big claws. Tony Impellizzeri looked at the iguana. The iguana looked at Tony Impellizzeri. Standoff.

He went around to his neighbors. Hey, you lose a big lizard? Nobody had, but everybody wanted to see it. One neighbor was so impressed that she called Channel Six.

Tony Impellizzeri was worried that the Iguana might fall into his bowling league party. He lassoed the thing with his pool skimmer and put it in a big garbage pail. That's where the lizard was living when it became a television star.

"I told them to use my name and phone number and everything," he told me. "I started getting all kinds of calls. Somebody lost one in Niskayuna, Saratoga, Clifton Park, West Sand Lake.

"All of a sudden, I started getting offers for two hundred, three hundred, five hundred. I said, 'Man, this thing must be worth some money.' One of the calls I got later on was from an enthusiast. He's a breeder. . . . He told me that this was a full-grown male, and it probably was worth about $2,500. . . .

"One guy offered me a thousand bucks. I told him, 'If we don't find the owner, we'll talk about it'. . . .

"So, the next day I had my party . . . I put the iguana in a big box in my bathroom with a heating pad, except he got out and ran all over. My wife almost had a heart attack."

Finally Rhonda Newcombe called. She lives a few blocks away. She said that her iguana, Bud, had escaped a few weeks earlier, chased away by her German shepherd, Spike. After all these calls, Tony Impellizzeri had turned into one suspicious guy.

Yeah, he said, prove it's yours. Somebody offered me a grand for the thing.

Rhonda Newcombe figured she was being shaken down. Tony Impellizzeri figured he could get into trouble if he handed over an expensive iguana to anybody who couldn't prove its ownership. They had words.

The next thing Tony Impellizzeri knew, Rhonda Newcombe was at his door with a picture of an iguana. And, incidentally, with a Colonie cop.

Tony Impellizzeri figures that, except to another lizard, all iguanas tend to look pretty much alike in photographs. He wanted more proof. But the cop had seen the big, empty iguana set-up that Rhonda Newcombe had in her house.

Give the lady the lizard, the cop said. Tony Impellizzeri says that the guy was pretty nasty, too, which the Colonie cops deny.

So, now Rhonda Newcombe has the iguana, and she's sure it's her old pal, Bud. Tony Impellizzeri is sore at the Colonie cops. He suspects that the iguana might actually be the one lost months ago by another woman in the vicinity. She called him after the cop relieved him of the lizard.

And here's the moral of this story: No, don't trust anybody. If you own a big lizard, paint your name on its side. Or have it tattooed or something. And, if a big lizard wanders into your back yard, ignore it. Just pretend it isn't there.

Tony Impellizzeri can assure you that life will be simpler that way.

—*July 22, 1997*

A Murder in the Family

Ralph Best, Jr., was standing yesterday in Penny Lane in West Sand Lake. A sturdy, gray-haired man, he wore jeans, a khaki jacket and the kind of grim, dazed expression you have when the shock still hasn't worn off—when you know that sooner or later the enormity of what has occurred will settle into your gut like a boulder, but that hasn't happened yet.

And when it does.... Oh, God, when it does....

Ralph Best, Jr. was gazing solemnly at a neat little red and white house with artificial stone facing. The late fall weather was bitter. Beneath early afternoon skies as gray and forbidding as a battleship, snow was hardening into ice. The wind chill stood at six degrees above zero.

"I'd been calling on the phone," he was telling me. "I couldn't get an answer. I got worried. So, I came over."

What Ralph had found when he'd arrived at his parents' home will be eternally imprinted on his brain cells. Inside the house on Penny Lane, he'd found the bludgeoned bodies of his parents—Ralph Best, Sr., 81, and Blanche, 78. Missing was their car, a 1996 Ford Escort wagon, green, and the family dog, a mongrel named Koda, black.

Missing also was Ralph Jr.'s nephew, the victims' grandson, Daniel J. Best., Jr. He's a bearded, bespectacled, tattooed high school dropout of 24 who'd lived in the Penny Lane house off and on for years, ever since his own father had died and he'd had problems getting along with his mother's new husband.

Is Daniel J. Best, Jr. a suspect in his grandparents' murders? Well, no, not exactly, the cops say. We would just like to know where he is, that's all. We would really, really like to talk to him.

"The way this works," I was told by a criminal lawyer I know, "is that the minute they put out a warrant for him and he gets picked up, they can't talk to him unless he has a lawyer present. This way, he's not even a suspect. So, if he shows up somehow, and if he decides to get chatty with the police without a lawyer around, they've got a good chance of getting that statement admitted."

"Do you have a warrant out for this guy?" I asked Rensselaer Sheriff Dan Keating back at the police command post in the West Sand Lake firehouse on Route 43.

"Oh, no," he told me. "We don't have enough evidence for a warrant at this point."

The cops are being as close-mouthed as possible about this vicious murder case. They don't know what happened for sure, although they have their suspicions, and this is not a case they want to blow. Here were two old people, in decent health and still with all their marbles, and this is how they leave life? Somebody smashes their skulls?

No, the cops don't want to make any mistakes here.

Penny Lane was in my ear and in my eye yesterday afternoon. You could hear the dull rumble of cops' and reporters' cars idling in the street. Everybody hopped in and out of the vehicles to stay warm as auto exhaust billowed in the frigid air. Around the Bests' house, you could see a slim, yellow and black police barrier tape deployed like a plastic fence.

In front of the place, a state police ID team was getting ready to enter the house again. This time they had Ralph Best, Jr., with them to help figure out what might be missing from the place. The ID squad dressed in white plastic coveralls from head to foot. Like them, Ralph Best, Jr. pulled plastic boots over his work shoes before he went through the front door. If evidence was to be had at this crime scene, nobody wanted it disturbed.

It would be scant consolation for Ralph Best, Jr., to know how unlikely it was that his parents would leave life in such a horrible fashion. Old people are seldom murder victims. Only three in 100,000 Americans 65 and older die this way, and that's almost half the rate of two decades ago. By contrast, nearly 21 Americans in every 100,000 between the ages 18 and 24 are murder victims.

When old people are murdered, however, they're disturbingly likely to die at the hands of family members. Only half of the nation's annual 20,000 murder victims are killed by strangers. When family members kill, half the time they're boozed up. One in four murderers who kills a parent has a history of mental illness.

Which in no way means that Daniel J. Best, Jr. did this vile thing. He might be a victim himself. He might be lying dead or injured in some stand of woods somewhere. For the police, the challenge here will be to get lucky. They have information that Daniel J. Best, Jr., might be heading to Florida, to Arizona, to Texas, who knows? But they also know that Daniel J. Best, Jr., might have gone to ground locally.

If he did commit these murders, though—and if he's running—then even if he'd had the sense to steal a new set of plates out of some parking lot somewhere he might still run some red light and get pulled over. With no drivers license and an all-points bulletin out for him in all 50 states, he would likely be detained.

But if Daniel J. Best, Jr., is on the run, he has a dependable car that gets good mileage, and he's apparently filling the tank with gas he buys with cash. So far, there's no evidence that he had a credit card issued in his name, and there's no sign in any police computer that anybody took any such credit card from his dead grandparents.

And with every day that goes by in a case like this, the odds of nailing whoever did the bloody thing diminishes. New cases come up and require attention. Cops can't stay on one case forever, no matter how horrific. Sure, violent crime is going down these days. Don't kid yourself, though.

Mayhem and murder remain daily occurrences in this society of ours.

—November 26, 1997

The New York State of Mind

A Display of Craftsmanship

The low-lying canopy of clouds was a grim, depressing battleship gray. Fat raindrops splattered against my windshield. Slowly, I eased my four-by-four truck across a little bridge that straddled a gushing stream.

"There it is," Bernadette Castro said. "There's our spouter."

There it was, too, off to the right of the stream—a slim spire of water shooting up maybe 20 feet from a cleft in the rock. It's the only geyser in the East, Bernadette Castro was telling me—a wondrous work of geothermal forces bubbling fiercely beneath the placid, pine-studded surface of Saratoga State Park.

This was one morning last week. The managers of New York's 151 state parks and historic sites were gathered at the park's Gideon Putnam Hotel for their annual conference. And Castro, George Pataki's parks commissioner, was taking me on a tour of the park.

We'd planned to do some walking, but a monsoon had descended on Saratoga Springs that morning. Instead—with me at the wheel, Castro in the passenger's seat and park manager Julie Stokes in the back, warning me repeatedly to honor the speed limit—we were cruising around the 2,200 rain-soaked acres of the park, one of the crown jewels in the system.

A good many things are wrong here in New York. Taxes are too high. Government is old, outmoded and wasteful. We have too much crime, too much poverty and too little opportunity. Politics is a bubbling pot of ill will at every level, meaner by far than in many other places.

But, once in a while, it's worth stepping back and assessing what's right about this huge state, with its 19 million people and 50,000 square miles of land mass. One of our premier assets is some remarkable real estate—the thundering plunge of Niagara Falls, the rolling grandeur of the great lakes, the emerald and azure vista of the wine country, the hearty, desolate wilderness of the Adirondacks and the vast, sea-kissed sweep of Long Island's glistening beaches.

God made it too cold for much of the year here, but Her magnificent craftsmanship is nonetheless on vivid display in New York. The trick is to manage it wisely and well. Against all odds, administration after administration has more or less done that.

Every year, about 65 million people use the 260,000 acres of prime park land Pataki placed under Castro's control—nearly as many as pass through California's parks. Bernadette Castro is determined to surpass California in attendance.

A trim, elegantly decked-out woman of 52—voted the best dancer of New York's delegation to the Republican National Convention in San Diego—Bernadette Castro is a shrewd merchandiser of this state's park system. A scion of the Castro convertible fortune, she's bent on peddling park usage the way her family used to peddle sofa beds—quality product, good customer service.

She presides over nearly 1,700 permanent employees and as many as 4,000 seasonal workers. Her department does not make a profit, but the $50 million or so in revenue it generates annually means that each New Yorker spends less than four bucks a year for a park system unparalleled in the nation.

As a kid growing up in the central part of the state, I used to swim regularly at the marvelous pond and waterfall in Ithaca's Robert H. Treman State Park. I went back there after 20 years absence. To my delighted shock, nothing had changed. Somehow, the politicians had failed to screw up the place.

For government in New York, positively amazing.

—November 27, 1996

The Simple Life

The tractor sat beneath a towering oak next to an old yellow farm house. It was a green and yellow John Deere with spiked steel wheels—a terror in dirt, a nightmare on pavement.

Mennonites don't use rubber tires on their tractors. With rubber tires, you might be tempted to drive down the highway into town. You might be tempted to pilot the tractor to a neighbor's farm instead of taking the time and trouble to hitch the horses to the buggy.

Yes, rubber tires would be a temptation. And Mennonites, by design, live uncomplicated lives as free of temptation as possible. The Plain People, they call themselves—simple and separate.

No television, no radio, no modern clothing. The scriptures, Menno Simons taught them centuries ago in Switzerland, require them to live apart from the lives of their more modern neighbors.

For the most part, they survive also without motor vehicles, with none of the corruptions of modern life. God demands simplicity, and the Mennonites oblige by living and dressing in an old-fashioned style, with straw hats and suspenders.

No T-shirts and shorts for the Mennonites. No designer labels. No Air Jordans. Their females, girls and women alike, wear long dresses and bonnets tied tightly beneath the chin. Their sons dress as their fathers do, in straw hats and suspenders.

To be a Mennonite means to dress and move about and to live and think a certain way—a plain, Spartan method of life distinct from the way of The Others.

It's because of this belief—that keeping faith with God requires a specific style of life and dress—that the 250-family Mennonite community of New York's Finger Lakes region has come into conflict with the thoroughly modern men and women who pass laws in Albany.

In Bluff Point, 220 miles west of State Street—in a world so different from the brown marble halls of the Capitol that it might as well be Mars—I was sitting one day in the shade of that towering oak next to that yellow farmhouse, the steel-wheeled tractor behind me, talking to two men of the Finger Lakes Mennonite community.

They begged me not to publish their names. The Plain People shun publicity on principle, but these men had practical reasons as well.

"There's people who are against the Mennonites," one straw-hatted man told me solemnly. "We get into trouble when our names appear in the newspaper. It could be because of the way we live. It could be that since we moved in here in 1974 that farm prices have gone sky-high. Some people are against us because we have steel-wheeled tractors that leave marks in the road.... We don't want people to harrass us."

They came from the Lancaster area, where farm prices had risen so high that young Mennonite couples couldn't get started in the Pennsylvania Dutch country that had been their stronghold for centuries. They'd been here for 20 years, raising families and crops and worshipping God in their own way, before they realized what it really meant to be New Yorkers—citizens of a state where legislators operate under the premise that you can never have too many laws.

Two years earlier, the Legislature in Albany had passed

an alteration to the Vehicle and Traffic Law requiring every child 13 and under to wear a helmet while on a bicycle. This was a law supported by the medical and insurance industries—and, probably, by the sporting goods dealers, too.

It was a well-intentioned law, as so many are. And it was a law that once again proves that, in the final analysis, nobody really cares or understands what anybody else is doing.

Mennonites tend to have large families. Their modest, black buggies hold only a few people. When the family goes to church, Mennonite kids depend on their bikes. So now every Mennonite child who climbs on a bike dressed as he or she believes God requires violates the law of New York state.

Ron Spike is the sheriff of Yates County, population 25,000 or so. He has had the job five years—as his father had it before him. Spike grew up in an apartment attached to the jail. When this law passed, he sent a letter to the Mennonite bishop, who was one of the men sitting with me beneath that tree the other day. Ron Spike said in the letter that he was sworn by sacred oath to uphold the law.

As a practical matter, the sheriff told me, the law is tough to enforce. It applies only when a parent or guardian is present. The ticket goes to the adult, not the kid. For two years, Ron Spike's department had issued no tickets to the Mennonites, only warnings.

There was a possibility that this law could be altered to exempt children who, for religious reasons, can't wear helmets on their bikes or off them. The Mennonites had spoken to Randy Kuhl, their state senator, about a religious exemption from the helmet law.

"What do you say," I asked the bishop, "to people who'll say that if these people really cared about their kids they'd make them wear helmets?"

"Well," the bishop said thoughtfully, "that's kind of a hard question to answer."

And then he answered it. If he were to be struck by a car, he told me, he would rather be in another car than in a plywood buggy. But the buggy is what God requires of him. And God requires the hat instead of the helmet, even if the helmet is safer.

After all, think how much danger the Mennonites would avoid if they stayed home on Sunday mornings and watched television.

Instead of going to church in the first place.

—*July 26, 1996*

Show Them the Money

Joe Bruno and Joe Lentol got the ball rolling this millennium.

Eleven days ago, on 2000 A.D. plus 10 days, the State Senate majority leader and the Democrat from Brooklyn held the first legislative fundraising events of the 21st Century.

(Yeah, OK, so some people figure that this is really the last year of the old millennium and not the first year of the new one. Please fight about that with somebody else; I'm producing a little poetry here.)

Anyway, for a mere thousand bucks, you could meet Sen. Bruno at the Desmond and wish him happy new year. You could enjoy the same enthralling experience with Assemblyman Lentol at the Crowne Plaza for only $300.

The next night came the 53rd birthday party for first-term Assemblyman Daniel Burling, Republican of someplace a lot closer to Ohio than to Albany. The lobbyists in this town must have been thrilled to cough up $250 to wish this guy happy birthday.

Ah, well, here we go again. The Legislature is back in session, and the annual shakedown is in full, grasping swing. Between New Year's Eve and the day of the presidential primary, March 7, our lawmakers have conducted 10 Albany fund-raisers and scheduled 22 more. The Brooklyn Democrats have scheduled one additional fund-raiser for April 13, nearly two weeks after the state budget is supposed to be adopted and at a time when much of the incentive for lobbyists to attend such gatherings supposedly has evaporated.

Which is an early sign that—even though the entire Legislature is up for election this year, and even though they've promised to produce a budget on time for a change—they won't. Why pass a timely budget—and abide by the law—when dragging out passage for many months is so lucrative?

For example, the longer you go without a budget, the more eager lobbyists are to kick in to your campaign war chest and influence the spending of state billions. Also, every day they're in session, lawmakers collect $110 a day tax-free in expense money—per diem expense, it's called. So, the longer the state goes without a budget, the more days the legislators can collect that $110.

Do we live in a wonderful state, or what?

In case you're civic-minded and would like to attend a fund-raiser for your local state lawmaker, know that you can shake the hand of Assembly Republican Leader John Faso of Kinderhook on Monday at the Fort Orange Club for only $400. If you want to be a Faso "sponsor" bring a cool grand. Assemblyman Jim Tedisco, Republican of Schenectady, will be receiving close personal friends with 200 bucks on Jan. 31 at the University Club. State Sen. Hugh Farley, Republican of Niskayuna, will be entertaining visitors with $250 at the Crowne Plaza on Feb. 7. The next night, a captivating interlude with Assemblyman Pat Casale, Republican of Troy, can be yours for only $175.

State GOP Chairman Bill Powers will be hosting a fun-filled get-together on the 31st for Assemblyman Bob Prentiss, Republican of Colonie, at the Sign of the Tree, only spitting distance from the building where the laws are made and the tax dollars are dispensed. Give Prentiss $250, and you can admire the tan he got on his recent trip to Cuba. While you're there, say hello to the special-interest lobbyists who really make the laws in this state.

Assembly Speaker Shelly Silver has a bill in that would ban legislative fund-raisers within 40 miles of the Capitol during the session. He figures that sometimes campaign money costs too much. Will this bill become law? Absolutely.

When pigs fly.

—*January 21, 2000*

Heady Times

> *"I think we still have a long way to go to control state spending."* —Gov. George Pataki
> April 13, 1995

The man is absolutely right. That's why the Pataki administration is firing state workers right and left. That's why the governor is going to chop another 10,000 state workers off the payroll next year.

Given that priority, though, I wish somebody would explain Evelyn C. Heady to me. I wish I could understand why she gets hired at Hudson River Psychiatric Center in Poughkeepsie for $69,500 a year while the state is eliminating 2,000 jobs in the state's 22 mental hospitals.

Evelyn C. Heady declined to explain that to me herself. I called her the other day, and she told me smugly, "You'll have to talk to somebody smarter than I am."

I said I didn't expect that to present much of a hardship.

Evelyn C. Heady is the Republican supervisor of the Town of Beekman in Dutchess County. Earlier this year, Hudson River Psychiatric Center, which has about 525 patients, cut its payroll from 1,122 slots to 986.

Hudson River Psychiatric Center also hired Evelyn C. Heady for an 18-month stint, which will have the effect of fattening her state pension considerably when she retires. As supervisor in the Town of Beekman, she makes only $13,500. She turns 55 on Jan. 6.

Roger Klingman, the spokesman for the Office of Mental Health, tells me that Evelyn C. Heady holds down a vital job. She's supposed to be a liaison with the Dutchess County business community, finding jobs for recipients of mental health services.

"We regard her as uniquely qualified for this project," Klingman assured me.

Yeah, sure. Well, that's politics, isn't it? New governors have a perfect right to hire party regulars as policy makers to alter the direction of state government. But Evelyn C. Heady doesn't make policy. She couldn't continue in her elected post as a town supervisor if she did. I'm also assured by my spies that she spends at least some of her time on the job reading novels.

I've written six novels. I'm all for people reading. But not when they're in high-paying state jobs while $20,000-a-year therapy aides, who care for sick people, are being bounced.

There's more to this story, by the way.

After Hudson River Psychiatric Center eliminated 136 positions, it hired 54 people as temporary employees. The administration there assures me they were different people. My spies assure me they were the same people.

Why did that happen? In late October, the hospital had to be evaluated by two agencies—the Health Care Financing Administration, an arm of the federal government, and the Joint Commission on Accreditation of Health Care. At stake was about $25 million a year in federal Medicaid and Medicare dollars. One of the things these agencies look at is the ratio of patients to keepers.

"The reimbursement streams for Medicaid or other federal dollars depend on those accreditations," I was told by Assemblyman Jim Brennan, the Democrat who chairs the Assembly's mental health committee.

He also said that staffing is a big issue at these hospitals. Two patients escaped from a mental hospital in Brooklyn last year and murdered people.

"Some of these patients are seriously disturbed," the assemblyman said. "Punching other patents out or punching out the staff is common. It's very difficult to maintain control with such low staffing."

But, if you have a friend or relative who's a patient at the Hudson River Psychiatric Center, you can relax about all that.

After all, Evelyn C. Heady is on the job.

—November 19, 1995

The Mad Mayor

On Thursday, I did what I've done every year now for nearly two decades. I took my daughter to dinner on our birthday. She was my birthday present 24 years ago.

This year, I had to drive to Utica to do it. She moved there a few months ago to do news for a TV station.

As I sat in the station's control room watching the 6 PM broadcast, on came a story about one Leon Koziol, Utica's corporation counsel. He was complaining that he'd just been fired by the mayor for talking to the press.

The mayor, Koziol was saying, is furious at the local newspaper, the *Observer-Dispatch*, and at two local TV stations. The mayor has imposed a total news blackout on them. No city employee is permitted to talk to the press, Koziol charged.

I thought that situation might make a funny column. I'm always looking for that. So, Friday, I started calling some people in Utica for guidance on all this—including the mayor, Ed Hanna.

I've found, I'm afraid, this situation isn't funny after all—not a bit. If anything, it's scary. And it's undeniably sad.

Ed Hanna is a shrewd, hard-driving, 74-year-old high school dropout who made millions years ago with some clever inventions—some sort of automatic carwash system and something to do with the chemical process you find in those photo booths. You know, the ones you pop a dollar into and the thing takes your picture four times and spits out the shots in just a minute or so.

He was mayor for a while back in the 1970s. He has been in office this second time about 14 months, having won a three-way race by fewer than 100 votes. He's a nominal Democrat, but he owes the party zippo.

He finances his campaigns out of his own pocket. He has appealed to voters over the years because he'd say precisely what's on his mind—usually a fetching trait in a politician.

Ed Hanna runs a troubled, post-industrial city of 64,000 that's losing population at the rate of about 1,000 residents a year. About 300 buildings are vacant, and landlords seem to be burning down properties at a snappy rate to collect the insurance money before the places lose more value.

Hanna has been undeniably right on a number of issues. He has fought to cut government costs and taxes to stem population loss. He has done righteous battle with city unions.

Early on, though, he declared total war on the paper—which supported him in his tax-cutting efforts—and on the two local TV stations. He'll talk to the paper in the neighboring city of Rome, which has little circulation among his constituents, and he communicates with Utica's citizens mainly via a rambling radio monologue he delivers several times a week on a station on which he buys time.

He agreed to talk to me Friday only after he determined that my newspaper isn't owned by the Gannett Corp., which owns what he calls the "Observer-Disgrace." He hates Gannett. I assured him that I have my own criticisms of Gannett—and a number of other newspaper companies, too, frankly.

The mayor then launched into a strident shout that continued unabated for the next hour. I tried to break in occasionally with a stray question, most of which he ignored. He simply delivered a furious, shrieking, screaming tirade unlike anything I've ever encountered from a public official.

I've been dealing with politicians for 30 years—from village council members to Presidents of the United States. Some of these people have been real whackos. But this was easily the most disjointed, maniacal, lunatic rant I've ever heard as a reporter.

At first, it struck me as funny. Ed Hanna has had a statewide reputation for eccentricity, and I like politicians with some style. But, as this conversation went on, all semblance of amusement on my part disappeared. I've interviewed serial killers who were conspicuously more lucid than the mayor of Utica, N.Y.

Over the course of an hour or so, I came to conclude that I was dealing with a man so consumed by his hatreds and his relentless insistence on total control of everything around him that Sigmund Freud would find Ed Hanna of more than passing interest.

I can't really tell you if his complaints against the newspaper and/or the TV stations make any sense because Hanna didn't make any sense. He kept screaming about lies and money-grubbing profiteers and slanted reporting. He said he would never talk to the local paper until he was given the right to proofread every story before it was printed.

At one point, I asked him to stop yelling at me—which he'd been doing for about 30 minutes straight. He flew instantly into a brand new rage, roaring that he'd never yelled at me, and how dare I accuse him of that?

I apologized just to settle him down, but the man remained wildly out of control. It was—to be direct about it—just an insane, demented performance on Ed Hanna's part.

Finally, Jim Roemer came on the line. He's a sharp, prosperous Albany lawyer who represents municipalities all across New York state on labor matters. He told me that the mayor figures he can't trust many people and is under a great deal of pressure. He assured the mayor that I was only trying to get his side, and then Ed Hanna came back on the phone. He said he loves his city and tends to get emotional. Then he resumed his tirade.

I finally just got off the phone with him. I checked with a few people around town. They made some guarded remarks about Ed Hanna's emotional health. One of them told me that some of Utica's major business leaders have expressed profound concerns about Hanna's continued tenure in office.

I certainly don't have a license to practice psychiatry, but I believe myself to have been in recent contact with a powerful local politician in the grasp of what any reasonable person would have to view as some sort of grand mal paranoid psychosis.

New York lacks a recall statute to remove public officials who've gone around the bend. But a petition is going around Utica to have George Pataki remove Ed Hanna from office under the state's Public Officers Law on grounds of . . . well, misfeasance, for want of a better term.

And I really wish that this column had turned out to be funny.

—March 3, 1997

The Lobbyist

"And you represent motorcyclists?" the woman in the state senator's office asked.

"That's right," Prospector told her. "We're bikers."

The woman gazed appraisingly at Prospector. She inspected the black, Harley-Davidson T-shirt, the tattoos on his thick arms and the half dozen or so memorial patches on his sleeveless denim jacket. One read "In memory of Dirty Dan, 10-20-93."

Then she glanced at me. I was in jeans and a brown leather jacket.

"You don't look like a biker," she said.

I shrugged. "Well, I'm trying."

Actually, I would never get on a motorcycle. You can kill yourself on one of those things. But the other day, when I went lobbying with Prospector in the Legislative Office Building, I ditched the usual suit and tie and tried to look inconspicuous.

I didn't want anything to get in the way of Prospector's rap to the lawmakers—or, on that day, actually, to the lawmaker's staff assistants. I drew the line, though, at getting tattooed.

Prospector is a retired airplane mechanic from rural Albany County named Bob Boellner, although nobody ever calls him that. He wants New York to repeal the 31-year-old law that requires bikers to wear helmets.

Prospector is pro-choice on helmets. And he's one of the more interesting of the lobbyists who haunt the LOB every week during the legislative session.

For one thing, his group—ABATE—doesn't contribute to political campaigns, although the bikers understand the power of money in the lawmaking process and are giving some thought to rewarding lawmakers who find their position congenial. For another, Prospector is dead right on the issue he's pushing.

"There's no helmet made that'll withstand more than a 13-mile-an-hour impact," he told the state senator's assistant.

"No company in this country even makes helmets any more because of the liability issue. Plus, if you're wearing one, you're more likely to have an accident."

"Why?" the woman asked.

"When you're on a motorcycle," Prospector explained, "you need to see and hear without interference. And on a hot day, the sun beating down on a helmet builds up heat and contributes to fatigue. To me, riding without a helmet is safer. But everybody ought to be able to make his own decision on that. That's ABATE's attitude."

The woman listened while Prospector explained that a four-pound helmet on your head can contribute to whiplash and cause more problems than it might prevent.

"Head injuries generally aren't bad," Prospector told her. "Unless a truck rolls over your head or something."

The woman winced slightly. Not many lobbyists at the LOB talk about trucks rolling over your head.

"The spinal cord injuries you get from whiplash is what you worry about," Prospector said. "A fractured skull generally isn't too bad. You can recover from that. You don't recover from a damaged spinal cord. That's wheelchair stuff. And wearing a helmet makes that more likely."

The woman said she would pass along Prospector's view to her boss. He thanked her and told her about the big rally ABATE is holding at the Capitol on May 18. Last year, the Albany cops busted a number of demonstrators for riding helmetless. This year, Prospector said, ABATE has made a deal with the cops.

"We want to be good citizens," Prospector assured the woman.

Then, as we were leaving, I realized that Prospector had left out a key part of his rap.

So, playing the straight man, I asked, "Say, Prospector, how many bikers in this state?"

"Oh," he said, remembering, "about 500,000."

"Five hundred thousand?" the woman said. "That's a lot."

Prospector smiled broadly through his gray beard. "Yeah," he said.

—April 10, 1998

When Fundraising Was Fun

It was about this time of year, maybe a dozen years ago. I was on State Street, just south of the Capitol, when I bumped into the late Dick Conners, then the assemblyman representing most of the City of Albany.

Dick was a jovial guy who loved to tell stories. He and another old-timer were reminiscing about a beefsteak they'd once attended in Saratoga Springs, during the racing season, many years before.

I said, "You guys went to a beefsteak? I thought a beefsteak is something you eat."

"It used to be a thing you went to, too," Dick explained. "And you got plenty of beefsteak at a beefsteak."

"And plenty of beer," the other old-timer said wistfully.

"Beefsteak and beer," the assemblyman told me. "That was the point."

At the time, I wasn't sure precisely what these guys were talking about. Then, not long ago, I came across an old piece from the *New Yorker* magazine. It was published in 1939 by Joseph Mitchell, one of the magazine's most gifted writers in its glory days.

Mitchell was writing about the decline of the beefsteak, which he described as "a form of gluttony as stylized and regional as the riverbank fish fry, the hot-rock clambake, or the Texas barbecue."

The beefsteak, Mitchell explained, had its roots in late 19th Century Manhattan. It had begun its decline the moment women got the vote and the process of democracy required female admission to these uniquely male-oriented political fundraising banquets.

According to Mitchell, when Dick Conners and his pal were young men, you got your money's worth at any beefsteak thrown as a political fundraiser. For five bucks, the usual pre-war price of admission, it was rare for any diner at a beefsteak to consume less than six pounds of grilled, sliced steak and 30 glasses of beer.

That didn't count the hamburgers and crabmeat salad that were served as appetizers, nor the slices of day-old bread on which the steaks were served. Empty beer barrels groaned beneath the weight of glass bowls of radishes and sliced Bermuda onions. Bands played raucously as diners warmed up on olives and scallions.

A butcher who prepared the meat for these affairs told Mitchell that the primary fare at a classic beefsteak was always the "short loin without the filet." Specially trained chefs would douse it with a sauce of meat drippings, butter and worcestershire.

Lamb chops and lamb kidneys wrapped in bacon were served on the side. No potatoes. They were deemed too filling.

At a classic beefsteak, Mitchell reported, you found no silverware, either. Nor were tablecloths or napkins in evidence. Tarps were placed on the floor beneath the dining tables while men ate with their hands, wiping away the grease on butcher's aprons they were issued upon coughing up their five bucks. Sometimes, at the end of the dinner, waiters had to forcibly remove the aprons from the rowdier drunks.

Beefsteak Tom McGowan, Mitchell reported, was Tammany Hall's organizer of these affairs. For his trouble, he had what apparently was a no-show job at the city water board. When Beefsteak Tom died, 1,000 tearful mourners followed his hearse to a Brooklyn cemetery.

The beefsteak faded away totally when World War II broke out and never returned as a fixture of New York political life. Today, political fundraisers tend to be cocktail parties, with pigs in a blanket, or picnics or coffee klatches. Or, on special occasions, catered dinners at hotels featuring wussy stuffed chicken breasts.

They always involve silverware or, at least, plastic knives and forks, and not a butcher's apron in sight. As the political process has gotten messier, fundraisers have gotten neater.

And, it would seem, a lot less fun.

—August 3, 1999

An Immortal Program

They were called *jibaros*. They were farm people no longer able to coax food from the Puerto Rican mud.

They streamed into New York City, as had the rural Irish and Italians and blacks before them. They hoped to trade futility and feudalism for pavement and prosperity.

Factory work had been there for the others. But when the *jibaros* arrived, those factories were moving south and west.

Without jobs, they settled into rent-controlled walkups in the South Bronx. The Jews and Italians and Irish saw these people as dangerously different—as they themselves had once been viewed. So they fled to Queens or Jersey. Or they migrated north, through Pelham and the Grand Concourse, to the shelter of Westchester.

As the *jibaros* fell unwillingly into the grasp of welfare—and as the only people capable of sustaining rent decontrol put down skid marks leaving the Bronx—rent control tightened its grip.

It had been instituted after World War II to protect returning servicemen searching for jobs and starting up families from landlord profiteering. Always, rent control was meant to be temporary. But, always, a compliant Legislature extended it.

Just a few more years. Only a few, the lawmakers said.

Now, with the working class fleeing the Bronx to be replaced by welfare recipients, well, this was certainly no time to lift rent controls. Then came heroin, the cruel curse of urban dwellers with too much time on their hands.

So, the Bronx landlords, seeing maintenance costs rise and stuck with the same artificially low rents, resorted to new, more desperate measures. They hired professionals with gasoline cans to build empty lots. Abandonment grew popular. Let the city government have the damned buildings.

And soon, the well-intended architects of rent control saw the South Bronx deteriorate into charred rubble, with broken windows staring darkly like eyeless sockets at the rest of this state.

This year's fight over rent control in the Legislature is the most vicious political battle in memory in this town. In all, 1.1 million units home to 2.7 million New Yorkers fall under the program. Another 2 million units don't.

The Democrats offer images of working-class New Yorkers being hit with huge rent increases and fleeing for the suburbs. The Republicans offer Mia Farrow, living in a palace on Central Park West at one-fifth the market rental.

Both are correct, but the story of rent control is best illustrated by the Bronx. There, compassion coupled with poverty and smack conspired to kill much of a borough of a million human beings in less than a decade.

Shelly Silver, the speaker of the Democratic Assembly, has passed a bill to extend rent control indefinitely. Joe Bruno, the leader of the Republican-controlled state senate, wants to decontrol rents over time. His argument is that rent-controlled apartments are subsidized by market-price rentals in the same building.

George Pataki has remained silent. Without senate action, rent control expires June 15. That, as our lawmakers put it, is when rent control goes over the cliff.

Sometime in the future, and it may be well after June 15, some tortured accommodation will be reached on rent control—some complex mechanism to phase it out. That will come after each party has managed to inflict maximum political damage on the other.

Ultimately, though, there's a right here and a wrong, too. For purely political reasons, the Legislature has for decades now perpetuated a bad system.

And, in the process, managed to destroy much of the world's greatest city.

—April 22, 1997

The Big Apple

Fresh off the train from upstate, I'm climbing into a cab at Eighth Avenue and 31st Street, and already the day is not going well.

I've just checked my voice mail in Albany. Mario Cuomo, who was supposed to see me in the afternoon, can't see me after all. He has, inconceivably, come up with something more important to do.

Plus, I have a cab driver who's not only surly—as only New York City cab drivers can be surly—but he's surly in a mystifying language. This guy is from somewhere extremely remote. He has no idea where my hotel is.

"Just drive down Lexington Avenue until you hit the park," I instruct him. "The hotel's on the right."

"Pomjeeb bobo queep," he snarls to me.

Then he jams the gas pedal to the floor, and I'm falling all over the back seat, suitcases flying in all directions. We reach a speed of roughly 165 miles an hour before he slams on the brakes for a red light at the next corner.

"Hey, take it easy," I urge.

"Eebee abba unto vorda," he responds.

So, here we are in the big city. I'm here for a week to write columns. Already, the first column has fallen through, and I figure I'm slightly less than even money to make the hotel in one piece.

The New York City Traffic Department estimates that the average speed of a vehicle crossing midtown Manhattan during the day is 5.3 miles per hour. The city's goal is to raise that to nine miles per hour. My guy here seems determined to do his part.

That's not easy, given how much time we spend going nowhere. A bunch of cops stops us because a movie company is shooting. Then a wino wanders in front of the cab and halts to commune with unseen spirits while my driver blasts his horn and screams from the window, "MEEJA BOOBA BOBBA, JOIK!"

Then there's traffic. I could have walked, I suppose, only I'm carrying suitcases, and I've read somewhere that you're 2.5 times more likely to be murdered in New York City than you are in Albany. If you look like you're from out of town, make that 487 times more likely.

I could have taken the subway, too. The only problem with the subway is that nobody from out of town has the slightest chance of figuring out which train goes where. Once you scrub away a few decades worth of soot and assorted crud, a typical subway sign reads more or less like this:

A-LINE c 4 2 bb MIDTOWN
CCC8 21 * LOCAL EXPRESS
GOAHEADFIGUREITOUTTOURIST

So, now my cab driver and I have hit a pothole, and this is some pothole. It is at 22nd and Park, and entire rural villages in Florida have disappeared into sinkholes smaller than this. We're in the midst of a burst of speed that has us up to, oh, maybe 150. We sail off one side of the pothole and, maybe 80 feet later, our front tires crunch alarmingly into the rim on the far side.

The cab emerges from this Evel Knievel maneuver with a blown front tire. The vehicle flops wearily to the curb. My driver explains the difficulty to me.

"Mamoo coom dorito," he says.

I pay him off and schlep the last few blocks with my suitcases. Nobody tries to murder me.

I figure the week is off to a flying start.

—September 20, 1995

The Uniquely Albany State of Mind

Your Tax Dollars at Work

If you live in the Town of East Greenbush and you're curious about the price of pettiness, you should know it's roughly $4.50.

That's the figure paid by each of that suburban community's 14,000 residents for the treatment accorded one Roberta Reno. She was a $26,600-a-year court clerk who was improperly fired last year by the East Greenbush Town Board in a rather breathtaking display of sheer, stone stupidity.

Here's the story:

Bobbi Reno, a Republican, had worked for two town judges. One was Charlie Assini, Jr., a Republican. The other was Anthony Maney, a Democrat.

Then Maney was defeated in an election by a Republican candidate for the part-time position. That was Catherine Cholakis, a member of a prominent Rensselaer County political family.

Almost immediately, Catherine Cholakis decided that Bobbi Reno was bad news. These two women did not get along at all.

Shortly after starting on the job, Catherine Cholakis turned in a signature stamp for Reno and the other clerks to use on warrants issued by the court. After she turned in the stamp, however, the new judge decided she didn't want it used.

When her stamped signature turned up on a couple of warrants, she was furious. She submitted an affidavit to the town board, which is controlled by Democrats, setting forth her belief that Bobbi Reno had used the unauthorized signature stamp.

Did she ask Reno if she'd used the stamp? No, Cholakis later told me. Did the town board ask Reno if she'd used the stamp? No, Town Supervisor Mike Van Voris later told me.

In fact, did the town board ask Bobbi Reno anything? Was she given a hearing? Was she given any chance whatever to defend herself?

Uh-uh. On the advice of the town's lawyer, she was simply fired—after 18 years on the job. Now, you can ask anybody who supervises anything in any workplace. Only bosses with heads full of faulty wiring fire people this way.

The sensible procedure is this:

You give the employee a hearing. You discuss performance problems. You ask the employee to participate in a program to improve performance. You ask how you, as a boss, can help. And, ultimately, if you can't get the performance the job requires, then you let that employee go.

Charlie Assini, Jr., the other judge, was appalled at what the town board did to Bobbi Reno, who swears that she never, ever used Cholakis' signature stamp after she was told not to. Assini disagreed with the firing.

And, ultimately, that was the basis of the suit that Bobbi Reno brought against the Town Board of East Greenbush. She won, too.

The last time I looked into this matter, back in November, the town board was appealing that decision. Then word came to me not long ago that Bobbi Reno had found a job in the Legislature and had worked out a settlement with the town board.

I called her. How much did they have to pay you, I asked? Can't tell you, Bobbi Reno said. As a term of the deal, everybody swore not to talk about it. But, she said, she's "very happy."

Well, the problem with that is that Bobbi Reno was paid off with tax dollars. Everybody is entitled to know how they're spent. So I filed a freedom of information request for access to the town's checkbook. Here's what's in there:

A check for $30,000 made out to Bobbi Reno. A check for $6,750 made out to her lawyer. And a total of 28 grand spent by the town on legal fees.

So, there you are, East Greenbushers. Those are your tax dollars at work. Moreover, given the terms of the settlement, nobody in town government can talk about this case.

Not even to say, like, duh.

—*August 1, 1997*

A Good Judge of Character

At this disillusioned stage of life, I have few heroes left—especially in government. After yesterday, however, I've added E. David Duncan to that short list.

He's the Albany City Court judge who listened for a day and a half as the prosecution made its non-existent criminal case against Joe Cavallaro. Then, Judge Duncan threw the whole shameful business out of court.

Paul Clyne didn't like that. He told me so yesterday afternoon. Joe Cavallaro is a criminal, Paul Clyne assured me. And, to Paul Clyne's credit as a professional advocate, he kept a straight face as he said it.

If you murder anybody in Albany County, you might get to know Paul Clyne. He's a smallish, bespectacled guy, the son of the late Judge "Maximum John" Clyne. Paul Clyne is one of the top guns in the district attorney's office. Paul Clyne's skills usually are reserved for nailing the biggest, baddest dudes in the criminal justice system.

He'd just spent a day and a half vigorously prosecuting a harassment case against a 49-year-old small businessman with no criminal history. This was a misdemeanor, strictly small potatoes. But Paul Clyne's presence in that tiny courtroom in the basement of city hall was proof positive that the power structure in this town was hell-bent on sticking it to Joe Cavallaro.

Why? Because Joe Cavallaro had gotten uppity. He'd tugged on Superman's cape. So, the lords of the political power structure were pulling out all the stops to stomp him into the ground.

This started last August, when Joe Cavallaro called the office of his assemblyman. That's John Faso, the smooth Kinderhook lawyer who leads the Assembly Republicans. Joe Cavallaro wanted a bigger sign for a nearby state park. He figured that would be good for his business. He has operated a general store and motel near that park for 25 years.

He got a Faso staffer he'd dealt with in 1996 about getting an ice skating rink for the park. The rink had never materialized, so Joe Cavallaro wanted to deal with somebody else—just about anybody else, actually—in his assemblyman's office. But Faso's staff director, Nancy Linehan, told him that he would deal with whoever she told him to deal with. When Joe Cavallaro tried to argue with her, Nancy Linehan hung up on him.

Joe Cavallaro then did what I would have done—and what most people would do upon encountering so lofty a level of haughtiness from the staff of an elected official. He got mad as hell.

Now, he wanted to talk to Faso himself. He not only wanted the sign, he also wanted to complain about Nancy Linehan. Over a three-day period, Joe Cavallaro called Faso's office about 30 times. The office staff hung up on him as soon as they heard his voice. Finally, Nancy Linehan had a state trooper threaten him with arrest.

Joe Cavallaro said: What? Because I want to talk to my

assemblyman? Hey, I voted for this guy. Is this America, or what? You want to arrest me, come do it.

Then, in desperation, he called Faso's house three times. Since Faso's home phone is listed, Joe Cavallaro figured it was OK to call him there. Wrong. Next thing he knew, Joe Cavallaro had a trooper in his store in Haines Falls, slapping him into cuffs.

The Albany City Court judge who'd ordered him taken into custody, Steve Herrick, simply could have issued this guy an appearance ticket for a charge like this. It was more fun, apparently, to have this insufficiently servile member of the great unwashed mob dragged off to arraignment in the company of hookers and drug dealers.

Then, figuring that they'd really shown Joe Cavallaro who was boss, the people who run the system offered him an ACOD—an adjournment of the case in contemplation of dismissal. If he didn't call his assemblyman again or annoy any other of his betters, the charge would be dropped in six months or so.

Joe Cavallaro was born and bred in Brooklyn—in a borough of a city where, at any given moment, you'll find eight million people standing up and demanding their rights. He told them all to go to hell.

So, this week, top gun Paul Clyne was drafted on short notice by the brass in the D.A.'s office to crush this little guy who had the temerity to believe that he has rights. New York State defines the crime of harassment as communication that causes the recipient distress, exempting "legitimate communication," which the statute doesn't define. That's left to the common sense of judges and juries.

This judge and jury watched closely as Nancy Linehan took the stand the other day. She's an attractive, well-spoken woman who bristled like a porcupine the moment cross-examination began. Nancy Linehan's prickly manner on the stand, at a time when she would be expected to be on her very best behavior, gave everybody a pretty good idea of what Joe Cavallaro must have encountered when he'd made that phone call.

Joe Cavallaro's lawyer, Mark Mishler, asked her: Why didn't she let Joe Cavallaro talk to the assemblyman?

"You do not just call the White House and speak to the President," Nancy Linehan explained. "It just doesn't work that way."

Yeah, well, the fact is that neither Tony Blair nor Boris Yeltsin will be calling John Faso anytime soon. Faso represents only 120,000 souls. He's supposed to be a creature of the village square. Even if he figures that a constituent is a fool, he has a certain degree of obligation to suffer that fool gladly—not have him busted.

On the day this trial began, Joe Cavallaro was already out five grand in legal fees. Just as it was clear that he's a guy with a short fuse, it also was clear that he'd been treated with contempt by people who are supposed to be public servants. Having him arrested and prosecuted was a breathtaking exercise in the sheer, naked arrogance of power.

The D.A.'s office could have dropped this. Faso certainly could have gotten it dropped. Instead, Faso displayed an uncharacteristic tin ear for the political consequences of trying to bully a guy constitutionally incapable of standing for it.

Too few of these imperious political people suckling at the public teat, it would seem, are able to resist the chance to punish an ordinary schnook who seems improperly impressed by their exalted status on the taxpayers' payroll.

But my new hero, the Honorable E. David Duncan, seemed to get the picture very quickly.

And he wouldn't let them get away with it.

—June 11, 1999

A Medical Marvel

Most freaks you can spot right away. They have six heads, three eyes or some other physical characteristic that sets them apart from the rest of humanity.

Not all of them, though. For example, Rachel McEneny looks completely normal. She's a pretty, blonde woman of 26—only one nose, no beard.

But Rachel McEneny is clearly a freak of nature. There's no other way to explain how her body sheds alcohol at such a stunning rate.

The Albany cops arrested Rachel McEneny last week and charged her with drunken driving. That happened the same night her father, Assemblyman Jack McEneny, handily fought back a primary election challenge by Gary Domalewicz, the candidate the mayor backed in that race. Mayor Jerry Jennings was eager to punish Rachel McEneny's father for his unsuccessful but annoying primary challenge against the mayor the year before.

The cops charged that Rachel McEneny, who managed both her father's campaigns, ran a stop sign at 2:17 a.m. while on the way home from her father's victory party. They said that she failed a sobriety test. So, they slapped her in manacles and dragged her off to the station. There, they gave her a breathalyzer test that recorded her blood alcohol content at .11 per cent.

Two hours later, though, after she was sprung, Rachel McEneny had a blood test conducted at Albany Memorial Hospital. The results of that test—.04 per cent blood alcohol content. Rachel McEneny's lawyer submitted results of that test to Albany Police Court yesterday.

Peter Gerstenzang, a lawyer not involved in this—but an acknowledged expert in driving while intoxicated cases—told me that the average human being sheds alcohol at the rate of .02 per cent per hour, tops. That makes Rachel McEneny a certifiable medical marvel, since her body manages to shed alcohol at twice the normal human rate.

Actually, though, some other possibilities exist to explain all this. One is that the hospital blood test was wrong. That is not a possibility that anybody should bet on, however. Another is that the breathalyzer was screwed up. The only problem with that explanation is that it was recalibrated only two days before Rachel McEneny blew into it.

Still another possibility is that Rachel McEneny was running a temperature, which would register a higher blood alcohol content reading on the breathalyzer. Also, just before her breathalyzer test, she might have used some mouthwash. Why she would do that I can't imagine, but I couldn't reach her yesterday to clear up that question.

Another possibility yet is that Rachel McEneny belched just before the test, which could throw off the machine. But the test was conducted by an officer specifically trained to watch for that sort of thing.

After all, no police officer would ever want to see anybody nailed for drunken driving—not even the daughter of a politician who has called for creation of a police review board—if that person wasn't really driving drunk.

So, it seems that only one reasonable explanation could exist for this bizarre turn of events in the Rachel McEneny drunken driving case. Jack McEneny has obviously fathered a fantastic genetic blip so far removed from the normal range of human physical response that she ought to be written up in the medical books in crimson ink.

Actually, Rachel McEneny's lawyer, Steve Coffey, wants to see his client written up in other literature. It's Coffey's fondest wish, once this case is dismissed, that his client appear in court reports as the recipient of the biggest false arrest damage award in the history of humankind.

For a lawyer, though, that kind of thinking is perfectly normal.

—September 23, 1998

A Private Place

It was a day when winter bared its fangs right up to the gums. Bullets of snow swirled around Peter Clouse's head and mine as we stomped through the slush and muck along the weedy shoreline of Lawson Lake.

"You should have worn different shoes," Peter Clouse noted.

He was in jeans and hiking boots. Genius that I am, I'd worn a suit, tie and dress shoes for this tour of Lawson Lake Park. I needed to see the place, though. I needed to see why no members of the public are allowed inside what's supposed to be a public park.

Lawson Lake Park is in Clarksville, high in the semi-rural Hill Towns in the mountains that are southwest Albany County. The county bought the 421-acre site in 1979 for nearly $600,000. It's a gorgeous place—with a glittering little gem of a lake and 20 or so rustic recreational buildings.

The problem is that, 18 years after the county bought the property, it remains the exclusive province of a summer camp for inner-city kids whose board of directors reads like a who's who of the Albany County Democratic Party.

Here are a few members of the Camp Opportunities board of directors: Former City Treasurer Ray Joyce, who serves as president; Polly Noonan, longtime confidante of the late Mayor Erastus Corning 2nd; County Coronor Phil Furie; Albany city council member Shawn Morris and Albany Police Chief Kevin Tuffey.

When the county bought the place, half the purchase price came from the federal government. In exchange for the money, the county pledged to open the land to the public.

A lot of things have happened since 1979. We've had

three governors, three Presidents and three county executives. The country has lived through two stock market panics and a war. Arsenio Hall came and went, and Johnny Carson just went. O. J. Simpson went from icon to outcast. Liz Taylor went through two more husbands. Bill Gates got rich. Mike Tyson got prison time.

Eighteen years. That's 80 per cent longer than the Vietnam War lasted.

And still, the issue of how to open Lawson Lake Park to the public continues, mysteriously, to befuddle Albany County Democrats. Every time a plan is proposed, it somehow gets shot down. And, somehow, this summer camp with its politically connected board of directors retains exclusive control over public land now worth a few million bucks.

This disturbs Peter Clouse. He's the county legislator from the district that contains the park. He's also a Republican, though, so nobody in Albany County government really cares what pleases or disturbs him.

The 1979 purchase was intended to bail out its owner, the Trinity Institution in Albany's South End. That's a venerable charitable organization founded by the family of Albany Alderman Jimmy Scalzo, who now heads it.

The Camp Opportunities people say they'll tolerate public use of the park as long as their use isn't disturbed. Jimmy Scalzo openly opposes public use, however. He doesn't want mere taxpayers skulking around near the summer camp to which he feels such strong ties.

And, watching the way every proposal to open the property to the public has been steadfastly stymied for 18 years now in the Albany County Legislature, it's difficult to avoid concluding that the real agenda here is to continue maintaining this public park exclusively for the benefit of the pet charitable project of a bunch of Democratic Party politicians.

Camp Opportunities is a fine and worthwhile operation, and nobody is even considering denying it use of the land. But when something like this sits around for 18 long years, it tends to develop a characteristic common to many taxpayer-financed projects in Albany County over the years. It starts to give off a definite smell.

—*November 19, 1997*

Politicians and Naked Ladies

So, there I was, minding my own business, listening to Janis Joplin's hoarse screech and watching this buck naked woman on stage wrap herself salaciously around a fire pole.

And here was this bearded guy in a Harley-Davidson cap trying to throw me out of the joint.

"You're making the girls nervous, Sir," he explained.

"Really? How am I doing that?"

"You were writing stuff down," he said. "We've had some trouble with the police in the past."

"Hey," I demanded, "do I look like a cop to you?"

He didn't even bother to answer that one. Turns out that the guy's name is Larry. He's an agent for a couple of the strippers at Goldfingers on State Street in Schenectady. After I handed him a business card, everybody suddenly became very cordial.

A public relations battle is being waged between the politicians who run the City of Schenectady and the strip club operators. Rule No. 1 in a war like this is make nice with reporters.

Al Jurczynski, Schenectady's mayor, is being hammered unmercifully in this war. First a federal judge threw out the city's ordinance banning nude dancing. The judge also has reservations about the city's ordinance to zone these joints into specific neighborhoods—which is moot at the moment, since everything is on appeal.

Plus, it turns out that somebody saw Jurczynski eight years ago in a suburban topless joint. He said he went for a bachelor party. Supposedly, Jurczynski's moral standing to criticize these clubs is impaired by the fact that he knows what naked women look like.

Frankly, I kind of like that in a politician.

The night I was in Goldfingers, I was part of a crowd of maybe a half-dozen quiet guys. No booze is served in the joint, so the audience contented itself with gazing slack-jawed at the ladies gyrating to Janis. The strippers sat along the rear wall, smoking and giggling when they weren't strutting their stuff.

One of the dancers came over to talk to me. Her name is Melissa, and her performance had been decidedly gynecological in tone. I already knew her more intimately than I felt comfortable with. I have kids her age. She said she's working her way through Hudson Valley Community College. I wished her luck. Tony DeMaria, who operates Goldfingers, said all these women could use some of that.

"A lot of these girls," he said, "they were in abusive marriages or relationships. With the money they make here, they can get out of those relationships. This buys them freedom."

"How'd you get into this line of work?" I asked him.

"I was working in the computer business. I thought that naked women would be more fun than computers. It is, too."

DeMaria explained that he operates Goldfingers as a private club. You buy a nightly membership when you go in. I asked him what his bylaws say and the date of the next club meeting.

"OK," he told me, "so, we're not too well organized. And we're a little lax in record-keeping."

The city probably won't manage to ban this outright. There's this thing called the U. S. Constitution. Like it or not, we're talking art here. With the right zoning ordinance, though, the city might succeed in moving nude clubs away from homes.

This dispute has become riotous material for radio talk shows, locally and nationally. Jerry Springer, TV freak show host, slithers into town in two days to capitalize on an old, fading city's fight against seediness.

The politicians have bobbled this flap. Now it's a circus.

And the clown acts are taking over center ring.

—February 4, 1997

A Contact Sport

Bathed in brilliant spring sunlight as the TV cameras pointed at him yesterday on Albany's State Street Hill, Jim Coyne must have been reminded of the old days, when he was the toast of local politics.

Then came his conviction on six counts of sticky fingers. And suddenly Coyne was the jelly—the highest-ranking Albany County politician ever shipped off to the slammer.

"I was away 46 months," Coyne was saying into the microphones. "That's more than most muggers get, more than some murderers."

Give him this; like Marion Barry in Washington, he did do the time. He still won't admit that he did the crime, however.

It was just a loan, Coyne maintains, not a bribe. He was guilty only of a little bad judgment, the victim of a railroading, a wronged guy, and yada, yada, yada.

The Uniquely Albany State of Mind

Well, that was then. Now, at age 53 and with a new wife and baby, Coyne is battling ferociously to elbow his way back into the spotlight. Outside the county office building at 112 State Street, he was announcing that he'll wage a primary fight this year for the county clerk's job, a post Coyne held early in his checkered career.

He'll challenge Tom Clingan, a man six years younger who spent 13 years as assistant county executive. Clingan was Coyne's right-hand man before winning his own election as county clerk in 1988.

With the cameras going and the microphones clustered at his chin, Coyne's old glow was undiminished. If politics is show business for ugly people, then you'll look long and hard before you'll come across a political performer more disarming, more appealing, than handsome, smiling James J. Coyne, Jr.

A little older? Sure. Grayer and more weather-beaten? After nearly four years in stir, who wouldn't be? And, yes, if he wins this election it'll be the greatest comeback since Lazarus.

But the Coyne pizzaz is still there—all the old charm, the old snappy patter and the well-practiced fancy footwork.

Tom Clingan is a sober, capable government technocrat with a master's degree in public administration. He lacks Coyne's name recognition. He's well aware that he's something of a nonentity to an increasingly anorexic news audience.

"There's a difference, though," Clingan told me later, "between being well-known and being notorious."

Still, on star quality, Coyne wins this race hands-down. When the TV cameras start to whir, he exudes warmth and good humor. Clingan is cerebral and well-spoken, but he once was given a gag T-shirt by county co-workers proclaiming him "Mr. Morose." On the few occasions he has made the TV news he has tended to come off like some guy making a hostage tape.

There is, however, more to this race than deft, practiced grace on the six and the eleven. This is a primary election—the only kind that counts in heavily Democratic Albany County. And Clingan is the consummate party man.

He's backed by the Democratic organization. The faithful also recall with some vividness the scandals that marked the last of Coyne's four terms as county executive—scandals that created a windfall for the Republicans.

After Coyne's conviction, Mike Hoblock, a Colonie Republican, won the county executive's job. Then Hoblock won a state senate seat drawn to be Democratic Party property. It took years and millions of campaign dollars for the Democrats to take back what they believed to be rightly theirs. And the most devoted Albany County Democrats know precisely who they can blame for that.

Moreover, there's this: Clingan is good at what he does. In the arcane world of county clerking, Clingan is a respected figure. He has headed the state organization of county clerks, and he has won the organization's top award.

His is not a sexy job. He's a record-keeper and a fee-collector supervising a staff of 40. But the job is important, and Clingan is an able, conscientious public official.

Mere competence doesn't count to the extent that it should in a world where half the voters, by definition, fall below median intelligence. But it doesn't hurt, either.

What's most interesting about all this, though, is that Coyne never had a more loyal deputy. When solemn, bespectacled Tom Clingan was dragged up on the witness stand in Coyne's corruption trial, his testimony tended to support the county executive. And I can tell you from personal experience that when his boss was under the gun because of this newspaper's hard reporting on Coyne's shady activities, the county executive never had a fiercer, more vociferous defender than Tom Clingan.

This is the thanks he gets. Coyne, out of work and eager for the 72 grand the county clerk's position pays, is looking to send Tom Clingan to the unemployment line. No good deed, it seems, ever goes unpunished.

Which only demonstrates that politics is a contact sport

in this town, and anybody who wants to play should make it a point to wear a cup. Clingan is well aware that a Jim Coyne eager to return to politics faced limited choices. He couldn't run for district attorney. He's not a lawyer. A convicted felon running for sheriff would quickly turn into a sad joke. Two other guys, one an incumbent, are already battling it out for mayor.

Given all that, Tom Clingan was simply the most convenient target for a Coyne comeback. So, Clingan was a devoted and loyal deputy. Like the conviction in federal court, that was then, and this is now. And loyalty is for golden retrievers.

They're the product of a careful, selective breeding process that accentuates positive traits and weeds out less desirable ones.

The breeding of politicians, however, is far less strictly supervised.

—*May 1, 1997*

Chimps and Chumps

Jimmy Carter was President. Elvis was barely cold in his grave. And I was an editor at another newspaper.

The photo department had given me a set on contact prints from which to select shots for the next day's paper. I'd gone back to photo with my choices. The photo editor occupied a desk in the middle of the room. I stood beside him as he bent over the contact prints, inspecting my choices.

What neither of us knew was that Zippy the Chimp was in the building that day for some advertising promotion.

Bored with it all, Zippy had gotten loose. As the photo editor and I studied the contact prints, Zip came roaring through the door. He wore a white sweatshirt with "Zip" emblazoned across his chest in red letters. Zippy the Chimp was on roller skates.

Three times, Zip furiously circled the desk in the photo department, grinning up at me with big, yellow, chimpanzee teeth. Then he rolled back out the door and disappeared down the hall.

I said to the photo editor, "What the hell was that?"

He glanced up from the contact prints he'd been studying with such intensity.

"What was what?" he asked.

I think of that guy every time I ponder the prospect of Sol Greenberg, the Albany County district attorney, investigating and prosecuting official corruption. The politicians could be selling off the Capitol, block by block, and Sol would be the very last guy to notice.

Or, if he were to notice, it would break the pattern of a lengthy professional lifetime. When Jim Coyne was Albany County executive and got such a bad case of sticky fingers during the construction of the Pepsi Arena, Sol failed to notice from his office four blocks away. When Davis Etkin was making so much money disappear at the Capital District Off-Track Betting Corp., Sol didn't notice.

Now, thanks to the members of the New York State Temporary Commission on Lobbying, Sol is supposed to investigate possible criminal activity during this town's most recent lobbying scandal—the one in which the Philip Morris Company violated state law with regard to reporting gifts to state legislators and perhaps by funneling cash to a third party to pay for the governor's trip to Hungary.

Instead of giving this investigation to Attorney General Eliot Spitzer, who needs a request from a state agency to look into this and has been positively drooling at the prospect, the commission's five members decided Monday to give it to Greenberg instead. After all, isn't Sol the D.A.? Isn't prosecuting crime in this county the D.A.'s job and not the attorney general's?

Republicans outnumber Democrats on this commission, but this wasn't a party line vote. With the exception of commission member Milton Mollen, a highly respected former Democratic judge, nobody really wanted this thing looked into. Neither the commission members nor their patrons in the Legislature and on the second floor want to know who in Philip Morris, other than the company's Albany lobbyist, knew about the lawbreaking. And, since Philip Morris has had similar problems in three other states, it's not unreasonable to suspect that somebody did.

The governor could fix this. He has the authority to supersede Greenberg and name a special prosecutor. He won't, though. They're all in this together, Democrats and Republicans alike. Everybody is loudly in favor of honest government until they have to actually do something to make it honest.

So, now Spitzer is shut out of this probe. Sol Greenberg runs an understaffed office and has spent a career ignoring just this kind of stuff. And he's supposed to investigate this lobbying scandal?

Even Zippy would be appalled.

—*January 12, 2000*

Memories of the Mayor

Like any sport, politics demands its heroes and villains. In Albany, where close proximity to both New York and Boston smothers any chance for any other big-time local sport, heroes and villains tend to be politicians.

That's why Albany *Times Union* reporter Paul Grondahl's biography of Erastus Corning 2nd has been greeted with such intense local interest since its publication a few weeks back. I say that not just because Grondahl is my colleague. I say it because I've seen the stir this book has caused in Albany.

For 41 years, Corning was the dominant public figure in the Albany metro area. As mayor of Albany, he held the most visible political job in town—not counting whoever happened to be governor at the moment.

Governors, though, came and went. Corning endured. If his power wasn't absolute during those decades—he deferred for most of that time to Dan O'Connell, the crusty political boss who'd put him in city hall—Corning's sheer star power was unmatched. As he aged, the matinee idol good looks faded. But the gracious charm only increased.

As Grondahl looked back over his career, it became clear that Corning, although a capable man, was not a great man in the sense that Nelson Rockefeller was great. Corning imagined no lasting monuments—like the state university system, for example. Corning was no builder. If anything, he could be faulted for presiding over long decades of stagnation in Albany.

He was, though, a master politician who saw party politics as a positive mechanism for improving peoples' lives. Grondahl's book makes that clear. So does a story I heard the other day from Bill Cunningham, now a banking executive but for much of his life a political operative.

Cunningham had been Gov. Hugh Carey's number two patronage dispenser. One day Corning called him. The mayor had heard that a job had come open in state government—chairman of the state Motor Vehicle Department Appeals Board. The job called for a lawyer and paid about 35 grand. I have just the guy for the job, Corning said.

Cunningham said he had to check with Bob Morgado,

the government professional who served as Carey's executive officer and who really ran the state day-to-day. Morgado said that the job was spoken for, that influential Bronx Democrat Herman Badillo had submitted the name of his own nominee.

Cunningham called Corning back and said sorry. Not acceptable, Corning told him. This had always been an Albany job. Besides, Corning said, at least a dozen families were counting on this job.

"He insisted I come down the hill to see him," Cunningham recalled the other day. "So, I went and sat in front of the metal desk in city hall. And the mayor explained it to me."

Corning said he wanted to give the state job to his city corporation counsel, who had kids in college and could use the extra $12,000 a year. The corporation counsel's job would go to his deputy, who would also get a nice raise. Then there was this lawyer on the payroll of the county legislature. He would get the assistant corporation counsel's job. Then there was this kid, just out of law school. . . .

"It was a political science lesson," Cunningham told me. "By the time he was finished he was down to a part-time road maintenance job in Westerlo. All these families, he told me, would benefit from this one state job.

"I went back to Morgado with all that. He said, OK, give the job to Corning's guy. That Badillo, he'd just screw us somewhere down the road anyway."

—*November 25, 1997*

On Broadway Hill

After Bob Nardelli pushed Al Jurczynski around, I made a call to Joe Battaglino.

Jurczynski, Schenectady's new mayor, had finally gotten a meeting with Nardelli, General Electric's top guy in the city. Jurczynski wanted GE to make available for development some of the vacant land at its main plant.

And, not only did Nardelli tell Jurczynski to go pound sand, he also warned him against discussing the matter with reporters—which, of course, Jurczynski did more or less instantly.

It was just more of the arrogance that Joe Battaglino has seen over and over. He's the assistant business agent, Local 301, International Electrical Union, and president of the Schenectady Area Central Labor Council.

I'd called to ask him about the 15 cents. This is how the AFL-CIO plans to raise political money this year. It'll assess each of its 78 unions 15 cents per member, per month. The unions figure to raise as much as $35 million to wage war on corporate mercenaries like Bob Nardelli.

That's nickels and dimes compared to what big business coughs up. Last time out, business outspent unions by 7-1. But Joe Battaglino says, his 14,000-member labor council will kick in $2,100 a month to the national effort.

He's 49. He went to work for GE in 1968 after getting out of the army. His father had worked for GE, and his grandfather. By the mid-70s, Local 301 had 14,000 members. Today, bloody from layoffs, it has 2,200.

Joe Battaglino told me, "I got a corporation I work for, they made almost $7 billion profit. I saw it in the paper today. And they still aren't making enough money. . . . It used to be, if you lived in Schenectady, you'd walk down Broadway Hill. You'd walk down to Building One, you got a job. And everybody in the family knew that.

"Now you can't walk down Broadway Hill. Building One is gone. And they're not hiring."

Sure, stockholders demand high returns. But aren't the stockholders working people—like you, Joe? What about the stock in retirement funds?

"Jack Welch owns eight million shares," Joe Battaglino said. "That's just one guy. Many times the union has gone to the stockholders meeting and tried to use our proxies. We'd been trying to get a seat on that board for the longest time.... With all our proxies pulled together nationwide, we still don't have enough....

"Look what they're doing to us. And it's going to eventually affect you. When we're gone—if the industrial workers go—what's left? Just state workers? And your taxes keep going up and going up. Somebody's gotta pay....

"I hear this world market business. But where's everything sold? In the United States. What's competitive is the labor market—because if you go to Taiwan, Korea, Mexico, South America, you can get workers for 50 cents an hour. But then you bring the product back into this country and you sell it for enormous money—the same money you were charging before and sometimes higher."

So the 15 cents will go to "educate" union workers—to persuade them to back candidates who'll support tariffs and to oppose free traders.

"We're for fair trade," Joe Battaglino told me. "But the American worker is getting killed with this free trade."

You can say it's more complicated than that. And it is.

But when a bloodless corporate shark like Bob Nardelli spits in your face on Broadway Hill, everything starts to look a lot simpler, doesn't it?

—April 12, 1996

Fall from Grace

When Davis Etkin went to work yesterday morning, the office was jammed with flowers from well-wishers.

"What's this?" he asked his secretary. "Did I die and nobody told me?"

Well, in a sense, yes. Politicians have constructed empires before, but few quite as deftly as shrewd, affable Davis Myron Etkin. As the founding father and reigning potentate of the Capital District Off-Track Betting Corp., Dave Etkin was lord of all he surveyed for more than a quarter century.

Governors came and went. So did the lords of the state Legislature, the county executives, the mayors and the party bosses. Etkin was there when they arrived. He was there when they left.

Now, in a little over two months, he'll be gone, too—ousted by the statewide leader of his own party. Etkin is scheduled to depart the empire he built on March 15—the Ides of March. That's the same day of the year that Julius Caesar ran afoul of some potent political opposition of his own. Etkin hopes to leave less of his blood on the floor than Caesar did, but whether he'll be able to manage that remains unclear.

Yesterday, at a corner table in the Blue Ribbon diner in Schenectady—where Etkin and his wife Lois eat several nights a week—this smallish, jovial, bespectacled man of 70 sat over a salad and a cup of coffee and reflected on his future.

He's working a deal to run some sort of off-shore off-track-betting operation, he was saying—a gig that would permit him to live here and fly back and forth to the job there. Hard feelings? Not at all. He had a terrific run as chief of the Capital District's Off-Track Betting Corp. He'll be delighted to help his temporary successor, Tom Cholakis, in any way he can.

Agreeable. That was Davis Etkin yesterday—the most agreeable guy anybody could ever meet.

But, he was saying, it just wasn't possible to be agreeable last spring, when the assassination attempt against him got rolling. Etkin felt he'd had to fight, even though he'd known deep in his heart that he had no real chance to win—although he wouldn't admit it at the time.

Sure, the members of his board were his friends, people he'd worked with for years. But when the state party chairman decides that you're going—and when the party he chairs controls all the immense machinery of state government—then sooner or later you're history.

Goodbye, adios, sayonara, au revoir, shalom, arrividerci, aloha, does vedanya. Don't let the door smack you in the butt on your way out.

Eventually, against truly serious opposition, you run out of directors willing to vote to keep you in. That's what happened to Dave Etkin.

The guy who pushed this was Bill Powers, the state GOP chairman. He'd listened to Albany County Democrats like Mike Breslin, the county executive, and Mike Conners, the county comptroller. They were howling loudly that Dave Etkin's lavish personal and promotional spending was cheating the counties in the Capital OTB area of revenue to reduce taxes. Powers watched them get on television with that relentless chant, day after day. And, ultimately, Bill Powers decided that they had a point. He decided that this was a Republican mess and that the Republicans had a duty to clean it up.

Moreover, Powers—who'd been Rensselaer County GOP chairman before he took over the state party—knew that 1997 would be a tough election year for Henry Zwack, the county executive in Powers' home county. No state party chairman will take lightly a possible loss in his home county. It's a simple matter of pride.

In his mind, Powers imagined Davis Etkin, a fellow Republican, as a giant albatross around Henry Zwack's neck. He imagined the Democrats taking Etkin by the ankles and using him to beat Henry Zwack like a gong right through November. Bill Powers imagined all that and had word sent to Etkin.

Time to retire, Davis. That was the word Bill Powers sent.

No deal, said Etkin—not unless I have assurances that my key employees, the team that has been so loyal to me over the years, will be protected. You are dictating no terms, Etkin was told. Then just try to throw me out, Etkin dared Powers. And, after initially losing a vote on the OTB board in June, Powers hunkered down and did precisely that.

The key weapon was a report by the State Racing and Wagering Board investigators that came out last week. The document was a grim, profoundly dangerous indictment of Etkin's management of Capital OTB—$4.3 million in unnecessary spending since 1991, nearly a million bucks in charitable contributions spread around the region at Etkin's discretion instead of going to the counties for tax relief, wretched controls over credit cards, cellular phones, shoddy accounting. Personal spending by Etkin and his family members that could prove troublesome down the road.

The state report just went on and on, a total condemnation.

Most significant from a political perspective, however, was the looming possibility that the state might remove certain directors—namely, Etkin's supporters—from their $1,200-a-year posts and sue them personally for what the state claimed was malfeasance in refusing to curb Etkin's spending.

That pretty much did it, and Etkin knew it. Personal liability of the part of the directors? That could have a fairly dramatic effect on board voting patterns, Etkin decided. On Monday, he tendered his resignation.

It remains an open question as to whether Etkin or his most loyal directors might be targets of civil suits by the state—or even criminal charges. Etkin figures he's probably covered. For years, he has been depositing money in an OTB account to reimburse the corporation in case anybody ever made a solid case that he'd personally misused OTB money.

He has about $44,000 in that account at the moment. In a real pinch, he could write a check for more. He'll collect a

$110,000 state pension after all these years. And he maintains a private law practice as well. For a public servant, Dave Etkin will be well fixed.

The problem here is that he has irritated a good many powerful people in his own party with his refusal to step aside quietly and gracefully when he had the chance. Moreover, state officials are hinting that 44 grand won't begin to cover Etkin's liabilities.

Also, Zwack is safely back in office now. There's no political reason for Republican prosecutors to exercise prosecutorial discretion and simply forget about the money that the state has accused Davis Etkin of misusing.

He'll say that this is all politics—and there's no question that politics played a powerful role in the state party's decision to drive Dave Etkin from public life. The real question is whether he'll be left to argue that position to rather inconsequential people like me over lunch in Schenectady diners.

Or whether, at some point, Davis Myron Etkin might be forced to make that argument to people in some jury box somewhere.

—January 14, 1998

After the Fall

He sat yesterday morning, dapper as always in a navy blue suit, on the rearmost bench of a wood-paneled courtroom, surrounded by family. In the judge's chambers, his lawyer, Steve Coffey, was doing battle with a government gladiator from the attorney general's office. I settled on the bench in front of Davis Etkin, turned around and said, "How's it going?"

"Well, you know what this is all about," Davis Etkin said.

Yes, in fact, I did. As a senior editor for the Albany *Times Union*, before I'd nailed down a terrific column gig, I'd supervised the work of a fine reporter, Mike Gormley, as he produced a multi-part series on mismanagement and woefully wasteful financial practices at the Capital District Off-Track Betting Corp. Davis Etkin had run OTB since its birth in 1972. Then I'd listened as radio talk show host Paul Vandenburgh, once an OTB employee, had railed day after day against Etkin's leadership of that public benefit corporation.

Then I'd watched Democrats like Albany County Executive Mike Breslin and Comptroller Mike Conners complain bitterly that Etkin's lavish salary, perks and corporate spending were cheating the county of cash needed to keep down local taxes. I'd watched State Republican Chairman Bill Powers finally decide that Etkin had become a liability to the GOP and urge him to step down. I'd watched also as Etkin unwisely had told Bill Powers to go to hell.

And I'd said to myself, "Uh-oh."

The State Racing and Wagering Board supervises New York's OTB operations. The next thing Etkin knew, the board was all over him with nosy, prying auditors. Moreover, Republican Attorney General Dennis Vacco was launching a criminal investigation into Etkin's management and spending. Pretty soon, Etkin's OTB board of dim-bulb political hacks finally had gotten the message: Yo, dummies, you can face civil and maybe even criminal penalties for Etkin's 25-year, unbridled spending spree. So, Etkin was out, Powers installed his own guy as OTB chief and that was it.

Until Democrat Eliot Spitzer was elected attorney general, that is—until Spitzer's people uncovered that bulging Etkin file. And, unlike Vacco, Spitzer was willing to actually prosecute Etkin.

Public integrity is no mere political platitude. In practical terms, in an operation like this, it relates directly to the ability of senior citizens in New York, the state with the nation's highest local property taxes, to remain in their homes and live out their lives in dignity amid familiar surroundings. Yet too much of what should have been profit from this OTB operation went not for tax relief but for what the prosecutors termed "a systematic, ongoing course of conduct to defraud the state...."

It's the firm suspicion of Spitzer's people that no small amount of that money also went offshore, to secret, private bank accounts. They want it back. Yesterday, Davis Etkin pleaded guilty to charges of scamming the government and of trying to bribe a witness in the attorney general's criminal probe. He'll be sentenced soon. He's a charming, gracious guy of 72, and it would be a shame to see a man that age go to prison for a non-violent crime. But Davis Etkin had better find some of that money, or that's what'll happen.

It's a sad story. Sadder yet, though, is this:

Pretty much, the whole town knew. The legitimate, establishment outfits that took OTB's influence-buying purchases, contracts and charitable contributions knew precisely whose money that really was. Etkin was steadfastly defended by people who should have known better.

So, yesterday, Davis Etkin copped a plea to "diverting" money that wasn't his. He had accomplices, though—all those good, solid citizens who took it.

And looked the other way.

—February 29, 2000

The Neighbor's Children

It's a neat, pleasant, brick house on a tree-lined section of Woodlawn Avenue in Albany, just a half-block west of Ontario Street. A metallic-blue Cadillac sat in the driveway yesterday. Parked in front was a gray Mercedes-Benz, a burgundy Lincoln Town Car and a white Volvo station wagon—all plush luxury vehicles.

Well, why not? This house is owned by a powerful member of the New York Assembly, Gloria Davis of The Bronx. And, according to Albany police, it figured heavily in a $20,000-a-week drug ring that operated for a minimum of six months.

Just before Thanksgiving, after a lengthy investigation, Albany police officers and sheriff's deputies arrested seven suspects at this site and at a house on Granito Drive in Colonie. Police also confiscated dozens of bags of heroin, three illegal pistols and a semiautomatic Uzi rifle.

One of the suspects charged in connection with the ring is Gwendolyn Gibbs, Davis's 42-year-old daughter. Another suspect arrested was Davis's niece, Jacqueline Davis, 19. Both are in the Albany County Jail at the moment.

Still another was Gibbs' husband and Davis's son-in-law, Fred Mays—a guy with a series of petty busts and who was permitted yesterday to plead guilty to use of drug paraphenalia. He was fined $150.

At the time of the arrests, Albany police issued a press release. But the release never mentioned that the Woodlawn Avenue house is owned by Davis—or that three of the subjects charged in connection with the ring are Davis's relatives. Moreover, according to police, they have no plans to recommend that the state or U.S. government seize the house, as has been done in several drug cases in Albany County over the past few years.

Davis is a big deal in the Black and Puerto Rican Caucus in the Assembly. Her assistant, Simone Lipscomb, said yesterday that Davis had no interest in discussing the arrest of her relatives at the house she owns on Woodlawn Avenue. Moreover, the police in Albany—one of New York state's most dependable Democratic party strongholds—were steadfast in maintaining that Davis and her relatives were accorded no special treatment in the arrests or in the release of information concerning them.

"We don't routinely put out the names of property owners when we make all these arrests that are taking place," said Lt. Bob Wolfgang, the police department's flack.

"Suppose it had been the governor?" I asked. "You wouldn't have mentioned his name?"

"Nope," Wolfgang said.

"Suppose Bill Clinton had owned property in Albany?" I asked.

"It wasn't part of the investigation," Wolfgang said. "She wasn't charged."

"All right," I said, "if Clinton owned a house in Albany, and Chelsea was operating a drug ring out of it, you guys wouldn't have mentioned it?"

"You probably would have," Wolfgang said accusingly.

Well, yeah, I guess I would have at that. You can decide for yourself if that little piece of information would have been relevant in a story about cops breaking up a $20,000-a-week heroin ring.

But, for whatever reason, the ownership of this house and the relationship of these alleged drug dealers to one of the state's most influential Democratic politicians wasn't worth mentioning, as far as the Albany police department was concerned. Go figure.

It's not all that unusual, when police break up a drug ring, that they recommend that the federal or state government seize property associated with the illegal activity. Federal RICO laws permit that. After all, local law enforcement authorities can realize 80 per cent of the proceeds of the seizure.

But Lt. Michael DeMarco, head of the Albany Police Department's narcotics squad, told me yesterday that he wasn't sure just who owned the house on Woodlawn Avenue. He also said that property is seized in drug cases only when that property has been purchased with drug money.

Which, according to Assistant U.S. Attorney Bill Pericak, isn't precisely correct. The feds can seize property when it has been bought with drug money or when it has been used in the drug trade—which would seem to fit the house on Woodlawn Avenue. And, he said, this is precisely the sort of case in which the feds might move for a forfeiture.

But, Pericak told me, the U.S. attorney's office isn't likely to move for the seizure of Gloria Davis's property on Woodlawn Avenue unless the city police and/or the county district attorney's office request it. And, according to Sgt. Thomas Fitzpatrick, the Albany police department's night narcotics supervisor, no such request will be made.

"The decisive factor," he told me, "would be demonstrating beyond a reasonable doubt an extreme knowledge or a participation in the criminal activity that was occurring there."

Now, nobody is even hinting that Gloria Davis—the mother of six and the grandmother of 11—is involved in the drug trade. And you can ask yourself if she could reasonably have been expected to have known that her grown daughter and company might have been using her house for drug dealing.

But a few things might have tipped her off. One might have been her daughter's drug bust in 1987 in New York City. Another might have been her daughter's arrest in Albany in April of this year on a drug charge.

These two items might have provided the assemblywoman at least a clue that her house on Woodlawn Avenue might be used for illegal purposes.

But, hey, I'm a parent, and I'm not a clairvoyant, either. I'm not about to make judgments about what Gloria Davis might or might not have known or suspected.

And, apparently, neither is the Albany Police Department.

Neighbors around the house on Woodlawn Avenue, however, are less sanguine about the whole matter. One neighbor I spoke to yesterday expressed concern that houses involved in the drug trade can become involved in violence. This is a mean business, and bullets from automatic weapons have flown around other Albany neighborhoods where the drug trade gained a foothold.

"We have a Little League field a block away," one neighbor told me. "And we have thugs with Uzis wandering around? She used to live there. She ought to sell the house or throw out the people who are doing whatever is going on there.

"She owes the neighborhood that much, at least."

—*December 3, 1996*

The Color of Disharmony

The Accused

He was dressed in jeans and a plaid flannel shirt—a dark-haired, dark-eyed man of medium height with the sturdy frame of a middle linebacker. The waitress recognized him and wished him luck. Steve Pagones smiled and thanked her.

"Most fair-minded people realize at this stage that the Brawley case was a hoax," he said to me. "But there's still some lingering doubt. I blame that lingering doubt on loose ends. And I call those loose ends Mason, Maddox and Sharpton."

We were sitting together yesterday afternoon in a diner on Route 9 in Poughkeepsie. At that moment, about 10 miles away in the 93-year-old Dutchess County Courthouse on Market Street, a white-haired judge named S. Barrett Hickman was in his chambers watching lawyers blow smoke. He was hoping, finally, to cut through that smoke. The judge was hoping, at long last, to get this case going.

For nine years, that smoke has hidden the truth of the Tawana Brawley case. It has been that long since Steve Pagones filed a $395-million slander suit against a porky, long-haired race hustler named Al Sharpton and two shrewd New York City lawyers named C. Vernon Mason and Alton H. Maddox, Jr. They're the men who'd accused Pagones of participating in the gang rape of a black teenager named Tawana Brawley.

A good many things have happened since then. Steve Pagones has spent roughly $120,000 in legal fees to clear his name. Maddox has been suspended from the practice of law for his conduct as Tawana Brawley's lawyer. Mason has been disbarred for misconduct in an unrelated matter. Tawana Brawley has moved to the Washington, D.C. area, where she got a job at a hospital and began calling herself Tawana Thompson and Marian Muhammad.

Most astounding, though, is what has happened to the Rev. Al Sharpton. He shed a ton of lard, got a decent haircut, bought a few new suits and has become nearly respectable. A few years back, he ran a credible race in a U.S. Senate primary. In September, he came within a hair's breadth of becoming the Democratic Party's nominee for mayor of New York.

But S. Barrett Hickman was planning yesterday afternoon on opening statements in this case today. Now, at long last, Steve Pagones will have a chance to get at the truth, the whole truth and nothing but the truth in open court.

"The only way you can convince people that the system did what it was supposed to do," Pagones was saying to me, "is by bringing these guys into court."

The Tawana Brawley case began when the teenager was asked why she'd failed to come home one day. Because, she explained, she'd been picked up in a car by some white guys —white cops, she was pretty sure—and they'd raped her. Then a part-time local cop named Harry Crist, depressed over a failed love affair and a stalled career, had killed himself. The Brawley lawyers immediately began charging that he'd done himself in out of guilt for the Tawana Brawley rape.

And Steve Pagones, a recent law school graduate from a politically connected family who'd just begun working as an assistant Dutchess County district attorney, had gone to his boss and explained that Crist had been with him and some other guys the day of the alleged gang rape. They'd all been shopping in Danbury, Conn., Pagones told the D.A.

The D.A. promptly recused himself from the case. Not long after that, the Brawley lawyers and their press spokeman, Sharpton, were accusing Pagones of being in on the rape.

They had evidence, they claimed. They had private lab tests of five different semen specimens. They had a confidential informant who'd told them that Pagones had admitted to the rape. But they refused to cooperate with a grand jury, maintaining that there was no point, that the fix was in for Pagones, whose old man had been a judge.

Bill Cosby stuck his nose into the case, offering support for Tawana Brawley. So did Mike Tyson. For seven months, the Tawana Brawley case rubbed raw every exposed racial nerve in this state. But the grand jury ended up ruling that no rape had taken place, that the whole business had been only smoke from the very start.

Which was when Pagones filed suit. Let's see your lab tests, he said to Sharpton, Mason and Maddox. Let's hear from your confidential informant. For nine years, the three accusers bobbed and weaved, ducked and dodged. Now it was almost time for everybody to take the witness stand in open court, to testify under oath and to undergo cross-examination.

"She made up a lie," Steve Pagones told me, "like every teenager does at one time or another. And that lie got out of hand. Instead of being surrounded by people who would help her do the right thing, she ended up with Mason, Maddox and Sharpton, who capitalized on her lie, who didn't care about the truth. They didn't care about her the exact same way they victimized me, the exact way they victimized the system."

At the time, with the air thick with accusations for seven full months, with Alton Maddox on TV recounting four centuries of American racial oppression, a poll was taken in New York City. Nearly one in three African Americans believed Tawana Brawley's story. After all, it wasn't as if black womanhood had never been violated by white cops. It had happened in the South, and many black families had stories to tell.

If it had happened in Georgia in years gone by, then why not now in Dutchess County, N.Y.? And here was Alton Maddox, who talked of being beaten by racist cops in his hometown of Newnan, Ga., two decades earlier, and he was assuring his brothers and sisters that this girl had indeed been raped and that the racist criminal justice system had covered up for the white cops who'd done it.

So, the demonstrators turned out then—just as they've been out on Poughkeepsie's Market Street off and on for weeks now, just as they were out last night in Al Sharpton's stronghold in Brooklyn to welcome Tawana Brawley back to New York.

And in Poughkeepsie, Steve Pagones, now a 36-year-old litigator for the New York State attorney general, was sitting in a diner and saying, "I got married in June of 1988. Because of the press and the death threats, I had to have armed guards at my wedding. My in-laws, they're very sophisticated people, but they came from Greece. Try to explain to them what this was all about. You know, like who are those guys over there with sunglasses on?

"Now I have a concern which is really the driving force in all this. I have three little girls. I have identical twins that are 3, and I have a 6-year-old girl. They're going to be confronted at some point in time with the fact that these men made some nasty allegations about their daddy. And I need for them to know that Daddy did everything he could do to hold these guys accountable, and he did everything he could do to bring them into court and show that they were lying."

Steve Pagones knows that he could lose this case. He's a public official, and it's tough for public figures to win slander suits. He has to prove not only that what was said about him was untrue, but that Sharpton, Maddox and Mason either knew it was untrue or exhibited a reckless disregard for the truth.

Regardless of the verdict, though, Steve Pagones is counting on sworn courtroom testimony to make his point—that he was cruelly, carelessly smeared simply so a political point could be driven home night after night on television.

And that whatever its other warts, we live in a world where the truth is the very first thing that matters.

—December 3, 1997

A Matter of Honor

This morning, after 11 years of warfare and an intense, seven-month courtroom ordeal, Steve Pagones will go back into the old courthouse on Market Street in Poughkeepsie to learn how precisely much money he'll never be paid.

"I'm hoping for a substantial judgment," he told me last night. "I hope the jury sends a strong message. We can't have this hate. We can't have guys like this running around spreading it."

Pagones sued Al Sharpton, Alton Maddox and Vernon Mason for $395 million. The jury proclaimed him the winner in this case yesterday, and it probably will award him well into six figures. But Pagones probably will never collect a nickel, and he has known from the start that he would never see dime one from these guys. For Pagones this was never about money—although money is the only remedy the law provides for the sins committed against him.

He has spent $330,000 in legal fees to prove that he never kidnapped and raped Tawana Brawley. The Steven Pagones Legal Fund, at Box 350, Beacon, N.Y. 12508, has raised about $150,000 for him to wage this fight. But he goes into that courtroom this morning in debt to the tune of 180 grand.

And for what? For the sake of what too many people consider a quaint and archaic concept. Steve Pagones went to war against these guys because their accusations had stained his personal honor.

This is Old World thinking—the sort you find in the solid, Greek-American community in the Poughkeepsie area that produced Steve Pagones. In communities like that, people exist who believe that values like honor still have sharp meaning even in a fuzzy world.

They believe that right and wrong are tangible commodities when much of the larger society views human activity through subtly tinted shades of relativist gray.

Most people wouldn't have waged this fight. After all, Pagones was exonerated by a grand jury that looked at the evidence and concluded that Sharpton, Maddox and Mason were only blowing smoke.

But these three men had made vile accusations against Steve Pagones. He had little girls. He had to be sure that no lingering doubt concerning their father's honor would ever exist in their minds.

From the beginning, Pagones faced two crucial problems, neither simple. One was that Sharpton, Maddox and Mason had made 22 separate statements, mostly on talk shows. They were lengthy statements, and some had defamed Steve Pagones in their entirety and some hadn't.

So, if you consider a statement that contains defamatory material, but not every word is an accusation, does that constitute slander? During deliberations, the jury asked the judge about that. You decide, he said.

The other problem was that Steve Pagones was a Dutchess County assistant district attorney when Tawana Brawley's lawyers, Mason and Maddox, and her press spokesman, Sharpton, branded him a rapist. As a prosecutor, he was a public figure. And for a public figure to collect in a defamation suit, he has to prove that what was said about him was not only untrue but that the person who said it either knew that or just didn't give a damn whether it was true or not.

That last thing is called a reckless disregard for the truth. It's the kindest interpretation of what Sharpton, Maddox and Mason were guilty of in branding Steve Pagones a kidnapper and a rapist—charges that Mason and Maddox repeat to this very day, without the flimsiest shred of evidence. The most charitable thing you can say is that the truth is utterly incidental to them.

What's probably more accurate is that they figured out, early on, that 15-year-old Tawana Brawley had been out partying for a few days and had cooked up the whole sordid story of kidnap and rape by white cops to dodge the wrath of her stepfather, who'd done time for manslaughter. And that unfortunate reality did nothing to bolster their contention that the criminal justice system discriminates against people of color.

So, the three of them simply ignored the truth. So, the facts don't fit the theory. A minor detail. So, this young white lawyer from a politically connected family is tarred as a rapist. So what?

Nothing personal, but he's white, so the hell with him.

Pagones figures that this defamation trial has been about nothing but the truth. In reality, though, it has been about a species of hatred that requires no truth for sustenance. It has been about a peculiar brand of hatred, born of pain and humiliation and generations of racial injustice, that feeds on its own flesh, with no other fuel necessary to burn brightly.

So, now this business is officially finished. As did the grand jury so many years ago, this civil jury in Poughkeepsie has made clear that Tawana Brawley was never kidnapped and raped by Steve Pagones or anybody else. She made that clear herself when she refused even to enter the courtroom to testify.

It also has been made clear that Steve Pagones was victimized through the sheer bad luck of having his picture appear in the paper and having a desperate, confused teenager point to it. And it has been made clear that race hatred, whether practiced by whites or blacks, remains humanity's largest, ugliest wart.

It also has been made clear that such hatred can poison even those who have devoted their lives to battling it in others. Somewhere along the line, as this case unfolded 11 years ago, Al Sharpton, Alton Maddox and Vernon Mason were transformed into what they were waging war against. They morphed into race haters willing to deny the essential humanity of those they oppose.

The hatred took over completely, burying any other

human impulse. Their only useful purpose now is to serve as bad examples.

They became what we all can become if we let hatred consume us.

—July 14, 1998

Songs and Tears

The warm-up act, those few dozen hardy Albany people who'd begun the chanting and sign-waving in Academy Park, had been milling around in the snow and the chill since early morning—since the first filmy rays of sunlight had filtered through the winter clouds canopied over the Albany County Courthouse.

Then, about 9:45 yesterday morning, the first of the buses from New York City rolled up to the sidewalk on Washington Avenue, on the park's west side. Al Sharpton's pros came through those bus doors and got down to business right away. The chant began the moment they hit the sidewalk:

"No justice, no peace. No justice, no peace. What do we want? Justice! What do we want? Justice."

"Where'd you come in from?" a big man in a black leather jacket and knit cap was asked as he moved through the slush toward the demonstration area that Albany cops had fenced off at the corner of Eagle and Elk.

"Flatbush," he said. "That's East Flatbush, where all the best folks live."

"You're here for Amadou?"

"We're here for Diablo."

"That's Diallo," he was told.

"Well, we're here for justice. Don't matter what name justice got."

As they moved along the freshly shoveled pavement to the demonstration area in the park's northeastern corner, directly opposite the courthouse, the signs were unfurled like battle flags. "Today it's Diallo; tomorrow it's me." And "A Badge Does Not Justify Murder."

Inside the old courthouse, secure behind its steel barricades and its ring of Albany cops, Judge Joe Teresi was presiding over the selection of a jury to decide if four New York City police officers had committed murder not quite a year ago when they pumped 19 bullets into an innocent, unarmed young man named Amadou Diallo. Was it murder, manslaughter or just a horrible, heart-wrenching mistake? That'll be up to the jury.

It won't be a jury to instill much faith in Sharpton's people. An appeals court decided that a fair jury could not be selected from 1.1 million mostly minority citizens of The Bronx. So, now the jury is being chosen here, from a population pool of fewer than 300,000 overwhelmingly white people—whom the courts view as just naturally fairer, apparently. You should know that, in case you're curious why The Rev. Al Sharpton is in town.

By midday, Sharpton was at the microphone in Academy Park, the courthouse looming up behind him as the TV cameras whirred. He was urging several hundred people to stay calm. No violence, he was saying. We're here because 41 bullets fired at an unarmed man is violence enough. He was leading the demonstrators in musical prayer.

"Sing it for Am-a-doo-ou," Sharpton sang in a rich, raspy baritone.

And the chorus rang back, "A-ay-ay-men. A-ay-ay-men. A-ay-men, amen, amen."

"Sing it for ju-us-ti-ice," Sharpton sang.

"A-ay-ay-men. A-ay-ay-men. A-ay-men, amen, amen."

As snowflakes swirled earlier in the day, Alice Green had stood quietly in the park, taking it all in. A longtime Albany activist in matters like these, she warmly greeted a smallish, smiling man in an elegant overcoat. He was Bojana Jordan, born nearly seven decades ago in Transkei in Africa, a former diplomat and college professor. He carried an ornately carved African walking stick. Bojana Jordan motioned to the falling snow.

"The gods of Africa are crying," he told Alice Green. "They are looking down on all this, and these are the tears they shed."

And well might they weep, too. This youthful corpse, this trial moved so far from home, this chanting, wounded, suspicious crowd in Academy Park.

Look at it all closely enough, and who wouldn't cry?

—*February 1, 2000*

Part of the Herd

It's called The Pen.

That's the pen as in the cops announcing, "The jury is coming out. Into the pen, you guys." Or, "OK, all media off the sidewalk and into the pen."

We media people always comply docilely, some of us mooing like cattle or bleating out an occasional, "ba-a-a-ah!" Then we're herded back into the steel corral the police have erected in the middle of Albany's Eagle Street to keep us from annoying real human beings who wouldn't recognize a deadline if it bit them in the butt.

What a glamorous business journalism is at this Diallo trial—freezing like Popsicles in The Pen outside the New York Court of Appeals building while a hardy corps of Albany cops, also freezing, clears the sidewalk so participants in the proceeding can move to and from the Albany County Courthouse without reportorial interference.

All along Elk Street on Academy Park's north side and Washington Avenue on the south, a towering steel forest of satellite antennas has sprouted from trucks emblazoned with the name of this broadcast news organization or that one. Media people from around the world have descended on this town to erect their tripods on the pavement of Eagle Street.

And to shiver and grumble and blow their noses and stomp their ice-numb feet inside The Pen.

When there's action, The Pen can be jammed with three dozen media people in parkas, knit hats, heavy boots and bad humors. In the old days, when I got started in this rotten business, press people trapped in similar circumstances would have passed around flasks of cheer to ward off the chill and to keep blood flowing dependably. Now, two out of three media people are Evian-sipping weenies who would be wearing jogging shoes if it weren't so freaking cold out there on the snow-caked pavement of Eagle Street.

On the trial's first day, as Al Sharpton's seasoned demonstrators from Brooklyn chanted in Academy Park, snowflakes swirled fiercely around The Pen. The street and sidewalk were awash in slush that hid a gorgon's head of thick electrical cables snaking between the demonstration site in the park and the steel enclosure on Eagle Street. The police department's huge horses pranced amid the snowflakes, steam billowing from their flared nostrils in thick, rolling plumes.

As you took it all in, you couldn't escape a mental image of one of those monster horses stomping on an electrical cable with a steel-shod hoof 10 inches across. Then you could watch all the media people inside The Pen dance crazily amid a wild shower of sparks while a thick cloud redolent of scorched flesh wafted skyward.

And the obituary in the local papers probably would lead with the horse.

At a quarter to one yesterday, Sharpton and company entered The Pen during a break in the trial to proclaim the prosecution's case a glorious success and the defense arguments to the jury nothing more than a transparent smokescreen erected to obscure a clear case of extreme police brutality.

When Sharpton left The Pen to lead his daily prayer in Academy Park, Tim McGan was waiting for him. McGan lives in Latham and works for the state comptroller's office in the Al Smith building. McGan shook Sharpton's hand and asked when The Rev is going to apologize to Steve Pagones. Not anytime soon, Sharpton assured him grimly.

Meanwhile, four white New York City cops are on trial on murder charges for gunning down an unarmed black man precisely a year ago today. Ordinary folks like Tim McGan are reminding Sharpton that nobody has forgotten the Tawana Brawley case. And no police horses have yet stomped on any electrical cables.

It's still early in this trial, though.

—*February 4, 2000*

Dousing the Flames

All hair and hubris and hustle, The Rev. Al Sharpton entered Academy Park as a sheet of winter rain poured down on the melting ice and snow. Hands in his overcoat pockets, he slogged through the ankle-deep mud to the makeshift stage.

Then, microphone in hand, he called out to the milling, chanting protesters, 100 strong or so, and urged them to stay cool.

"No violence," Sharpton shouted into the mike. "We're the victims. We cannot become the victimizers."

This was Friday evening, just after the verdict in the Amadou Diallo case had come down. It was just after that drenched, furious crowd had learned that an Albany jury had found four New York City cops not guilty of all criminal charges in a horribly botched stop-and-frisk incident in the Bronx in which an innocent, unarmed man had been cut down by 19 police bullets.

The protesters in the park weren't Sharpton's people. As the jury had deliberated, The Rev had made it a point to keep his busloads of 60ish church people, trained to demonstrate peaceably, at home in Brooklyn. Albany Mayor Jerry Jennings—in his best, assistant principal voice—had essentially told The Rev, "No trouble in my town, Al. You have political ambitions? Well, I control a few votes upstate, so don't screw around with me."

Jennings was so confident that his message had been delivered that he'd been in Aruba Friday night, on his honeymoon, while Sharpton had been slogging through the mud of Academy Park, urging restraint. This crowd was composed largely of local folks, most of them much younger than Sharpton's seasoned professionals. Even Sharpton, apparently, wasn't sure how they might conduct themselves.

As it turned out, about 15 members of the Capital Region Justice for Diallo group did manage to get themselves busted in the drizzle, but nobody got really out of hand. Nobody got hurt. This town has never seen real trouble like that. I have, though.

More than 30 years ago, in New Jersey, on my first day in the newspaper business, I found myself covering a race riot. A white cop named Jimmy Gleason had been killed, literally torn apart, by a minority crowd in Plainfield, N.J. The next day I'd been a passenger in a car that had ventured into the riot area and roared out, in reverse, as bullets flew.

The Color of Disharmony

Friday night, as I watched that outraged crowd in Academy Park, chanting, "Murderers! Murderers!" As the cops left the courthouse, I couldn't help but reflect on the lingering, seemingly immortal intensity of racial hatred in this country—hatred of whites for blacks and of blacks for whites, too, generation after generation of it.

A few days earlier, I'd found myself on the phone with a young woman who was in that park that night. I have a daughter her age. I told her: You have no idea—just no idea at all—how horrible this stuff can become. You're angry because cops everywhere profile and stop and frisk and hassle minority folks. And that's a valid concern.

The New York City Police Department's Street Crime Unit did that to 56,000 minority people last year, most of them totally innocent. To be stopped and searched is degrading and dangerous, as the Amadou Diallo case demonstrates.

But this killing was a mistake, not murder, I told her, and you know not what you do. You do not understand what horror you can create when you ignore the words and focus instead on the music.

I spoke to that young woman harshly, and I made her cry, and I didn't mean to. And I apologized. Tears, however, are what's called for here.

Not rage.

—February 27, 2000

The Four Seasons

The Ice Storm

It started as a mild winter rain. Then, as evening fell on the second drizzly day, a blanket of frigid air slipped in from the west and settled ominously over the ground below the pregnant gray clouds.

And still the rain drenched down. Only now it splattered into ice. The coating thickened, drop by drop, on trees and power lines all across the six northernmost counties of New York and much of the Canadian province of Quebec. In another day or so, with rain still weeping from leaden skies, New York state's North Country began to choke in the tight, murderous grip of ice six inches thick.

Encased in hard glitter, trees started to snap from the weight. Celine Paquette, the Clinton County legislator who represents the quiet village of Champlain, population 1,500, said she could lie in bed and hear the sharp crack of branches torn from tree trunks. Power poles swayed and snapped and crashed to earth. As the night wore on, the North Country began to slip into a Stygian hell of ice and frigid agony.

And still the rain fell, splattering down relentlessly. Glassy coatings on roads grew to thicknesses of 14 inches. Fallen branches froze across the pavement. Tire ruts grew so deep that no vehicle, once caught in the tracks, could hope to break free.

In a matter of days, the fragile electrical framework of civilization was obliterated in much of Canada and upstate New York. In greater Montreal, one of North America's precious gems, a million people were without heat, power or water. And an hour to the south, in tiny Champlain, Joe Perreault was trying to keep his neighbors alive by building a perpetual motion machine.

A truck mechanic who doubles as the village's volunteer fire chief, Joe Perreault is a trim, smallish man with a feel for machinery. As the ice thickened, the only power in this village was in his firehouse, supplied by his fire company's generator truck.

Only the truck's alternator had died. So, Joe Perreault hooked a charger to the truck battery. The battery kept the truck going. The truck kept the generator going. The generator provided power to the firehouse, which provided power to the battery charger, which kept the truck battery charged.

None of which, technically speaking, is supposed to work for long. He'd had it going about a week on the day I slid across the icy parking lot into his firehouse. In all of recorded history, ice had never inflicted such grievous injury on this part of the world, so it wasn't surprising that none of the old rules seemed to apply any more.

When the North Country went dark, taking the heat with it, pipes froze and burst in thousands of houses over hundreds of square miles. By yesterday, nearly two weeks after the rain began falling, about 85,000 North Country customers remained without power. Dairy farmers, unable to milk their cattle with the electric machines they'd come to count on, watched cows die in agony with milk sacks swollen impossibly large.

Those with the means and the will to flee headed for shelters set up in American legion halls, firehouses and other community buildings. Churches fed them; preachers consoled them. When they can go home is anybody's guess.

Others decided to tough it out in their ice-encased houses, struggling to survive with heat from gas stoves and kerosene heaters. Some fell victim in fairly short order to carbon monoxide poisoning as they consumed all the breathable air in the tiny, tight spaces into which they'd retreated from the ice and the blackness.

At first, as the scope of this disaster slowly grew on everybody's consciousness, local authorities and volunteer firefighters bore the entire burden of preserving life and clearing roads for emergency vehicles. When I visited this little village, Joe Perreault had been on the job 10 straight days. But his gallant, exhausted company had been joined by volunteers from Colonie, Rhinebeck, Beacon, Orange County and from elsewhere around the Empire State.

And, not incidentally, by busloads of solemn-faced inmates from North Country prisons in knit hats and neat khaki uniforms. Peddle snow on 125th Street; battle ice in Champlain—rehabilitation all around.

The sun shone down brightly on Champlain Wednesday. The ice was receding. But it will be some time before this village can rejoin the 20th Century. They need generators, plumbers, electricians, food, cots, chainsaws, you name it. They need heavy vehicles to clear roads.

And rescue workers need sleep. Joe Perreault has slept maybe two hours of each day since this nightmare began.

"We need federal help here," he was telling me. "I don't know why they're not flying in big planes full of generators and other gear to the old air force base in Plattsburgh."

I suggested that somebody call Al D'Amato for help. Senator Pothole is up for reelection this year. He always valued his reputation for community service. I gave Joe Perreault a phone number and the names of a few people in D'Amato's office. He asked pleasant, bearded Marty Picard, one of his emergency medical technicians, to handle it.

"I called like you suggested," Marty Picard told me later. "They said it was the press office, and they couldn't help. They gave me some woman in resource management. She said I should write the senator a letter. No fax. It had to be a real letter.

"I told her, 'Ma'am, we don't even have a post office going here. You don't understand.' She said, 'Oh, yeah, I understand. Just send a letter.'"

All of which might help explain why Joe Perreault and

his people, like volunteer rescue workers all across the North Country, are hugely frustrated with what they complain is a slow response to their crisis by politicians and government. In fact, though, state government has thrown everything it has into this emergency.

The problem is the sheer, epic scale of this disaster. The state simply doesn't have enough—not enough people, not enough generators, not enough of anything to make all this go away anytime soon.

For mile after mile north of the Adirondacks, you can gaze at the forests that line the Northway. You see trees half their original height. It's as though God swung a machete over this part of the world. In some places, it looks like He used a power mower.

Eventually, they'll get it back—their electricity, their heat, their houses, their roads, their lives. But with that recovery will come a new appreciation of just how dependent we all are on the luxuries that humans did without for 40,000 years—until just this century, really.

And of how easily a winter sneeze from Nature can obliterate it all.

—*January 16, 1998*

The Man on the Street

"Ah," he said to me, "you look like an Irishman."

He was a bum—a guy about my age who clearly has lived a tougher life than I have. He caught me the other day, as I was coming out of a shop on Central Avenue.

"Oh, yeah?" I said. "Which Irishman do I look like—Pierce Brosnan?"

He blinked for a moment, thrown off balance by the question. But he recovered rather nicely.

"You do look a bit like him," he said. "You're better looking, though. Could you spare some change?"

I laughed. "For you, I can spare a full buck."

I handed the bum a bill. He blessed me and all my progeny. Then I headed across the street to my car. As I climbed behind the wheel, I saw the bum approach some other guy. Like me, the bum's target wore a suit and trenchcoat. As I put the key in the ignition, I watched the bum start his patter with this guy.

Who put out his arm and basically stiff-armed the bum aside.

The bum was surprised. And, in my car across the street, I was surprised, too. OK, you don't want to give the guy money, fine. Just say no.

What was going on was clear enough. The bum was begging in the hope that he could scrape together enough for a bottle. Thunderbird is big on the street—or Richards' Wild Irish Rose. A lot of these guys have worn out their livers. They can't handle spirits any more. The fortified wines run maybe one-fifth alcohol, and they have enough sugar to make up for a missed meal.

Yeah, I know that you should say no. If you want to help, send a check to a homeless shelter, instead. But if a bum has a good patter, and if he's not threatening, I usually cough up a buck or two.

OK, so, I'm a sucker. Given all my character flaws, it's not my worst trait.

After that, I sat in the car and watched the bum for a while. He was staked out in front of the Blue Note Record Shop. It was midday, and foot traffic on Central Avenue was fairly substantial. I sat there long enough to watch the bum approach 14 people—most of them men, most of them well-dressed. Not one gave him a dime.

One guy actually stopped for a moment. He gazed at the bum and sneered. He had the same look on his face he'd have had if he'd been forced to lick a piece of porcelain in a public restroom. Then he went on his way.

Zero for 14—that was the bum's total during the 10 minutes that I watched him. You want an indication of the national mood these days, just watch some bum on the street trying to hustle a few bucks for a jug. We live in a hard-hearted time when nobody displays the slightest shred of sympathy for human frailty.

After a while, the bum shuffled off toward Townsend Park at Central and Henry Johnson Boulevard, a few blocks to the east. That's sort of a gathering place for bums in this town. On decent days, they sit back on the park benches and watch the straights in their cars as they cruise back and forth between the Capitol complex and their homes in the suburbs.

For the straights, El Nino has made this a cold season that North Carolina would envy. For them, Saturday and Sunday were days for T-shirts, shorts, sandals and for wiping a few months' dust off golf clubs.

Not for the bums, though.

For them, this is still a long, cold winter.

—March 31, 1998

That Time of Year

I schlepped out some garbage the other morning. A neighbor strolled by with her dog.

"Well," she said brightly, "Warm weather is pretty much behind us now, isn't it?"

Until she'd said that, I'd been in a fairly decent mood. But my neighbor's greeting forced me to confront a grim, disheartening truth. The upstate New York winter looms malevolently before us with its icy scowl. Damn.

I don't know about you, but I once again let the glorious upstate summer sucker me. Every year, in the deepest pit of winter, I ask myself why I continue to hang on here, where the temperature can dive 130 degrees between July and January. We must be demented, all of us.

Then, one morning in May, a seductive summer breeze always reaches out, takes me in its arms and nibbles salaciously on my ear. It's always a warm, gentle breeze, soft and rich with the tremulous trill of songbirds.

And, like a fool, I forget. I forget that summer in this part of the world is gone in an eyeblink or two while winter lingers with a dogged, diabolical determination for at least 15 months every year.

Oh, sure, it's still relatively balmy, but the days are growing shorter. And, as of two days ago, autumn came upon us—a sad, dying season that forms a short bridge between warm, sunsplashed mornings and bitter, frigid darkness as we leave for work.

Soon, the leaves will paint themselves yellow and red, then fade to an indistinct brown before fluttering to the pallid grass below. Winter will swoop down on us like a mugger with a blackjack, clutching at warm flesh with cruel fingers as we wrestle snow shovels in a still blackness broken only by the wheeze of snow blowers and the ominous rattle of frozen engine valves.

Then, for months, winter will rap on our teeth with hard, uncaring knuckles. The wind will roar and bellow and bite through our clothing like a crocodile. Snow will spill from the sky to turn gray and muddy and form treacherous ice.

Car batteries will gasp to their deaths. Triple-A will be too busy to show up, so we'll be out in the silvery wasteland, struggling with frozen fingers to bend stubborn tools to our will.

The Four Seasons

Then, as winter drags on, the snow will deepen with new belches from the leaden clouds. We'll shovel; we'll plow. We'll drip as we enter the house, ice clinging steadfastly to boots and eyebrows.

The cat will refuse to go out any more, so now there'll be a litter box to clean and a distinct aroma of ammonia in the house that'll linger until the windows are once again opened. Streets will be deserted. Communities will be transformed into ice-crusted ghost towns.

During the brief interlude of daylight, we'll blow on our hands and tighten our mufflers and lift our coat collars. At night, we'll huddle throughout the endless darkness beside hissing radiators. We'll brood and mutter and eat too much at dinner. Later, we'll drink to excess by the fireplace—waiting, praying for all this to end.

Meanwhile, parks will lie deserted beneath a blanket of snow that'll resemble the set of "Dr. Zhivago." Golf clubs will gather dust in closets. Body shops will put on extra help to mend fenders that fall victim to ice and stupidity on the highway.

Yes, I know that we still have a few weeks before the decent weather deserts us. Then, however, the interminable chill will settle over us like a shroud.

And I bet it'll be another bitch of a winter again this year.

—September 24, 1996

A Day in Washington Park

The dog was small and yappy. It seemed to be living proof that dachunds and labrador retrievers, if they're determined about it, really can manage to be more than good friends.

The kid had a stick. He winged it into the lake in Albany's Washington Park. The dog paddled frantically in pursuit, as though the thing was a chunk of knockwurst.

"What kind of dog is that?" I asked the kid, who was about 12.

"A swimming dog."

"Yeah, I can see that much."

"Well, that's what he is."

It was late one afternoon last week. I'd been in downtown Albany, politician-watching. That sun-drenched day marked the first time in seven months that the temperature in this 300-year-old snowbelt town had topped 70.

As I drove back to my office, I pulled into the park, took off my suit coat, locked the car and treated myself to a stroll. What a place this is—one of the capital city's great treasures.

Washington Park is 90 acres of rolling meadows and towering trees. And it's studded with gems like the elaborate statue of Moses and the lake and the lakehouse theater beside it.

The park was created mostly between 1869 and 1882. It was designed by two engineers, John Bogart and John Yapp Cuyler. They'd worked under Frederick Law Olmsted in building parks in New York City.

Oddly, Olmsted's own plan for Washington Park had been rejected by the city. His thinking on the mission of public parkland, though, is evident in the work produced by Bogart and Cuyler.

Olmsted was utterly untrained as a builder of parks. He'd been born into a comfortable Connecticut merchant family. He took a brief stab at Yale, lost interest and ended up farming on Staten Island.

Not yet 30, he journeyed to England and wrote a book on British farming methods. On the strength of that effort, he landed a job with the *New York Times* covering the American south.

The result of those years was a huge book on southern agricultural feudalism, a tome he called "The Cotton Kingdom." The book made Olmsted enough of a celebrity that he was appointed New York City park superintendent. Working with an architect named Calvert Vaux, he came up with the plan for Manhattan's Central Park in 1858.

To Olmsted, a park in an urban setting should be a tangible manifestation of life in a democratic society. He designed Central Park as a series of independent elements, with no single feature distinguishing it. Washington Park is like that, too.

Something for everyone; that was Olmsted's goal—a park that would serve rich and poor alike as a gathering place for fun, frolic and placid reflection.

The park he built in Manhattan, like the park built later 150 miles north in Albany, was a uniquely American creation. It differed dramatically from tightly structured European parks. Olmsted envisioned urban parkland as a great leveler— as a potent mechanism for obliterating, if only temporarily, stubborn social divisions.

It works, too.

There I was, a middle-aged white guy in white shirt and tie. And there was this little black kid with his swimming, yapping dog. And there was a teenager bopping by with a boom box blasting out N.W.A.

There was a young mommy and her kids, flying a kite. And this older guy sat on a bench beside the lake, leafing through his newspaper.

All of us were there together, sharing the beauty of the place, escaping the concrete and the noise and the stench of car exhaust.

Frederick Law Olmsted has been dead for 94 years. But his egalitarian philosophy is not.

On that balmy, blissful afternoon, I saw it alive and well in Albany's Washington Park.

—May 6, 1997

Invasion of the Yuppies

They're not fancy.

They're modest little cottages squatting on a wooded hillside in the Finger Lakes. They're high enough off the water that a mountain goat could get shin splints clambering back and forth to the shoreline.

At water's edge, I've built some crude, shaky docks. Every few winters, ice crunches the docks into kindling. If Al Gore is right about global warming I won't have to put up with that forever.

I run there every chance I get, dodging semis on the Thruway for four hours each way. My reward—a few days in the peaceful place I knew as a child. Sometimes, when I have work to do, my only companion is a golden retriever. I sit on the dock and read while he paddles after ducks. I sit on the porch and write, as I'm doing now, while he wanders the woods behind the cottage, terrorizing squirrels.

Keuka is a slim, elegant, glittering ballerina of a lake— 23 miles long, 180 feet deep and maybe a mile wide at the hips. A glacier retreating north created it 140 centuries ago. Today, the lake nestles between rolling hills studded with oaks and maples and carpeted with lush vineyard. The Finger Lakes region is wine country. Images of grapes are everywhere—on municipal signs, on tourist T-shirts, in restaurant windows.

My family has been on Keaka Lake for six decades. In an attack of spendthriftery, my grandfather shelled out 600 bucks for a sagging, battered shack that was the scene of my childhood's most glorious moments—huge, surging clan gatherings marked by raucous laughter and odd adventures.

Then my father died, and the place was sold out of the family by my uncles—over my vehement objections and my older brother's. We handled this family dispute in traditional American fashion. We sued their butts.

Ultimately, the suit was settled and familial harmony restored—a decade or so later. Now the uncles are dying off at a snappy rate, and my brother and I have these little cottages, side by side, a few miles down the road from the scene of our fondest early memories.

Summer camps are a uniquely northern tradition. Southerners, for whom winter is less arduous, tend not to have them. Here, though, for many people, a summer camp represents a crucial psychological weapon against the ice and snow and the rigid routines of winter working life.

Until recent years, an unpretentious summer shack on some lake was within the reach of most working people in upstate New York. Now, high real estate prices and towering property taxes are driving ordinary folks off my lake, at least. They're being bought out by brain surgeons in Lexus 400s who stomp down the old, shabby cottages and replace them with lavish mansions of glass and cedar—monuments to the glories of third-party payment.

For some time now, Keuka Lake has been Beemered and jet-skied into full-blown yuppihood, and nobody can do much about it.

Labor Day weekend is summer's last gasp. This year we had the usual mob of friends and family members joining us for a few days of farewell to the season. Now, school has started again for my wife, the teacher, and I have an election to cover.

There'll be a few more weekend trips to Keuka—to throw sheets over the furniture and blow water out of the pipes as golden leaves float down on the porch. Then winter will dig its frigid fingers into our hillside once again. For long, dismal months, the cottages will sleep beneath a blanket of snow.

While, at least once a day, I'll maintain my sanity by thinking about next summer there.

—September 8, 1998

Snow Country

It's depressing to confront the reality that a disturbingly high percentage of my fellow upstate New Yorkers seem somehow to believe that we live in the tropics.

And, when reminded that we do not, proceed to plunge into unseemly panic.

Yesterday was a perfect case in point. For two days, weather forecasters on television and radio have been issuing the usual dire, dramatic, doom-laden warnings about a Nor'Easter roaring up the coast and dumping a load of snow on us. As of last evening, the high-end estimate was four inches.

Four inches of snow is not exactly a rarity in upstate New York in February. We do not reside in Key West. I've lived most of an ill-spent life in this part of the world, and I do not regard four inches of snow in February with the same level of gravity with which I might regard, say, a nuclear missile sailing into my back yard.

That is to say, it snows here all the time in February. What's the big deal?

Yesterday afternoon, however, I journeyed to a supermarket to see how consumers might be responding to the news of an impending snowfall. I watched one woman at the dairy case load five—count 'em, five—gallons of milk into her cart.

"You must run a day care center," I said.

"There's supposed to be snow coming tonight," she told me.

I saw another couple load up on 48 rolls of toilet paper. Yes, I counted. And I saw this other guy with eight six-packs of beer.

"Gee, must be snow coming," I said as we got into line together.

"Yep," he said. "Stocking up on the necessities."

The same mindset was in evidence as I stopped for gas on the way home. Cars were three deep at every pump. Can you imagine what this must be like in Syracuse, where blizzard warnings come on Halloween?

I'm not sure who's to blame for all this, but television weather people will do for starters. Somehow, some way, local television news operations got the idea decades ago that a weather forecast is worth 25 per cent of a newscast.

Hey, forget famine; forget war. There's a cold front creeping in on Utica.

On every station, the person who tells you whether it'll rain tomorrow is a huge local celebrity on the order of Madonna. He or she also goes through this spectacular arm-waving, Macarena routine in front of a gaily lit weather map with arrows flashing and cartoon clouds zipping in from this direction or that.

Every night the person giving us the weather on TV manages somehow to come across like Gen. Norman Schwartzkopf briefing us on the bombing of Bagdhad—only the weather guy has more advanced radar.

John Madden at the Super Bowl doesn't swamp us with so many arrows and sweeping lines. And what he tells us is important. Some very nice people have serious money riding on that.

So, if you're looking for some explanation for the panic you see at every gas station and supermarket just before any snowstorm, I think you can probably blame the television weather people. Too bad. Except on the rarest of occasions—say, an impending shower of meteors the size of Lincoln Navigators—the likelihood is that the weather forecast really isn't all that important. Nothing you'll learn there is likely to affect your life in any crucial way.

If the forecasters are right, though, snow will be falling when you pick up this newspaper. Well, what do you expect? We don't live in Algeria.

So, chill out and leave a little milk for somebody else, OK?

—February 24, 1998

The Canadian Factor

Skiing is only for people who love the feel of broken bones, and you can spend only so much time sitting in front of the fireplace reading before cabin fever sets in, but there is one nice thing about the arrival of winter in upstate New York. It means no more Canadians roaring along the Adirondack Northway or the New York Thruway threatening the life, limb and emotional security of everybody else on the highway.

It means a winter's respite from Canadians in general, and that's almost worth the 80-odd inches of snow we can expect between December and the time we all have to venture back out on the highway and resume dodging whizzing minivans with Quebec plates.

I have to be honest; I don't know many Canadians. The ones I do know seem pretty nice. But they are, of course, here and not there, so they presumably have been subjected to some sort of civilizing influence. In fact, I've never been to Canada except for a weekend once in Montreal and going over to their side to look at Niagara Falls. All I really know about Canada is what I learned as a kid from watching Sergeant Preston of the Yukon on black and white TV and from observing the MacKenzie brothers slurping beer and burping with merry abandon on cable.

But, like all upstate New Yorkers, I've also seen plenty of Canadians whipping along upstate highways without regard to their own well-being or for that of the residents of the United States, which is foolish enough to permit them across the border without first administering saliva tests. It's nerve-wracking enough to spot some pickup with green Vermont plates coming up behind you on the highway—Vermonters are not renowned as particularly skilled drivers, either—but it's downright chilling when it's a Canadian in a Winnebago lurching along like Jabba the Hut on wheels. Is it, I'm forced to wonder, a requirement of citizenship in Canada to own a Winnebago with your name and the names of all your kids plastered across the rear end?

Since my personal experience with Canada is pretty much limited to contact with its driving tourists, I'm unavoidably left with the impression that the whole place is sort of a frozen Texas filled with people who consider Midwesterners exotic and who gaze longingly southward at relatively balmy spots like Fargo, N.D., where everybody enjoys so much wild nightlife. It's my guess that Canadians spend most of their time watching grizzly bears catch salmon, oiling up their snow blowers and watching televised demolition derby on TV. They watch that stuff all winter. Then, during Canada's two weeks of summer, Canadians finally forget about hockey players with

French names and head south to stare goggle-eyed at a place with no tundra while they roar along our roadways at speeds that blow down billboards.

Maybe they do that sort of thing as a joke. Maybe Canadians think this sort of thing is funny. After all, they laugh uproariously at jokes about people from Newfoundland, and nobody down here even knows where that is. You've got to wonder, after all, about the overall level of Canadian humor. Think of the comedian Howie Mandel. He's from Canada. This, apparently, is what passes up there for scintillating wit.

Now, it's true that the Canadians have been helpful to us on occasion. They did sneak some of our diplomats out of Iran in 1980, and they do brew Molson's. But they also gave India the technology to build a nuclear bomb, and from what I've seen and read they truly are a boring nation. Next to Canada, I'm sure, Kansas must seem positively compelling—although I've made it a point never to go there, either.

Now, I don't want anybody to get the idea that I'm being hard on Canadians—even though they seem bent on destroying as many of us as they can manage on our highways every summer. No, this is merely a little constructive criticism, and I would hope it would be accepted in that spirit by anybody who's truly fond of Canadians despite their demonstrated lack of concern for human life once they get into their cars.

It's just that every summer—when I know they'll soon be emerging from hibernation, shedding their mukluks and wool plaid coats, piling into their cars and sweeping southward like Exocet missiles—I start thinking of going to confession, just in case. Canadians on upstate highways are a bigger hazard to your health than a nuclear power plant next door.

It's difficult to figure out how an entire nation can survive with so many outrageously reckless drivers moving like blurs over its roads. And it's hard to imagine what factors could be responsible for making Canadians such horrible drivers.

The only explanation I can come up with is this:

Canadians are horrible behind the wheel because they're more accustomed to dog sleds.

—*October 19, 1986*

The Festival

Late morning, August 17, 1969. A few months out of college, cruising north on Route 17 in a pale blue Mustang. It's my first new car, bought just a month earlier. For precisely 24 hours, I've been married to the woman in the passenger seat. This will be our first full day of facing an uncertain world, hand in hand.

Summer sun splashes down on the highway. Aretha Franklin shrills out at us on WABC's 50,000 watts, insisting on a little "R-E-S-P-E-C-T; found out what it means to me."

Our destination is a modest honeymoon cottage in the Finger Lakes, well northwest of the concert site, but we're toying with the idea of stopping somewhere along Route 17 and checking this thing out. We have no tickets. WABC assures us, though, that most of the people on site haven't bothered with them, either.

Hundreds of concert-goers have spilled out of the concert site and onto the highway in the Town of Bethel. Pup tents squat along the roadside. Cooking fires flicker in the grassy median strip. One girl in a flowered headband sits in front of one of them, stirring a pot of something or other. It's a hot day, and she's naked to the waist. Nobody seems to notice except goggle-eyed, real-world motorists whizzing by on either side of her.

Somewhere, well off the highway, there's a stage and a mountain of sound equipment. Somewhere a supremely stoned Joe Cocker is croaking into a mike and Hendrix is wringing the national anthem out of a supercharged Fender. But Woodstock—the Woodstock that capitalists will try vainly in just a few days to recreate a quarter century later on another site—is right out there on Route 17 this morning, personified by a semi-nude free spirit stirring her cooking pot as the straights roll by in their station wagons.

If you're young today you live in a world of jocks, preps, metalheads, cyberfreaks, vegans, burnouts, skateboarders, druggies and any number of minutely sliced subgroups. The Woodstock generation was less intensely defined. We generally fell into one of three classifications—greasers, hippies and everybody else. Woodstock was a hippie happening, with all that was implied by that now defunct sociological classification.

We never did stop that day. If you pulled your car far enough off Route 17 to ensure that it wouldn't be smacked into, you stood a terrific chance of being blocked in by somebody else's car. That would mean spending the first few days of your honeymoon in a muddy farmer's field listening to Richie Havens and Wavy Gravy and trying to locate a porta-john. At the time, it didn't seem worth it. In retrospect, it still doesn't.

If you wanted to know what Woodstock was all about, all you had to do was cruise up Route 17 that warm summer morning and keep your eyes open. You saw thousands of teens and twenty-somethings gathered to revel in music their parents hated and to celebrate a value system that their parents hated even more than they hated the music.

Sex, drugs and rock and roll. Peace and love. Brown acid, Melanie, Maui Wowie and the Grateful Dead. It was a three-day camp-out designed in large measure to infuriate Ozzie and Harriet, Ward and June, Jim and Margaret Anderson and anybody else who might have voted for Richard Nixon. The anarchists had organized for a weekend of frolic. Well, more or less organized. It was chaos, but placid chaos. Two people died at the festival; two were born. Everything came out even in the end.

If you weren't around then—or have cheerfully forgotten—those were brutal years. National political figures were being assassinated every 15 minutes or so. Race riots in big cities had become regular summer events. The country was torn apart over a misguided war half a world away. I knew one guy who volunteered and came back missing an ear and part of his shoulder. I knew another who slept with his girlfriend's cat the night before his draft physical just to aggravate his asthma.

It was the best of times only because we were young; it was the worst of times because the times were truly rotten.

It was in that context that the original Woodstock Festival ended up as a shimmering ray of sunlight in a generally dark era. That's why the rock festival in Max Yasgur's field has managed to achieve almost mythic status over the years. In one of the angriest and most profoundly bitter moments in our national history, 450,000 youthful rebels surging with hormones and God knows what else in their bloodstreams gathered in a sea of mud to thumb their noses at their elders. And, in an era when mayhem was commonplace, it all unfolded without a hint of rancor.

The Woodstock II event will bear almost zero resemblance to the original. It'll be held in a different world in which all the people who went to the first festival are different, too. Overwhelmingly, they've gone straight—trading in their bongs for briefcases and their VW microbuses for mini-vans. The first Woodstock Festival turned out to be a warm and fuzzy showcase for cultural upheaval. This second one is bound to be nothing more than a a trip down memory lane for graying post-yuppies with designer labels on their clothes and cellular phones in their pockets and purses.

I can't help but wonder if that girl I saw at the cooking pot that day will be one of them.

—August 7, 1994

The Twister

There were two of them, a man and a woman. They were huddled last night beneath a single umbrella on a rain-soaked hillside where, just a few hours earlier, God had let loose with a ferocious snort.

"I heard it before I saw it," Joe Thomas was telling me. "It sounded like a train coming through. Then it came right down this street. There are trees here, they're a hundred years old, and it just picked them up, pulled them right out of the ground."

As he spoke, a jagged ribbon of lightning flashed across the leaden sky. It bathed the wreckage that was Mulberry Street in a brief, eerie glow. Joe Thomas wrapped his arm more tightly around his wife, Maryann. She was worried about rain pouring through a ragged, gaping wound in the house in which they had lived for 32 years, before a tornado had touched down in a part of the world where tornadoes aren't supposed to exist.

Twisters are supposed to be creatures of the prairie. They're supposed to come to life in flat, rectangular states where tiny farming towns field five-man high school football teams.

But this one touched down last evening on a hilltop in Mechanicville, an old mill town on the west bank of the Hudson just north of the state capital of Albany. It leveled the hill's crest, spraying the remains of the houses it consumed for thousands of yards in every direction, snapping power poles, picking up cars as if they were made of Styrofoam. Then it tore down the hill and toppled one of the two towering brick smokestacks of an old paper mill before it whirled across the river to die as it hit the woods on the Hudson's eastern shore.

The Four Seasons

Miraculously, in its life of only a minute or so, the twister killed no one and injured only a few. It left that hillside mangled and bleeding, but it took no lives—only the possessions that people accumulate as they live.

The red Mustang, for example. I found it up the hill on Stillwater Street last night. Imagine a car with its roof flattened as if by a huge, almighty fist. It sat there in the street, electrical wires wrapped around it like pythons, its headlights still gleaming in the darkness.

"There had to be two of them," Joe Thomas was saying. "You look here at Nassau Street, and you can see what it did. Well, it did the same thing one street over. And the street in between wasn't hit at all. But up the hill, way up, My God. The houses are just gone."

Joe and Maryann Thomas weren't supposed to be on the hill last night. Rescue workers had come through to evacuate everybody after the tornado had touched down. But this was home, and they were hanging around, hoping to get back inside.

I'd been blocked as I'd driven into Mechanicville from the south. A rescue worker directing traffic told me I would have to walk to the scene, a distance of several miles, in a downpour. When I got there, I found TV vehicles all over the place and a checkpoint of cops keeping people off the hill.

So, I walked down the road, found the path of the twister and followed it in the darkness. It led behind a shopping center and across a set of railroad tracks surrounded by chain link fencing—until the twister came through.

I crossed the tracks and found two fire hoses hanging down a muddy bank at the foot of the hillside. I grabbed one hose and climbed hand over hand up the bank until I reached a flat site. Gazing around in the darkness, I realized I was standing where a 30-foot travel trailer had been picked up by the twister and thrown aside as though it were no more than a tin can.

The power of a thing like this boggles the mind. And, oddly enough, I'd actually seen another one, a miniature version, only a few days before. On Friday afternoon, traveling west on the New York Thruway, I'd found myself in a driving rain and buffeted by strong winds. Then, next to the highway just as I passed the spot, a flying collection of dust and dirt swirled into a distinct funnel.

The wind hit my two-ton vehicle with a ferocious thump. For a brief moment, I felt the two right wheels leave the pavement. Then I stomped on the gas and watched in my rearview mirror as the mini-twister evaporated. And now, two days later, a vaster, larger, meaner version of the same thing had ripped through a community only miles from where I live.

So, what is this—the Northeast's balmy winter, a vicious January ice storm in New York's North Country up near the Canadian border, a towering tornado in a rolling Northeastern community where none has ever formed before?

Is this the product of Global Warming? El Nino? Who knows?

Although, I did read where some guy in California named Al Nino got 100 phone calls when the weather got weird out there last fall. People were demanding to know why he was doing this horrible thing to them.

That explanation makes as much sense as anything else.

—June 1, 1998

Animal Companions

An Old Friend

It had to have happened this month. He had to have been born in May.

He was six or seven weeks old that sunny morning in early July. I'd just left *Newsday* on Long Island and begun duties as managing editor of the Albany *Times Union*. My wife and I and our two little children were moving into a new house.

That's when he wandered out from the bushes into our new driveway, skinny and scared. He meowed piteously. Can we keep him, the kids asked?

The family menagerie at that point consisted of a large and good-natured Siberian husky, a burly yellow rabbit, a fuzzy guinea pig, and two—count 'em, two—cats. And my kids wanted this one, too. Wonderful.

"Uh, I don't think so," I said.

"Please?" the kids begged. "Please, please, please, please?"

OK, so now we had three cats. Since the new kitten was black and white, like a pinto horse, the kids named him Tiger. It made sense to them.

My toddler, Kevin, was nuts about this new cat. This one was his personal property. He took Tiger to bed with him that first night. And for every night for years after that.

In the family album, I have a marvelous photo of Kevin, in his Spiderman underpants, heading upstairs to bed with the little black and white cat slung over his shoulder like a towel.

From the start, Tiger was high maintenance. Once, he climbed up under the hood of a car during cold weather. He was peacefully sacked out there when somebody got into the car and started it. The fan clipped him. He dragged himself home with a broken hip that cost me a fortune.

Another time he bounded up on my chest in the middle of the night. He stuck his face an inch from mine and let out with a ferocious yowl. When my heartbeat settled down, I managed to figure out what he was telling me. He had a urinary tract blockage. It took surgery to fix that, too.

Then there was the time a rear claw fell off. The wound wouldn't heal. Another trip to the vet. Toe cancer. Luckily, they got it all during that surgery.

Tiger came through every impoverishing health crisis just fine. As time went by, the other beasts slipped away to their eternal rewards. And the kids grew, of course. My little girl is now a woman of 26 with a career in television news.

And that little boy who loved his black and white cat so desperately? Next month, he graduates from college.

Meanwhile, Tiger is still here, essentially unchanged in two decades. The vet says his kidney function seems to be slowing, but he's still feisty enough to bat around that upstart golden retriever whenever the whim strikes him.

Three years ago, I moved Tiger indoors. He was losing a step or two. I didn't trust his judgment in dodging cars. Like many pro athletes and some politicians, cats don't always know when it's time to retire.

Now he sits on my lap at night as I watch television. Routinely, he sneaks into bed when I'm deepest into sleep to run a sandpaper tongue over my face at 3 a.m.

Sometimes, he's a bit confused. He'll start howling frantically. Apparently, he's asking, "Where the hell am I? What's going on?"

When Tiger was born, the President was a guy named Jimmy Carter. That President is long gone, just like the little kids who fussed over that terrified kitten in that driveway so long ago. So, when Tiger howls like that, I pick him up. I stroke him and assure him that everything is fine.

After 20 years together, he always takes my word for it.

—May 12, 1999

The Gray Ghosts

They built the comfortable, brick-faced house 50 years ago. That was when Waite Road was a rutted ribbon of mud in the spring, back when Clifton Park was farmland and forest instead of sprawling, upscale suburbia.

Now Harold and Betty Keefner have neighbors—nice, modern houses nearby. Even newer neighbors live in the woods behind them.

Harold Keefner is a tall, trim, white-haired man of 80, a retired carpenter. The other day, we stood in a frigid breeze outside his house. He was saying, "The coyotes came, oh, probably seven, eight years ago. You could hear them howling. Five, six years ago, there were four of them right by my back door."

Which would be fine, generally. Coyotes don't attack humans. Cats and small dogs, however, enjoy no such immunity.

"We used to have three little poodles," Harold Keefner was telling me. "We've got two now. Well, more like one and a half."

Bummer went first. He was gray and good-natured, Harold Keefner's special pal. One day last August, Betty Keefner let him out the back door.

"The little dog went down to the edge of the woods

there," Harold Keefner was saying. "He was barking. Then all of a sudden he stopped barking, and we went looking for him. We looked all over, couldn't find him. They got him.

"They got a few of the dogs along this road. Mrs. Kopacki across the road from us, she was out hanging up clothes. She had her little dog out there. He went over by the bushes, and she went to call him and he was gone. She saw the coyotes in the bushes."

Then, just a few weeks back, Betty Keefner let the two surviving poodles out. Buttons, the black one, hung near the house. Tonia, the chubby white one, ranged farther afield. Harold Keefner gazed through the kitchen window, keeping an eye on things.

Then there was a lithe shadow, the color of fog, moving in on Tonia.

"I started banging on the window and yelling, 'Coyotes!' My wife went running out right away. The little guy got right in. But the coyote had already got the white one. So, Betty ran about 200 feet. From her hollering and everything, the coyote dropped Tonia. Jeez, her neck was all torn up. She was all torn up to hell."

Nobody knows how many eastern coyotes live in this state—tens of thousands, anyway. They're serious carnivores. Males can approach 60 pounds.

Some apparently came down from Canada decades ago, as forest gave way to farmland up there. Others may always have been here, scraping by shyly as bigger, bolder predators like wolves were exterminated.

For years, however, more efficient farming has returned New York fields to forest. Songbirds thrive. Turkeys are back in abundance. And whole families of gray, amber-eyed phantoms have settled into stands of woods in the suburbs, running rabbits on golf courses and stalking squirrels in back yards. To coyotes, a small, yapping dog is a territorial intruder, like a fox.

Which means it's also lunch.

All across this country, as conservation efforts bear fruit, humans and wildlife are getting to know one another all over again. And, as family members end up on predators' menus, ancient animosities are being rekindled.

With a state license, you can hunt coyotes legally in winter. But if another gray ghost slinks into Harold Keefner's yard even during warm weather, he'll have his shotgun handy.

Harold Keefner has diabetes. Sometimes it gives him double vision. If another coyote shows up at his door, he'll just blast away at both of them. He'll protect his poodles.

"And I'll bear the consequences," he said.

—December 16, 1997

Going It Alone

In case you haven't noticed, we live in a world where we're increasingly on our own in solving all but the most monumental of problems. Take what happened to Debbie Zotto, for example:

One day last week, Debbie Zotto went into the garage behind her house in a nice, tree-shaded neighborhood of 75-year-old homes in Troy, right near Rensselaer Polytechnic Institute. She was greeted by bright eyes, a ball of black and white fur and a distinct odor.

"It was a little skunk," Debbie Zotto told me, "and it wasn't at all afraid of me. And skunks are pretty much nocturnal. They're not out during the day. And they're certainly not friendly. But, this guy, he wasn't afraid of me. . . .

"Now, skunks walk with a waddle. But he was falling over and listing and, you know, not right. . . . So, now the skunk is in the back yard, and he won't leave. So, I called the county health department. I said, 'Do skunks get rabies?' And they said, 'Yeah. Stay away from him.'"

That much Debbie Zotto had figured out for herself. But she has two little kids. The neighborhood is jammed with other people's kids, too. She wanted desperately for somebody to come and take this animal away. When she called Troy's animal control officer, though, all she got was a recording.

I later asked Mark Pattison, Troy's mayor, why somebody with a potentially rabid wild animal in her back yard couldn't get a live human being when she called for help. Well, Pattison said, he has only one guy on the city payroll doing this kind of work. Besides, there's always 911. You can always call the police.

"Meanwhile," Debbie Zotto told me, "the skunk was now in a neighbor's yard, where my neighbor is getting ready for his 6-year-old's birthday party, which he can't have because the back yard has been taken over by Pepe LePew. . . . I called the police. They told me to call animal control. . . .

"The policeman was so nasty to me. He said, 'Hey, lady, what do you want me to do?' I said, 'I want you to come shoot it.' He said, 'We're not going to do that.' I said, 'Can I have your gun? I'll shoot it. . . .'

"Finally, they did send a patrol car. . . . The guy wouldn't even get out of the car. I said, 'Why don't you just shoot it and we'll be done with it?' Well, he didn't want to shoot it because he didn't want to get sprayed. So, I said, 'Sir, what do you want us to do?'

"And one of the neighbors said, 'If you hypothetically had a gun, you could shoot it, right?' And the officer said, 'Well, you can't shoot a gun in the City of Troy.' But he would look the other way if we wanted to shoot it."

Troy's public safety commissioner, Mark Whitman, told me that Debbie Zotto probably spoke with a civilian dispatcher, not a cop, and that his department has no procedures on handling calls like this, even though rabies has been a pretty grim problem in this state for a few years now. Every cop is on his or her own in working out what to do in a case like this.

Finally, Debbie Zotto and her neighbors decided they had no choice but to act on their own.

"I didn't see it get shot," she told me, "so I can't say who did it. . . . I guess that maybe somebody had a bullet and maybe somebody else had a .22, and that was that."

After that, she put on gloves, shoved the little skunk's corpse into a big coffee can and put it into her freezer overnight. The next day, she took it to the state health department lab.

No rabies. Distemper.

"Who knew?" said Debbie Zotto.

And, more to the point, who cared?

—August 28, 1998

A Love Story

He'd been born Carroll E. Van Ginkel, an Iowa farm boy, but when he entered the Marines he figured he would knock out a few letters. So, his first name became Carol.

For decades thereafter, people would see the name, and they would assume this was a woman. But he was really a large, powerful man—six-foot-four and 200 pounds—who made his living in law enforcement as a member of the U.S. Marshals Service, the U.S. Border Patrol and the U.S. Customs Service.

When he retired, he settled in Hanover, Pa. That's where he was living when his wife, Dorothy, died seven years ago. Shortly thereafter, he came to live with his daughter, Carolyn Horton, in Delanson. She's a nurse.

That's when Carol Van Ginkel fell in love again. Twice, he fell in love, in fact.

The objects of that affection were two small, mixed-breed dogs named Pookie and Mollie. From the moment Carol Van Ginkel moved in with his daughter and her husband, Jerry, their two little dogs latched on to him.

They would fuss over him, follow him around. He was an old man in failing health, deprived of the companionship of the woman with whom he'd shared life for 55 years. But Carol Van Ginkel still had love to give. Somehow, these two small creatures sensed that and responded in kind.

Dogs are like that. Anybody who has shared quarters with one for any length of time knows what stunningly empathic qualities they can exhibit. There are those who find dogs annoying, and those who believe that keeping a pet of any kind is somehow akin to slave ownership. But there also are those who understand that the bond between a person and a non-human companion can be every bit as compelling and emotionally fulfilling as any link with another human being.

Carol Van Ginkel was 75 when he moved to Delanson. His heart was failing, and they soon found cancer in his lung. They removed the lung, but it took two operations. The ordeal left him drained and weak.

Carolyn Horton told me, "He always said the reason he recovered was those two little dogs. They sat in his lap every day, comforting him and making him feel good."

But as he was recovering, one of the dogs, Pookie, jumped up on the bed one night and died.

"My father was a typical old Dutchman," Carolyn said. "He was very undemonstrative and stoic. But when Pookie died, he sat at the kitchen table and cried and cried. He didn't cry any near as much at my mother's death, even though they'd loved each other very much. He wouldn't allow himself to do that then.

"He really started to deteriorate about six weeks ago. He told me he was having trouble breathing. He was standing by the bookcase, and he passed out."

Carol Van Ginkel was in and out of the hospital for the next few weeks, fighting for breath and growing progressively weaker. Finally, earlier this month, he entered St. Peter's for what he knew would be the last time.

"He told me that we have to talk," Carolyn said. "He knew he was dying, and we went over his will. And he cried just one more time—because he knew that he'd never see Mollie again. And we cried, too."

Carol Van Ginkel died on Monday, Nov. 16. He was 82. His last years had been arduous because his wife was gone and his body was betraying him. But tomorrow, on Thanksgiving, his daughter will reflect on those years and on her own gratitude for Pookie and Mollie, the little dogs who'd loved her father so deeply.

And made his last years worth living.

—November 25, 1998

Family Matters, and the Stuff That Truly Counts

Fathers and Sons

When Wayne Jackson, the sergeant-at-arms of the New York Assembly, asked him to stand yesterday, Herman Johnson wasn't sure what to expect.

He stood anyway, an elegantly dressed man of 82 with short gray hair and a gray goatee, back in the roped-off visitors' section in the rear of the chamber. The eyes of the New York's lawmakers turned toward him. Then, out on the floor, Jack McEneny began to speak.

We have in our chamber today, said Assemblyman John J. McEneny, Democrat of Albany, a uniquely distinguished man. Herman Johnson of Kansas City, Mo., is a graduate of Cornell University and the University of Chicago. He's an immensely successful businessman in his own community. He served as a major with the Tuskeegee Airmen during World War II. He served two terms in the Missouri Legislature. He has made this world a better place for his presence in it.

And, McEneny added, Herman Johnson is the son of Henry Johnson, Albany's great hero of World War I—a hero whose valor has yet to be properly recognized by his country, but we hope to change that very soon.

As Herman Johnson stood in that chamber next to his wife, Dorothy, only a few blocks from where his father labored as a railroad worker and drank himself to death in despair, the members of the New York Assembly formally greeted him.

The lawmakers are black and white, male and female, Democrat and Republican—people who disagree with one another on every significant aspect of the human condition.

Family Matters, and the Stuff That Truly Counts

271

Upon meeting Herman Johnson, however, they broke into applause—unanimously.

Somewhere in the mysterious vastness of the cosmos, the ghost of Henry Johnson had to be gazing down on yesterday's scene in the Assembly chamber with at least some small measure of satisfaction. Henry Johnson never got the applause he had coming. But his son did.

Herman Johnson is in town during Black History Month to work with the 369th Veterans Organization. They're trying to bring to his father in death the recognition denied him in life. On May 15, 1918, near Verdun, France, Henry Johnson performed an act of conspicuous gallantry in hand-to-hand combat that saved a comrade's life.

The French, with whom he was serving, awarded him the Croix de Guerre. But, like all 500,000 African Americans who served in that bloodbath 70-some years ago, Henry Johnson was denied his own country's highest award, the Medal of Honor.

He was, in fact, awarded nothing. He came home, horribly banged up. He took to drink. He died young, laid to rest in a pauper's grave that has never been found.

Herman went on to lead a thoroughly admirable life. Now, in that life's twilight, he works with Albany politicians and veterans groups who fight to win for Henry Johnson in death the proper level of recognition denied him in life.

Yesterday, Herman Johnson met with lawmakers. Today, he will lay a wreath at the statue in Washington Park honoring his father. Tonight, he will meet with the governor at the state museum at a reception to kick off Black History Month. Tomorrow, he will receive the key to the city from Mayor Jerry Jennings at the "When You Need a Hero" breakfast at the Omni Hotel.

"I can't help but think," Herman Johnson said yesterday as he stood in the Senate chamber with State Sen. Neil Breslin, "what my father might have been if he'd been given that medal. It all might have turned out differently for him."

But Henry Johnson lived in a world where justice was

hard to come by for black folks. He never lived to see it. His son prays that he'll see it for him.

—*February 9, 1999*

(*Author's note: Several years later, Henry Johnson's grave was discovered—not in a pauper's cemetery in Albany but in a racially segregated section of Arlington National Cemetery, just outside Washington. The Pentagon re-opened his case and posthumously awarded Sgt. Johnson a distinguished decoration for his bravery in World War I. As of the publication of this book, Albany veterans groups were continuing the battle for the award of the Medal of Honor to Henry Johnson.)*

Sins of the Father

Here's cheery news for anybody interested in clean campaigning in this year's political season:

Eliot Spitzer says that he wasn't responsible for spreading the word that Catherine Abate's father had been a capo in the Lucchese crime family. And Spitzer will never do it again, either.

In case you missed this, State Sen. Catherine Abate, a 50-year-old New York City lawyer, announced her candidacy the other day for the Democratic nomination for attorney general. Only a heartbeat later, old newspaper clippings were circulating detailing allegations that her late father, Joseph Abate, had been a vice president in the New Jersey mafia.

Which, apparently, is true. Or, at least, New Jersey authorities believe it's true. Joseph Abate died last year after a decade or so of dementia from Alzheimer's Disease, so nobody can ask him. I did ask his daughter, however.

"This is very painful to me," Catherine Abate said. "You're talking about my father, someone I absolutely adored.... I was raised in a wonderful household. I grew up in a little place called Margate, N.J. It's a wonderful little beach resort, and my parents' friends were doctors and lawyers and business people....

"The emphasis when I was growing up was on going to school. And I ended up going to Vassar, and my brother ended up going to Princeton—which is pretty amazing, right, for a father who's a first-generation immigrant?"

Joseph Abate's official occupation was manufacturing uniforms for the Army and the Air Force. His daughter says the mob rumors first surfaced in the 1970s. She didn't really confront them until she became New York City corrections commissioner in 1992.

"I read as much as I could then," she told me. "Do I believe it? I still don't believe it. I believe it's only allegations. But I'll never know.... And there was nothing in my home life—no persons who came to visit, nothing—that would lead me to believe that this is true. But I'm in no position to prove or disprove it."

"Which of your three opponents for the nomination circulated the clippings?" I asked.

"I don't know who's circulating them. But two people called my campaign to say they had nothing to do with it, and that was Ollie Koppell and Evan Davis."

"That kind of narrows it down, doesn't it?"

"It does," she said. "Eliot hasn't called me."

I got Spitzer on the phone. Did you do it, I asked?

He said, "I will not talk about that issue, have not spoken about that issue and have given people strict directions that that is not an issue that we talk about."

"So, if somebody from your camp did do this thing, it was without your OK?"

"That's correct," Spitzer said.

For the record, it was somebody from Spitzer's camp. For the record also, the mob connections of Joseph Abate are stunningly irrelevant to this campaign. If you were to lose your mind and run for public office, how would you like your parents' backgrounds raised as a campaign issue?

"What my father did or did not do I'll never know," Catherine Abate told me. "I've spent my whole life trying to do the right thing. I'm devoted to public service. I love the work I've done. The values I have, the things I believe, they come from somewhere, right?

"I will love my dad to my last dying breath. And I will always have the most wonderful memories of him."

Unfortunately, however—and early in this campaign— some steps have been taken to ensure that everybody else remembers the late Joseph Abate, too.

—*March 16, 1998*

Keeping Your Eye on the Ball

We've been friends for 30 years, ever since we pledged the same college fraternity.

I was a dirt-poor Irish kid from upstate New York with an affection for books and football. He was a Jewish kid from a financially comfortable family in New Jersey with a passion for commerce and female companionship.

We had this in common: each of us liked to laugh. It was enough to bind us together.

After graduation, each of us got married, had kids and followed our careers. I went into the newspaper business as a

Family Matters, and the Stuff That Truly Counts 275

wage slave, moving from city to city. He went into the electrical supply business as an entrepreneur, opening his own operation in his home town and prospering right from the start.

We stayed in touch even though we lived some distance apart. There were phone calls, notes in the mail. The friends you care about most deeply are generally the ones you make early. No matter what you might become as years go by, you remain who you were. When you do get together, the years melt away. That's just the way it works.

That's why it was so jarring last summer when he called to say that his wife had a blood disease related to leukemia. She needed a bone marrow transplant.

This was just what they needed at the moment. He'd sold his business not long before. The guys who'd bought it had made three or four payments then declared bankruptcy. My friend was out nearly a million bucks and fighting a bank for the equity. He was working as a salesman in somebody else's electrical supply operation and trying to hold everything together financially. And, meanwhile, going into hock to his lawyer to the tune of 50 grand.

And now this. Wonderful.

"What can I do?" I asked him. "Can I get tested to see if I'm a bone marrow match?"

"Well," he said, "not yet. She's in the hospital now, and they're working on some things."

These are smart people. When she'd first gotten word that she was sick and where this might go, she'd had some of her own bone marrow extracted and saved. This past fall, the doctors pumped in the healthy bone marrow. The improvement was immediate.

Now she's home. She seems to be doing well. And they're making plans.

"She loves Florida," he told me last summer in that telephone conversation. "If she gets through this, I'm selling this house, and we're moving down there. The hell with the business. The hell with all the money. What's going to happen with all that is going to happen, and it doesn't seem so important now. I'll just get an ordinary job down in Florida and spend as much time as I can with my wife."

That's what they're doing. One kid is out of college, and the younger one is planning his future. The house is on the market. As soon as my friend and his wife get a decent offer on the house, they're off for warm weather—and for a life that'll give them more time than they were able to savor together during the hectic years, when making money and launching kids into the world was the unavoidable focus of their lives.

There's a lesson there, and you don't need to be in Mensa to figure it out. You can never predict what'll happen or when.

So, you truly need to hone in constantly—like a laser beam—on what really counts.

Instead of getting hung up on what's just jive.

—April 2, 1996

Paying the Debt

Today is the day.

For most of you, this'll be just another Sunday—maybe church services in the morning and then some lawn work or some golf. If the weather holds up, maybe a barbecue in the back yard.

For me, though, this is a special Sunday. It's the day I fulfill half the bargain I made with my father 30 years ago when I went off to college. Today is the day the elder of my two kids gets her bachelor's degree.

Family Matters, and the Stuff That Truly Counts

277

When I left for school, the old man's financial condition was pretty much what it had been his whole life. If he had a nickel in his pocket that day, it was lonely.

My older brother had been a science whiz—a certifiable genius in math and physics. He'd gotten through college largely on merit scholarships. I was neither that bright nor that dedicated a student. My grand plan was to pay my own way through college with a football scholarship—a strategy derailed by an unfortunate shortage of size, speed, talent and durable knee tissue.

Consequently, my college career was financed through student loans and with every dime the old man could scrape up during those four arduous years. It wasn't until I was a junior, home on a holiday break, that I had any clue as to what this was really costing him. We were at the dinner table. I noticed him chewing with great caution.

"What's the matter?" I asked him.

"This upper plate is shot," he said, wincing.

"So," I advised casually, "get new teeth."

"When I get around to it," he told me.

He didn't manage to get around to it, however, until after he'd written that last tuition check. It wasn't until then that I fully realized that the cost of my college education had included intense pain in my father's mouth every time he sat down to eat. Three times a day for four long years he did torturous battle with that worn-out dental plate.

I tried one day to find the words to let him know how much I appreciated what he'd done to help me get through. He told me, "Don't worry about it. Just make sure that when your kids go to college you do everything you can to give them a clean, solid start in life. If you want to thank me, that's how to do it."

So, that was the deal we made. He has been dead 20 years this coming December, and I'm just now making the first payment. My daughter, as of today, will be an educated woman. And her younger brother will be 25 per cent of an educated man. Three more years to go with him, then I'll be square with my father.

I wonder how I'll feel when I watch Kelly cross the stage in her cap and gown. I'll feel pride, certainly. But I'll also be thinking, remembering....

... a chilly winter morning 22 years earlier in a mint-green hospital delivery room when she made her appearance on the planet. She never cried. They gave her to her mother for a while and then placed her in my arms. We studied one another. She had swooping eyelashes and tiny, incredibly delicate fingernails that captivated me. Somehow, I hadn't expected all that flawless detail in somebody so small and so new.

She was the perfect child—good-humored, loving, funny, as bright as the morning sunlight. I treasured every stage of her growth—the Raggedy Ann stage, the baton-twirling, Wonder-Woman-bathing-suit stage, the time of no front teeth, the designer jeans phase.

She started to change in the fifth or sixth grade. I recall driving her to school one morning. We pulled up in front. A swarm of kids surged all around the car and into the building. I waited for my hug and kiss, our unfailing morning ritual. She gazed out the window at the other kids and then up at me, trying to figure out how to say it.

Then she told me, "I'll kiss you goodbye when I see you at home tonight."

That was the day she began to grow up and broke my heart.

That little girl soon vanished, replaced by somebody who lapsed into a bad mood and stayed like that for six or seven years. After that morning outside the school came the cheerleading and the boys with no necks in varsity jackets. And rotten music. And pictures clipped from magazines and taped to the walls and ceiling of her room. And secret diaries. And more boys. And more cheerleading.

And then college.

I'd always promised her that she could go to any school she could get into—an option that hadn't been open to me. She picked a private college where the tuition bill could stop your heart. And, although the college was close to home, she wanted to live on campus, too.

My wife and I told her, "Okay, we'll find a way to pay for it."

Which we have. Our solution was bondage. There'll be stiff monthly payments to a bank for years to come, but Kelly emerges from college debt-free—for which she can thank a man she can't recall and the bargain to which he bound me so many years ago.

Her degree will be in English. Television news, that's her goal—the only business imaginable that's tougher to get started in than newspapering.

Well, good luck, Sweetheart. You really are a big girl now. My father told me once that parents are obligated to provide their kids with both roots and wings. The roots you've had from the start.

You'll pick up your wings today.

—May 21, 1995

Another Link in the Chain

Always, he'd worked hard, fighting the tide, day after day.

Miraculously, he'd gotten both his sons through college. Now, his last kid, my younger sister, was close to graduation. That was all the old man cared about—getting us all educated—somehow, some way.

This was a few years ago. My older brother and I had gone to school poor. He'd gotten through on academic scholarships. I hadn't been that smart, so I'd had to work my way through as a clothing salesman, as a security guard and as a bouncer at block dances. And, later on, as a scribbler for newspapers.

Our baby sister, though, she went to a fancy private college in Pittsburgh, like some rich guy's daughter. She was the last one, so the old man shot every nickel to send her through in style.

When her graduation arrived, my brother and his family drove up from Washington. I flew in from New York. My wife, extremely pregnant, was warned against getting on a plane, so she couldn't make it.

The old man drove down to Pittsburgh from his home in New York's Finger Lakes region. Just outside the city, his treasured old Oldsmobile—the Batmobile, we called it—blew up. Somehow, he got there, though. He had no car and not dime one left in his bank account.

I have in the family album a photograph of him sitting at a table in the motel the family occupied during that graduation weekend. We'd celebrated my sister's degree with pizza, rowdiness and a case of beer. The old man was dead broke and happier than he'd ever been in his life.

Seven months later, a blood vessel burst in his chest. He was dead before the doctors figured out what had happened.

I mention all this only for this reason: On Friday, amid the jagged peaks of the Rocky Mountains, that baby my wife was carrying that graduation day so long ago will walk across his own college graduation stage. My Kevin saw his grandfather only once, at the very beginning of Kevin's life—and within only weeks of the end of the old man's.

My father didn't live to see what I saw. He never saw the little boy hug his beloved pet cat with such desperate affection. He never saw Kevin beat out a grounder in tee-ball. He never saw the kid bounce a quick and clever pass in a CYO basketball game. He never saw the stiffly dignified, long-haired deadhead in a tux heading off for a prom with a gorgeous teenage goddess in a flowing dress. Believe me, this kid always dated well.

The old man also never saw my Kevin's hard-fought transition from uncertain adolescence to the glowing grace of early manhood. He never saw Kevin slowly develop the steely, singleminded desire to achieve.

For some reason, though, whenever I think of my father or my son, I always think of them standing side by side. All of us, we're links in a chain. The old man wanted every link stronger than the one that came before it. It was his mission in life—all that really mattered to him.

So, this Friday, I'll be in Colorado, watching this latest link receive the degree that his grandfather never had a chance to earn. Then my son heads further west, to L.A. He'll fight to break into the movie business as a writer.

A long shot? OK, sure. But Kevin seems to figure that if life is about anything, it's about dreams. It's about doing whatever it takes to make those dreams come true.

My son, the dreamer. And the old man? Well, Kevin represents his dream come true.

Mine, too.

—May 30, 1999

A Little Advice

Yet another year has gone by in which nobody asked me to deliver a commencement address.

They usually ask people like federal judges with lifetime jobs. Either that or people so rich and powerful that they don't have to face the day-to-day challenges most graduates are likely to confront. Instead of inviting speakers who have it made, wouldn't school administrators be wiser to seek out speakers of more modest accomplishment? I'm thinking here of somebody who might give the graduates a clue to what they can do to make out better in life than the commencement speaker.

Since I finished school, I've learned a few things through painful experience that I wish somebody had tipped me off to at my graduation. Instead of selecting somebody to offer practical advice, though, the rulers of my college asked Theodore Sorenson, John F. Kennedy's adviser and ghost writer. To this day, my most vivid memory of Sorenson's speech was that he was quite tall.

If somebody had asked me to deliver a commencement address this year, this is what I would have said:

"Greetings. I come to you as an advance scout from the real world. It's filled with pitfalls, injustices and disappointments. Here are some tips on how to make your way in it with a minimum of hassle:

"Remember that there's no law that requires you to say whatever pops into your head at any given moment. Always change your oil at three months or 3,000 miles. Never become romantically involved with anybody you suspect might be crazier than you are. Don't let anybody talk you into paying retail.

"Be polite even when you're dealing with jerks. Keep your tires properly inflated. Always give any job about 10 per cent more effort than you think it really deserves. Start saving money early. Never eat at a place called 'Mom's.' If you have any doubt whatever about telling a joke in a particular circumstance, don't tell it. Just assume that nobody has any sense of humor any more.

"Be nice to old people; they'll be gone sooner than you think. Tape movies on extended play; that way you can get three films on every tape. When somebody tells you a secret, keep it. If you have to speed, stay out of the left-hand lane.

Family Matters, and the Stuff That Truly Counts

"Never play pool with somebody who carries a personal cue in a case. Never play poker for money with anybody who says, 'Gee, I'm not very good at this game.' Eat fresh fruits and vegetables. Never take an elevator when you can climb stairs. Lock your doors at night. Go easy on the anchovies; they'll give you gout. Don't listen to Howard Stern; he really is a bad influence.

"Don't bother to get even; it seldom works out, and when it does it's not worth the trouble. Buy in bulk. Always bear in mind that, for better or worse, tomorrow will definitely arrive. Use your turn signals. You don't have to win every argument. Eat slowly and chew thoroughly. Try to be thoughtful. Never, ever say anything like, 'Go ahead; you wouldn't have the guts.'

"You get older every day; that's a law. Don't buy dented canned goods. Get to work on time. Try to avoid telling people that they're dead wrong, even when they are. You'll never convince anybody of anything by making him or her mad. Whenever anybody says, 'Go ahead and tell me the truth; you won't hurt my feelings,' don't believe it, and lie shamelessly.

"Whenever somebody asks, 'How do I look?' or, 'How did I do?' the only sensible answer is, 'Terrific.' Bread crumbs make hamburger meat go farther. A little garlic gives it more flavor. Don't drink every day. Count your change. Don't use a radar detector; the cops get seriously annoyed when they pull you over and see one. Don't confide in anybody unless you're absolutely, positively certain you can trust that person. Never agree to be a guest on *The Jerry Springer Show*.

"Do it now; there's not always time later. If it really doesn't feel right, then don't do it at all. Don't sweat the small stuff. Your coffee tastes better if you keep the can in the refrigerator. Your car has a parking brake for a reason. Make it a point to really listen. People are seldom as impressed by your anger as you think they should be. Go easy on the desserts.

"Always dress a little better than you think you should have to. Don't hog the remote. Stay away from coffee after nine at night and alcohol before noon. Always remember that life is in session, right now and until they lower you into your grave.

"You can have too little schooling, but never too much. Dream big dreams for yourself and then act on them with a single-minded intensity, even if people think you're crazy. Be willing to defer gratification if you expect to find any at all. Wear seat belts. It's never too late to do anything worth doing.

"Try harder to be nice to people, especially if you get to be a boss. The higher up you go, the more juice is packed into your thunderbolts. Check your antifreeze level at least once a week. Make sure you turn off the oven right away when you pull something out of it.

"When you realize that you're having a really good time, pay close attention; you'll want to remember it. Go out of your way to stay in touch with people you like. Don't push anybody into a corner. Turn off the lights when you really don't need them.

"Shine your shoes. Don't smoke. If it's over with, don't worry about it; just get on with things and remember the lesson. Don't make the same mistake twice, however tempting. Never make it a third time. Stop at red lights.

"Whenever you hear a little voice in your head saying, 'But what if somebody finds out?', then don't do it, because you can count on somebody finding out. Never offer advice unless you're sure it's right and the person asking for it is likely to follow it.

"Now, go forth in the world and do your damndest to become somebody really special. You might just get there, and you'll really kick yourself later if you don't try."

—May 28, 1995

ABOUT THE AUTHOR

Photo by Donna Lynch

Dan Lynch is a veteran newspaperman, author, and television and radio commentator. He worked at the *Philadelphia Inquirer* as chief political writer, was an editor for New York's *Newsday* and served for 16 years as managing editor at the Albany *Times Union*. He became the newspaper's featured columnist in 1995 and his opinion column was distributed to 660 North American newspapers by *The New York Times* News Service.

Lynch received multiple awards for his column from the Associated Press and the New York Newspaper Publishers Association. He was twice selected by a *Times Union* reader's poll as the New York State Capital Region's "best print journalist." Lynch is the author of six novels, a book of short stories, and two works of nonfiction. He has also written many articles which have appeared in a wide variety of publications including *Reader's Digest, Cosmopolitan,* and *American Journalism Review.* Lynch has taught journalism at Temple University and Long Island University.

His live radio talk program, *The Dan Lynch Show* is broadcast weekdays on WROW, Albany's leading news-talk radio station.